corrigible docile
costard a large apple
coulter plough-blade
counterfeit portrait; to pretend
Counter-gate gate of debtors' prison in London
coystrill knave
cozier cobbler
crabbed harsh
crack small boy
cracker boaster
cranks winding paths
crants garlands
crescive increasing
crisped closely; stiffly curled
cross-row alphabet
crotchets whims
crow-keeper scarecrow-boy
crown imperial the cultivated fritillary
cullionly rascally
culverin type of cannon
cunning skill; informed, clever
curious careful
curtal dog dog with a docked tail
curtle-axe short sword
customer prostitute
cuttle cutpurse
cypress crape

daff put off, thrust aside
damask blush-colour
darnel a weedy grass
darraign prepare
date span of life
daubery pretence
debile feeble
debonair gentle
defunctive funereal
deliver disclose
denier small copper coin
deracinate weed out
dern dark
derogate debased
derogately disparagingly
digest assimilate, amalgamate
dimensions bodily parts
discandy melt
disguise drunken state
disponge drip
distressful earned by toil
disvouched contradicted
dog-apes baboons

dole lamentation
dotage infatuation
dout extinguish
dowlas coarse linen
dowle feather
down-gyved fallen to t
draff swill
drawer tapster
drench medicinal drink
drift scheme, meaning
drumble to move slowly, loiter
dry-beat cudgel fiercely
dudgeon dagger handle
duello duelling code
dump slow mournful song
dup to open

eager sharp, biting, desiring deeply
eale evil
ean to give birth
eftest quickest
eisel vinegar
elder-gun toy gun for child
elf tangle
emboss swollen, foaming at the mouth
empiries quacks
emulous seeking glory, engage pledge
engine weapon of war, plot
enseamed greasy
ensign standard or standard-bearer
enskied dwelling in heaven
entertain take into service
eruption unnatural calamity
escoted maintained
estate to bequeath, settle
estridge goshawk, ostrich
evitate avoid
exigent crisis
exsufflicate puffed up
eyas young hawk

facinerous wicked
fadge turn out, succeed
fairing present (noun)
falchion curved sword
falling sickness, epilepsy
fan to winnow
fang to seize
fantasy imagination (adj. fantastical)
fap drunk
farced stuffed

fee-grief priva
fere spouse
festinate speedy
fet derived from
fettle make ready
file list
fill-horse carthorse
firk beat
flaunts ostentations, finery
fleer sneer, grimace
flewed having large chaps
flote sea
flux secretion
foin thrust
foison harvest
foppery folly
forfended forbidden
forgetive shaping, inventive
forthrights straight paths
frampold unpleasant
frank sty
frantic mad
freestone-coloured brownish-yellow
freshes freshwater springs
frieze coarse cloth
frippery old-clothes shop
frontlet headband; a frown
frush to batter
fulsome rank
furtherance aid

gaberdine a cloak
gad sharp metal point
gage pledge
gallimaufry a wild mixture
gaskins wide loose breeches
gaudy night feast
gear business
geck butt, dupe
gennet (or jennet) small Spanish horse
german blood relation
germen seed
gib tomcat
gig whipping-top
giglots harlots

**glaze** glare
**gleek** gibe, jest
**gloze** use flattering but specious words
**gnarling** snarling
**goodman** husband
**goose** tailor's iron; prostitute
**gorget** throat armour
**grange** lonely country house
**grate** vex, annoy
**gravelled** perplexed
**great morning** broad daylight
**green sickness** a form of anaemia among young girls
**groat** four pence
**guard** trimming on a garment
**guerdon** recompense
**guidon** pennant
**gust** taste
**guttered** jagged

**hackney** prostitute; horse for hire
**haggard** wild hawk
**hale** drag
**handfast** marriage contract
**handsaw** dialect form of "heronshaw" (heron)
**hardiment** valour
**heady** impetuous
**heaviness** drowsiness
**hectic** fever
**heft** hearing
**hempseed** gallows-bird
**herb of grace** rue
**hilding** good-for-nothing
**hive** straw hat
**hoboys** oboes
**holland** fine-quality linen first made in Holland
**hood** jealous, a jealous woman
**hoodman blind** blindman's buff
**horn beasts** cuckolds
**horn-mad** mad as an angry bull
**horologe** clock
**hoxes** hamstrings
**hoy** small coasting vessel
**hugger-mugger** secretly
**hull** to lie at anchor
**hurricano** hurricane
**hysterica passio** hysteria, choking

**imbar** lay bare
**imbrue** shed blood
**immoment** unimportant, trivial

**immures** walled confine
**impawned** staked
**implorator** one who begs
**imposthume** swelling, abscess
**impresa** device, crest
**incarnadine** redden
**inch** small island
**incony** fine
**indifferency** reasonable size
**indigest** shapeless
**indign** unworthy
**indue** endow
**inkle** tape, thread
**inland** cultured, civilized
**inly** inwardly
**insculped** engraved
**intendment** intention
**intenible** unretentive
**intituled** displayed
**intrenchant** invulnerable
**intrinsicate** intricate
**Iris** goddess of rainbow
**iwis** assuredly

**jack-dog** mongrel
**jade** inferior horse; treat with contempt
**jar** discord; tick of clock
**jaunce** going back and forth
**jesses** straps on a hawk's legs
**jet** strut
**journal** daily
**juggler** buffoon

**kam** nonsense; crooked
**kecksies** weeds (like hemlock)
**keech** roll of fat
**keel** to skim; cool
**kennel** gutter
**kern** light-armed Irish soldier
**kersey** plain woollen fabric
**key-cold** cold as metal
**kibe** chilblain
**kindness** natural instinct
**knapped** knocked sharply; gnaw, nibble
**knot-grass** plant thought to check growth of animals
**knotty** gnarled

**lade** to empty by ladling
**landrakers** thieves
**lank** to shrink

**lapse** arrest, delay
**lark's-heels** larkspur
**latten** a brass-like alloy
**laund** clearing in forest
**lavolt** high-leaping dance
**lazar** leper
**league** friendship
**leaguer** camp
**leasing** lying
**leather-coat** russet apple
**leiger** ambassador
**leman** sweetheart
**leviathan** whale
**libbard** leopard
**liberal** gross
**light** wanton
**limbeck** alembic for distilling
**limber** flabby, limp
**linsey-woolsey** cloth made of linen and wool; hence mixture or medley
**lisp** with foreign accent
**lockram** cheap linen fabric
**loggats** game in which small logs of wood are thrown at a stake
**long purples** kind of orchid
**loof** luff, sail away
**looped** full of holes
**love-in-idleness** pansy
**lozel** rascal
**lubber** clumsy, stupid fellow
**luce** pike, freshwater fish
**lugged** baited (of bears of bulls)
**lumpish** low-spirited
**lurch** deprive, bear off the prize
**luxurious** salacious
**lym** bloodhound

**machine** body
**maculation** impurity
**maiden strewment** flowers scattered on grave of unmarried girl
**maim** punishment
**malapert** impudent
**malkin** slut
**mallard** a wild drake
**maltworms** ale drinkers
**mammet** doll
**mammock** pull in pieces
**mandragora** opiate made of the mandrake root
**mandrake** narcotic plant with forked root

# The
# Shakespeare
# Companion

with a foreword by
## DAME JUDI DENCH

J.C. TREWIN Revised by Stanley Wells

CASSELL
ILLUSTRATED

John Courtenay Trewin (1908–1989), a renowned stage historian, theatrical biographer, and drama critic, was author of 50 books, editor of 50 more, and Literary Editor for the *Observer*. He lectured on Shakespeare in Britain, Europe, and North America and was President of the Shakespeare Club of Stratford-upon-Avon.

Author's note: Shakespeare wrote his plays to be acted, and no dramatist in the history of the world has been performed more often and in more languages. Though the book's emphasis is upon the theatre, it does also, I hope, answer concisely many questions about Shakespeare himself, the origin and history of his work, and of the characters he created. I am most grateful to Wendy, my wife, for her watchfulness, and to Susannah Read, Ken Hewis, Halina Tunikowska, and Keith Spence for their help and care in editing.

J.C.T 1981

for Wendy    *Love's Labour's Lost*, IV.3, 340–1

In revising this book I have been indebted at every turn to researchers and critics. Indebted also to those many theatre-workers whose labours this volume modestly seeks to illuminate. And indebted to the late J.C. Trewin, the guide's "onlie begetter", to whose memory I and the publishers wish to dedicate this revised edition.

James Brown  1994

J.C. Trewin was among the best-informed and most perceptive of Shakespearean theatregoers (and among the kindest of men). His succinct, pithy, and good humoured commentaries retain their freshness, and it has been a pleasure and a privilege to prepare this updated edition of his invaluable book.

Stanley Wells  2005

# The
# Shakespeare
# Companion

CASSELL
ILLUSTRATED

An Hachette UK Company
www.hachette.co.uk

First published in Great Britain in 1981 by Mitchell Beazley,
a division of Octopus Publishing Group Ltd
Carmelite House, 50 Victoria Embankment, London EC4Y 0DZ
www.octopusbooks.co.uk

This edition published in 2017 by Cassell, a division of
Octopus Publishing Group Ltd

ISBN 978-0-7537-3276-2

A CIP catalogue record for this book is available from the British Library

Printed and bound in China

10 9 8 7 6 5 4 3 2 1

For the Cassell edition
Publisher: Lucy Pessell
Designer: Lisa Layton
Design: Ummagumma Graphic Design Services
Editor: Sarah Vaughan
Production Controller: Sarah Kulasek-Boyd

# FOREWORD

When I was sent a bulky parcel containing the manuscript of this book I thought how wonderful it would be if you could *really* carry all this information around with you in your pocket or bag (because you certainly can't keep it all in your head, even after a lifetime of working in the theatre). It would act as a guidebook for visitors to Stratford, introducing them to Shakespeare's work through its historical context; it would give you the background to programme notes while you waited for a play to begin; unravel the complications of even the most elaborate of Shakespeare's plots; and provide instant reference for Elizabethan words no longer used, the name of the character that had slipped your memory, or the star of a past production.

Somehow the bulky manuscript has become this compact little book which you *can* actually take to the theatre with you or keep close by you to consult on every aspect of the plays. I know that it will be invaluable to all theatregoers but it will meet a wider audience as well: professional and amateur actors and actresses alike will certainly use it — I wish I had had the benefit of John Trewin's succinct synopsis of *The Comedy of Errors* before I started rehearsing for it; students will find it essential background reading; and even children coming to the plays for the first time will be able to benefit from his marvellously accessible text.

In fact, one of the most enjoyable aspects of my work is the letters I receive and some of the best of them come from children who write, "I was dreading coming to see your play but I never knew Shakespeare could be like that." So many people, less open than the children, come to Shakespeare with the fixed idea that the language will be archaic and incomprehensible, the plots difficult to follow and the whole performance lacking in relevance to contemporary life and thought. For those who are not already converted I think that this little book will do as much to promote the richness and relevance of Shakespeare's work as any good production can. John Trewin, whose gentle and constructive criticism has provided inspiration and guidance for over half a century, has written this book with a freshness and enthusiasm that cannot fail to communicate his lifelong love and appreciation of Shakespeare to all his readers.

*Dame Judi Dench*

# WILLIAM SHAKESPEARE
## 1564–1616

Not much is known of William Shakespeare. Human curiosity cannot abide a vacuum, and so speculation and legend have made good the lack of fact — even to the point of speculating that Shakespeare did not write the plays attributed to him, but was part of an elaborate conspiracy to conceal their real author. But such a lack of information is not unusual in this period. John Webster, for example, is an even more shadowy figure.

This is partly because materials which might have filled the void (such as correspondence and journals) have not survived or never existed. But it is also inherent in the nature of writing. There is a Monty Python sketch which imagines Thomas Hardy sitting down to write *The Return of the Native* in a packed sports stadium, with the crowd cheering his every word, and a breathless running commentary. The joke is that no matter how high the subsequent public profile of the finished work, the actual process of writing is unexciting; the works may enter the public world, but their creator doesn't necessarily follow them.

Shakespeare of course did enter the public world: six times a week in the season, as an actor. But despite the best efforts of Victorian scholarship to discover (or invent) a unity between his life and work, the images each gives us of Shakespeare differ.

**Life: Stratford** William Shakespeare was born in Stratford-upon-Avon, the eldest son and third child (of eight) of John Shakespeare, a glover, who also traded in wool, property, and occasionally lent money at interest (for which he was fined, usury being an offence at the time). His father's affairs thrived for a while, and John Shakespeare became an alderman, holding office in local government. The family who took the infant William to be baptized on 26 April 1564 were prosperous, middling people — roughly what we'd call middle class today. But economic conditions were bad and prosperity did not last. There are signs of John Shakespeare getting into difficulties from the mid-1570s onwards, and, though never destitute, by 1591 things reached such a pass that he did not dare go to church for fear of being arrested for debt.

It is likely that young William was educated at the local grammar school. He never went to university, and his younger contemporary and fellow-dramatist, Ben Jonson, would later speak disparagingly of his "small Latin, and less Greek" in the eulogy prefaced to the First Folio. But, as the American scholar T.W. Baldwin has demonstrated, the curriculum of the grammar school would have provided a formidable linguistic and literary education. Shakespeare could certainly read Latin, and probably French and

Italian as well. There was heavy emphasis on learning by rote, but there were also compositions to write, involving, for example, devising speeches appropriate to famous historical figures. Eloquence was highly prized, and rhetoric occupied an important place in Elizabethan education and society.

The spoken word may have been even more important at home. It is possible that John Shakespeare was illiterate: on official documents he made his mark (a cross or a pair of glover's compasses), rather than sign his name. The 16th century was crucial in the development of attitudes to literacy: in 1500 writing was a skill which it was no more expected everyone should master than we would today expect everyone to be able to do their own plumbing. By 1600, though literacy was still confined to a minority, anyone with any pretensions would be likely to read — and not just English, but Latin, and possibly Greek. A classical education was a badge of status.

This transformation in attitudes to learning needs to be seen in the context of the broader cultural changes of the 16th century. The Reformation swept away or suppressed much traditional culture — notably the mystery plays; humanist education thrived on the opening up of the world of the classical past to new investigation. It was Shakespeare's good luck or shrewd judgement to find himself, in the midst of rapid cultural change, with a foot in both the old and the new.

After his baptism the next certain thing known about Shakespeare is his marriage. On 27 November 1582 he secured a licence to marry Anne Hathaway without the reading of the usual banns. He was 18, his bride 26. They may have had reason for their haste; their first child, Susanna, was baptized just six months later on 26 May 1583. The twins, Hamnet and Judith, followed in February 1585.

For the next seven years Shakespeare drops from sight entirely. These are the so-called "lost years", though in truth we're not much better informed about the years that preceded them. According to one story he was a schoolmaster; another has him turn soldier; yet another puts him with a group of private players in Lancashire. There is no way of knowing. However, somehow by 1592 Shakespeare had got from Stratford to London, and embarked on a career in the theatre as actor and playwright.

He seems to have maintained his links with Stratford throughout his life. He was both born and buried there. It appears that his family stayed in Stratford while he worked in London.When he started to make money it was in and around Stratford that he invested it. It was in Stratford that Hamnet was buried in 1596. Richard Quiney, a fellow-Stratfordian, wrote to Shakespeare in October 1598, asking to borrow money from "my loving good friend and my countryman Mr Wm Shakespeare" [one's "country" at this date commonly meaning one's locality, rather than one's state or nation]. Subsequently he was remembered in the will of John Combe, a Stratford landowner from whom he had purchased property in 1602. The marriages of Shakespeare's children are recorded in the Stratford register: Susanna to John Hall, 5 June 1607; Judith to Thomas Quyney, 10 February 1616.

It would be nice to be able to read particular emotional import into Shakespeare's continuing association with Stratford, given that he worked and made his money in London, but never settled there. Certainly his loyalty to his home town sets him apart from other writers, such as Marlowe, who quit his native Canterbury for London. But Shakespeare's was a common pattern at the time. Local loyalties were strong and many people lived in London as temporary residents to earn money, without ceasing to regard themselves as natives of whatever part of the country they haled from.

The 17th-century gossip, John Aubrey, recorded that Shakespeare used to go back to Warwickshire at least once a year. After his mother's death in 1608 (his father had died in 1601) it is possible that his business interests there claimed more of his attention; they were certainly successful. It would be interesting to know with what feelings he recouped the family fortunes and secured for his father, and therefore for himself, the status of gentleman, which was granted by the College of Heralds in 1596. Was it very important to him? Was he a snob? Or was he just being conventional? One cannot tell. Perhaps the most one can say on the little evidence available is that there seems to have been a large part of Shakespeare's life which was conventional by the standards of his background and time. Possibly this side of him suggests a stability which contributed to the one feature of his character that is generally attested to: his sweetness of temper. But it was also bound up with his sense as a businessman. However much burdened we have become by Shakespeare's genius, he appears to have been more concerned for his property and the continuance of his family line, which the tortuous provisions of his will sought (and failed) to secure.

Setting aside apocryphal tales, such as that relating to Shakespeare's alleged poaching from Sir Thomas Lucy's property as young man, or the possibility of his having been a Roman Catholic, little else is known of Shakespeare other than in connection with his work. Though highly regarded in his own lifetime, he did not inspire the kind of adulation that has been accorded him since. No one kept special records of him in the way that Boswell later captured Dr Johnson — or if they did they have not come to light. On admittedly scanty evidence, the picture that emerges of Shakespeare outside his artistic work is that of a well-liked and successful businessman.

# WORK: LONDON

By 1592 Shakespeare was an established figure in the London theatre, both as actor and playwright, for in that year he attracted the envious bile of another writer, Robert Greene. Greene, who was university educated, wrote a pamphlet warning his fellow graduates in the literary scene that their rights were being encroached upon by a mere actor. Greene warns his colleagues that the players are out to exploit and replace them:

Yes, trust them not; for there is an upstart Crow, beautified with our feathers, that with his *Tiger's heart wrapt in a Player's hide*, [an allusion to 3 *Henry VI*, I.iv.137] supposes he is as well able to bombast out a blank verse as the best of you: and being an absolute *Johannes Factotum*, is in his own conceit the only Shake-scene in a country.

Greene wrote this (on his deathbed, as it transpired) towards the end of 1592. Shakespeare had clearly made a name for himself by then.

Many writers, such as Ben Jonson, wrote for several different companies. The diaries of Philip Henslowe, the entrepreneur and theatrical impresario, suggest the kind of frenzied conditions under which a lot of work must have been produced. There was a huge turnover of scripts, many of which were written at high speed and collaboratively. Shakespeare, by comparison, enjoyed an unusually stable relationship with one company. In the earliest stages of his career he worked with different companies, but by 1594 he was one of the leading members of the Lord Chamberlain's Men, for over Christmas they performed at Court, and warrant for payment specifically names Richard Burbage, William Kempe, and Shakespeare. Burbage and Kempe were the leading tragic and comic actors of the company respectively. Shakespeare (unlike Molière, another actor-dramatist) never seems to have done leading business as an actor, so it is fair to infer that it was his writing that had won him this status. Possibly by 1594, but certainly by 1599, when the company moved its London base from the Theatre, north of the City, down to the Globe, south of the river, Shakespeare became a sharer (i.e. part-owner) in the company. This may reflect his talent, or it may simply be that he was able to raise the cash to buy his share. He remained with the company (renamed the King's Men in 1603 when James I brought it under royal patronage) for the rest of his career.

There is some indication of whereabouts he lodged in London: in St Helen's, Bishopsgate, near the Theatre in Shoreditch, and later on south of the river, probably to be near the Globe. A lawsuit of 1612 indicates that he lodged for some time around 1604 with a Huguenot called Christopher Mountjoy in Silver Street. Their apprentice, Stephen Belott, married their daughter, and later quarrelled with his in-laws over the dowry. Shakespeare was called as a witness because Mountjoy "did send and persuade one Master Shakespeare that lay in the house to persuade the plaintiff to the same marriage", and it was hoped that he would be able to testify what had been agreed. Diplomatically perhaps, having attested to Belott's good character, Shakespeare proved unable to recall the terms of the financial agreement.

We know he acted in plays other than his own, for editions of Jonson's *Everyman In His Humour* and *Sejanus* list him among the actors. But at some point before 1610 he probably stopped acting. His output as a writer also slowed. He may have spent more time in Stratford. But in 1613 he bought a house in the Blackfriars area of London, and he continued to make money as a sharer in the King's Men.

These are the bare bones of Shakespeare's London life; the meat of it is to be sought in his works. But tracing his development as a writer is difficult because it is impossible to be certain of the chronology of his output. E.K. Chambers reviewed the evidence in 1930, and generally his conclusions were accepted until the recent re-evaluation by the editors of the Oxford Shakespeare (see Stanley Wells and Gary Taylor, *William Shakespeare: A Textual Companion*, Oxford, 1987). That has resulted in a few significant revisions. But even so, it still makes sense to divide Shakespeare's writing career into roughly four stages.

The first starts with Shakespeare's earliest plays, whenever they were produced, and is brought to an end by the plague. Stanley Wells remarks that his earliest extant plays show such verbal power that Shakespeare may have been writing for some time by the time he produced them. Possibly he had a hand in some of the many collaborative works which the Elizabethan theatre churned out. His earliest works show great ambition. It is not certain that the English History play existed before Shakespeare worked in the genre. But if he did not invent it, he made it his own.

This first period is dominated by his dramatization of the Wars of the Roses. Though he probably did not set out to write a tetralogy, by the time he finished *Richard III* he had created an extraordinary sequence which had a formidable impact upon his contemporaries. The tetralogy (consisting of *Henry VI Parts 1, 2, & 3* and *Richard III*) ends with victory of the future Henry VII, the reigning queen's grandfather. These were events in which Shakespeare's spectators felt implicated. Shakespeare's own forebears may have passed down personal recollections of the events of this period; the grant of a coat of arms to John Shakespeare recorded that his "parents and late grandfather for his faithful and valiant service was advanced and rewarded by the most prudent prince, King Henry the Seventh...".

The other works of this period are a little more tentative. These are Shakespeare's earliest experiments in comedy with *The Two Gentlemen of Verona* and *The Taming of the Shrew*, and in tragedy with the bloody *Titus Andronicus* (*The Comedy of Errors* is now thought to come later). The artifice of the first and last of these plays can make them difficult today, though they have all been produced successfully; while the *Shrew*, funny as it is, needs to be interpreted with ingenuity if Petruchio's taming of Katharina is not to give offence.

Having made such a promising start, Shakespeare was forced to abandon the theatre. Plague was an ever-present threat, and London, with a population many times that of the next largest towns, and equipped with inadequate sanitation, was particularly vulnerable. When the number of plague deaths rose beyond a certain point (usually 30 a week), the theatres would be closed. Plague orders were imposed in June 1592 and the theatres closed; they did not reopen until the summer of 1594, by which time approximately 11,000 Londoners had perished.

Anyone who could, got out. The players set off on lengthy tours. Shakespeare was probably in Lord Pembroke's Men, whose tour petered out. It was no use writing new plays, so he turned to poetry. While the plague raged he wrote the narrative poems, *Venus and Adonis* and *The Rape of Lucrece*. Maybe he also wrote the earliest of the Sonnets. This meant moving into more obviously literary territory, and it also meant moving upmarket. As the dedications of the narrative poems indicate, Shakespeare secured a patron for himself: the Earl of Southampton. It is possible that he spent some of his enforced absence from the stage moving in aristocratic circles.

The plays of the next stage of Shakespeare's career reflect the influence of his excursion into non-dramatic poetry. His language is now capable of lyrical, courtly refinement. In this respect *Richard II* forms a striking contrast with the earlier history plays. It is self-consciously fascinated by language: by what it makes possible and by what it conceals.

*Romeo and Juliet* also belongs to this period. The language here is more varied, with surging lyricism often giving way in an instant to more earthy language. As

Shakespeare fused different idioms, so he juggled different genres. *Romeo and Juliet* may be a tragedy, but it flirts with its opposite. It was normally expected that tragic characters be princes, or rulers; the Montagues and the Capulets are just well-to-do. The whole set-up — two young lovers, opposed families — is the natural stuff of comedy.

Tragedy is still nothing like as important to Shakespeare as comedy. This is the period of *Love's Labour's Lost* (probably), *A Midsummer Night's Dream*, *The Merchant of Venice*, *The Merry Wives of Windsor*, *Much Ado About Nothing*, possibly, early in the period, of *The Comedy of Errors*, and *As You Like It*. Most of Shakespeare's comedy is in a loose sense romantic — both in its subject-matter, but also in that he uses little satire. He was also disinclined to write directly of the contemporary world. *A Midsummer Night's Dream*, *The Merchant of Venice*, and *As You Like It* all take their characters away from the everyday world where laws apply, into other worlds of freedom and self-discovery: the two forests and Portia's Belmont. Shakespeare tends to press beyond the normal limits of the genres he uses, but always there is the possibility of the final limit of death. It is one of the features of Shakespeare's comedy that it often needs to invoke the possibility of death and loss.

In some of the comedies the negotiations between law and everyday life on the one hand, and the libidinous, pleasurable world of imagination and love had been strained. *The Merchant of Venice* in particular anticipates the disturbing qualities of the later comedies in the way the legalistic Old Testament values of Shylock are played off against Portia's magic at Belmont and her plea for mercy. It's not Portia's values that win the day for her, but her ability to outwit Shylock on his legalistic terms. But the most complex, sustained treatment of this central issue is to be found in the two parts of *Henry IV*. Henry finds himself ruling a fallen world, in which he can never establish his authority definitively because of the means by which he got it. The orderly development of a political plot gives way as the rest of the life of the kingdom crowds onto the stage. We see the rebels and Hotspur with his dream of honour, we see the Welsh, we see Justice Shallow caught up in the leisurely rhythms of rural life, and above all we see Falstaff, the Lord of Misrule, presiding over festivities down in Cheapside, while the King, his sour, disappointed counterpart, paces his palace, unable to appease heaven, and struggles to hold the kingdom together. The variousness of the life on display is an artistic triumph, but the mere fact of its claiming so much attention in a sense registers the fractured, flawed hierarchy which ought to regulate this world. Caught in between

Falstaff and Henry, Hal has to find some way through to the throne and to redeem the time. In *Henry IV, Part 2* the problem has become urgent. The same range of life is there, but its vitality has given way to old age and disease: Northumberland, Falstaff, and the King are all sick. In some way it is a play about waiting for the end.

Hal chooses rule over fellowship and festivity, and rejects Falstaff. His own play, *Henry V* seems to bring fruition and to confirm his success. He has unified his kingdom — figured in the way his army includes Welsh, Scots, and Irish as well as English. He can beat the French. The play ends like a comedy with his wooing of Katherine. But if we've seen *Henry VI* we know it will not last. Shakespeare uses a chorus before every act, almost as if trying to shape the material and our response to it. A sense of an ending has to be forced out of the material, for history by its nature, as Henry Ford put it, is just one damn thing after another. There is no reason for it ever to stop, so the conclusion of a history play can only be contingent.

The Lord Chamberlain's Men moved to the Globe in 1599 (see "Shakespeare in the Theatre"). Also in 1599 the Privy Council banned the publication of verse satire, so the theatre reaped the benefit as the satirists, popular with the public, turned to drama. This changed the theatrical scene, as did the resurgence of the children's companies from 1600 onwards.

For the first eight years or so of the new century Shakespeare worked mainly in tragedy. English history no longer figured, unless one counts *King Lear*, set in ancient Britain; it had proved politically awkward, and in any case Shakespeare had used up the best material.

But he continued to work with history in a broader sense. Although the First Folio divided Shakespeare's plays into tragedy, history, and comedy, the dividing line, especially between the first two, is far from clear. *Macbeth* and *King Lear* both owe something to Holinshed's *Chronicles*, from which Shakespeare had culled material for the English histories, while the three Roman plays, *Julius Caesar, Antony and Cleopatra,* and *Coriolanus*, can be regarded as Roman histories. In watching the Roman plays, the contemporary spectator would have to make allowances for cultural differences between his world and the represented world, especially between English monarchy and Roman republic. Such clashes of values are central to these plays, as Rome shifts from being a republic towards being an Empire (in *Julius Caesar*), and its values are set against the very different culture of Cleopatra's Egypt in *Antony and Cleopatra*. In *Antony and Cleopatra* we are presented with utterly irreconcilable images of the central characters: Antony and Cleopatra are both a strumpet and her fool, and also an heroic couple. Disconcertingly, they are both of these things — at opposite ends of the scale of values — simultaneously.

In other plays one encounters full-blown conflict between utterly different systems of values. In *King Lear* all the characters are forced to take sides in the struggles that follow Lear's abdication: on the one hand there is the self-seeking politics of Edmund, Goneril, and Regan; on the other, the bonds of traditional loyalty of Kent, Edgar, and Cordelia.

Even in the comparatively domestic world of *Othello* there is such polarization. Iago is opposed to the love of Othello and Desdemona and all that it stands for. It is Iago, the native-born Venetian, who proves to be the real alien, while Othello, the "extravagant and wheeling stranger of here and everywhere" is set against him. The terrifying thing about *Othello* is that the alien, destructive quality lurks within; Iago, an insider, contains an evil that infects the whole play.

*Hamlet* is set entirely in Elsinore, yet Hamlet's mind quests beyond the physical limits of his world into realms of speculation, and beyond the old-fashioned role of revenger which the ghost imposes on him. The conflict is most powerfully felt within the protagonist, who, like a discontented actor, quarrels with the part assigned him. This gulf between Hamlet's sense of himself and what his society and duty require of him is part of the play's exploration of the vexed relationship between appearance and reality. Hamlet can only reconcile the conflict in the terminal silence he speaks of in his final line.

The other vein of Shakespeare's work at this stage is, if comic, then blackly so. As with the tragedies, the conflicts of the comedies are deep — too deep, it sometimes seems, for their resolutions to be plausible.

For example, *Twelfth Night*, depending on the company and the director, can either emerge as an engaging mixture of romance and farce, or as a bitter comedy which, even in its apparently happy ending, can never quite shake off the possibility of loss and isolation. Other plays are obviously blacker. *Measure for Measure*, for example, returns to the tension between law and desire which proved so unsettling in *The Merchant of Venice*. *Troilus and Cressida* presents a world locked in sterile conflict.

The last phase of Shakespeare's work comes after the acquisition of the indoor Blackfriars theatre by the King's Men; it is defined by four plays which overlap to some extent with the preceding phase, but which have notable similarities which invite one to see them together: *Pericles*, *The Winter's Tale*, *Cymbeline*, and *The Tempest*. Resolution is now achieved by art or magic. Prospero uses his magic to avert disaster in *The Tempest*, and presides like a master of ceremonies over the play. *Cymbeline* is likewise magical. *The Winter's Tale* resorts to art; Leontes thinks he has killed his wife, Hermione, by the violence of the fit of jealousy which dominates the first three acts. Then years pass. Leontes' lost child proves to have grown up as a shepherdess. She is restored to him. But the world of pastoral life and renewal that Perdita represents is not sufficient to resolve the play. Hermione must ultimately be restored to Leontes and her long-lost daughter by posing as her own statue, which then miraculously comes to life. There is an element of wishful thinking in these late plays, but also a poignant expression of the human sorrows that make such resolutions so intensely desirable. Paulina's solemn injunction to Leontes just before she makes Hermione come to life might stand as the motto for the whole group: "It is required you do awake your faith."

It is common to end surveys of Shakespeare's work by drawing a parallel between Prospero's renunciation of his art to return to his duties in the human world, and Shakespeare's final retirement to Stratford. But Shakespeare had never really left Stratford and, at the time of writing *The Tempest*, though Prospero might have been ready to abandon his art, Shakespeare was not quite finished. He was to work on three more plays: the lost play *Cardenio, Henry VIII* (know in its own time as *All Is True*) and *The Two Noble Kinsmen*. In all of these he collaborated with John Fletcher, who was to take over as main playwright for the King's Men. This is perhaps the truer, if less sentimental, parting image of Shakespeare: the theatre professional continuing to work with his colleagues. It is certainly easier to reconcile it with our earlier image of the Stratford businessman. But both images leave the mystery of his talent and artistic achievement intact — as finally it must be.

# Henry VI, Part 1
### 1589–90

**THE CHARACTERS**

King Henry VI
Duke of Gloucester, uncle to the
King, and Lord Protector
Duke of Bedford, uncle to the King,
and Regent of France
Thomas Beaufort, Duke of Exeter,
great-uncle to the King
Henry Beaufort, Bishop of
Winchester (afterwards Cardinal),
great-uncle to the King
John Beaufort, Earl (afterwards
Duke) of Somerset
Richard Plantagenet, son of Richard,
late Earl of Cambridge; afterwards
Duke of York
Earl of Suffolk
Richard Beauchamp, Earl of
Warwick
Earl of Salisbury
Lord Talbot, afterwards Earl of
Shrewsbury
John Talbot, his son
Joan la Pucelle, commonly called
Joan of Arc
An old shepherd, Joan's father
Edmund Mortimer, Earl of March
Sir John Fastolfe, a cowardly knight
Sir William Lucy
Sir William Glansdale

Sir Thomas Gargrave
Mayor of London
Woodville, Lieutenant of the Tower
Vernon, of the White Rose or York
faction
Basset, of the Red Rose or Lancaster
faction
Charles, Dauphin, and later King of
France
Reignier, Duke of Anjou, and titular
King of Naples
Margaret, daughter to Reignier
Duke of Burgundy
Duke of Alençon
Bastard of Orleans
Governor of Paris
Master Gunner of Orleans; and his
Son
General of the French forces in
Bordeaux
Countess of Auvergne
A Lawyer, Legate, Warders of the
Tower, Herald, Officers, Soldiers,
Messengers, a Porter, Attendants,
Watch, Servants, Fiends
appearing to La Pucelle

**THE SCENE**
England and France

# SYNOPSIS

This is a play of battles in France (where the English try vainly to hold their possessions) and of a perilous breakdown of order in England. Internal dissension, fatal to a campaign abroad, presages civil war.

At the Westminster Abbey funeral of Henry V news arrives that the French have beaten back the English; Talbot, the valiant general, has been captured, and the

Dauphin crowned. At home Gloucester (Lord Protector, the gentle young Henry VI's uncle) and Beaufort, Bishop of Winchester (Henry's great-uncle), are dangerously at odds. In France Joan La Pucelle, seen here not as the saintly Joan of Arc but as a harlot and witch in league with the powers of darkness, raises the siege of Orleans. Talbot (Act II) regains the city.

In London, a feud between the ambitious Richard Plantagenet, claimant to the crown, and the Earl (later Duke) of Somerset, moves to the symbolic plucking of roses in Temple Gardens: a white rose for Plantagenet, a red for Somerset. King Henry (Act III) makes Richard Duke of York and goes to be crowned King of France in Paris. La Pucelle captures, then loses, Rouen, but wins the support of the Duke of Burgundy. Henry, seeking to make peace among the English factions (Act IV), puts on a red rose, saying:

I see no reason, if I wear this rose,
That anyone should therefore be suspicious
I more incline to Somerset than York.

Talbot dies, beleaguered with his son outside Bordeaux where no reinforcement has reached him from the quarrelling nobles. But (Act V) La Pucelle is taken prisoner before Angers, deserted by her familiar spirits, and sent to the stake. A "solemn peace" is patched up between France and England. The unscrupulous Earl of Suffolk, entranced by his captive, Margaret, beautiful daughter of Reignier, the Duke of Anjou, plans for his own benefit to have her married to the King; Henry, influenced by a "wondrous rare description", breaks a previous diplomatic betrothal and orders Suffolk to bring back Margaret as his Queen.

# IN PERFORMANCE

Probably acted at, appropriately, the Rose on Bankside, and manipulated, in many short scenes, from the history by Edward Halle, *Henry VI, Part 1* has puzzled scholars. It is probably a collaborative play and may have been written in part by Thomas Nashe. In general, its characters all use the same kind of serviceable blank-verse grandiloquence and good mixed invective. Highly popular in its time, it had no real restoration until the 20th century, though there had been various muddled conflations of the *Henry VI* plays in which Part 1 had little share. It did have a single performance (Covent Garden, 1738) for some unspecified "Ladies of Quality".

Curiously, Osmond Tearle chose Part 1 for revival at the old Stratford Memorial Theatre in 1889, maybe 300 years after the play was written. It was left to Frank

Benson, whose Talbot was "a rugged dog of war", to stage the entire trilogy (Stratford, 1906). Robert Atkins, a Talbot among directors, did Part 1 (also with cuts) at the Old Vic in 1923, the First Folio tercentenary year; his enterprise had surprisingly little critical response. In the early 1950s, the Birmingham Repertory under Barry Jackson, with Douglas Seale as director, presented the three plays superbly, opening with Part 2 (1951) and ending with Part 1 (1953): Jackson joined it to Shakespeare's earlier chronicles by opening with the final Chorus of *Henry V* ("Henry the Sixth, in infant bands crowned king"). The trilogy was later done in chronological order at the Old Vic in the summer of 1953, and Seale revived it in 1957.

The next adventure was *The Wars of the Roses* at Stratford (1963). Here John Barton — cutting, rearranging, and vigorously adapting the seven history plays more than most people realized — provided a new trilogy: *Henry VI, Edward IV,* and *Richard III*. The opening play covered Part 1 and the first half of Part 2. Returning to the original text, Terry Hands directed the trilogy, practically uncut, on consecutive nights at Stratford in 1977. He included the hitherto seldom-played scene (II.3) where the Countess of Auvergne seeks to entrap Talbot.

Michael Bogdanov won an Olivier Award for Best Director for the English Shakespeare Company's touring *The Wars of the Roses* (1988), in which the three parts of *Henry VI* became two; *The House of Lancaster* and *The House of York*. Michael Pennington was Henry. A year later the RSC presented their history marathon, *The Plantagenets*, in which *Henry VI, Parts 1, 2 & 3,* and *Richard III* became three plays. Adrian Noble directed Ralph Fiennes as Henry (Stratford/Barbican, 1989–90).

A landmark in the production of the history plays from *Richard II* to *Richard III* was the RSC's "This England" (2000–2001), in which the eight plays were staged in various styles by four different directors in The Other Place (*Richard II*), the Royal Shakespeare Theatre (*Henry V*), and the Swan (*Henry IV* Parts 1 and 2, *Henry VI* Parts 1, 2, and 3, and *Richard III*), in London, and in other locations. Michael Boyd's innovatively athletic productions of the first tetralogy, seen to best advantage in the Swan, which was reconfigured as a traverse auditorium, was given by a single company led by David Oyelowo, as a dignified and beautifully spoken Henry. Many of the actors took several roles. As often, *Richard III* was less impressive as the last play of the series than when played on its own. Edward Hall, who directed a lively *Henry V* for the RSC, also produced *Rose Rage* (2001, Watermill Theatre, Newbury, and on tour in England and overseas). Set in an abattoir, this was a vivid conflation by Hall and Roger Warren into two two-hour shows of the Henry VI plays.

In the United States the play had probably its first American performances during the summer of 1935, at the Pasadena Community Playhouse, where all ten histories were done consecutively under the direction of Gilmor Browne. Although *The Wars of the Roses* has seldom been performed in the United States, it appeared at the Palace Theatre, Stamford, Connecticut as part of the 1988 Stamford Shakespeare Festival. Barry Kyle directed *Henry VI, Part One: The Contention, Part II, The Civil War* for Theatre for a New Audience in New York, 1995. Michael Boyd's RSC productions were performed at the University of Michigan in 2001.

## IN OTHER TERMS

The trilogy was included in Peter Dews's television sequence, *An Age of Kings*, for the BBC (1961), which spanned the histories from *Richard II* to (and including) *Richard III*. Jane Howell's 1983 production of the Henry VI plays and *Richard III*, filmed over a period of six months on a set resembling an adventure playground, was among the most successful contributions to the BBC television series.

## CHIEF CHARACTERS

**Henry VI** Very young, gentle, and unequal to the demands of kingship.

**Richard Plantagenet, Duke of York** Self-centred, ambitious, and a sensualist.

**Lord Talbot (later Earl of Shrewsbury)** A gallant soldier betrayed. The longest part in the play. We recognize the voice of Shakespeare in Talbot's elegiac couplet over his son "Poor boy! He smiles, methinks, as who should say, "Had Death been French, then Death had died today." Thomas Nashe wrote in his *Pierce Pennilesse* (1592): "How would it have joyed brave Talbot (the terror of the French) to think that after he had lain two hundred years in his tomb, he should triumph again on the stage, and have his bones new embalmed with the tears of ten thousand spectators at least (at several times) who, in the tragedian that represents his person, imagine they behold him fresh bleeding?"

**Duke of Somerset** There are three in the *Henry VI* trilogy. In Part 1 it is the third Earl, and later first Duke, John Beaufort; in Part 2 it is the second Duke, Edmund Beaufort, John's younger brother; and in Part 3 it is the fourth Duke, another Edmund.

**Earl of Suffolk** Woos Margaret for the King, and for himself. He has the play's final lines: "Margaret shall now be Queen, and rule the King;/But I will rule both her, the King and realm."

**Duke of Gloucester** The Lord Protector, a man free from all cunning, whose last line is ominous: "Ay, grief, I fear me, both at first and last."

**Joan la Pucelle** After an opening (I.2) in the heroic manner, her treatment — derived from Holinshed — is scurrilously anti-French, the Tudor idea of Joan as a harlot and witch. Even so, in her first scene (I.2) she has three of the most quoted lines. Joan's part is the second largest, 260 lines. Charlotte Cornwell (Stratford/ Aldwych, 1977–8), recoiled prophetically at the sight of a torch held by a soldier.

**Margaret** A single scene (V.3) for the wilful and alluring princess who develops into the tigress-Queen, one of Shakespeare's great full-length portraits.

---

# Henry VI, Part 2
## 1590–1

**THE CHARACTERS**

King Henry VI
Margaret, his Queen
Humphrey, Duke of Gloucester, his uncle, Lord Protector
Eleanor, Duchess of Gloucester
Cardinal Beaufort, Bishop of Winchester, great-uncle to the King
Richard Plantagenet, Duke of York
Edward and Richard, his sons
Duke of Somerset
Duke of Suffolk
Duke of Buckingham
Lord Clifford
Young Clifford, his son
Earl of Salisbury
Richard Neville, Earl of Warwick, son of the Earl of Salisbury
Lord Scales
Lord Say
Sir Humphrey Stafford
William Stafford, his brother
Sir John Stanley
Sir William Vaux
Walter Whitmore, a pirate
Margery Jourdain, a witch

John Hume and John Southwell, two priests
Roger Bolingbroke, a conjuror
Thomas Horner, an armourer
Peter, Horner's man
Clerk of Chatham
Mayor of St Albans
Saunders Simpcox, an imposter
Wife to Simpcox
Alexander Iden, a Kentish gentleman
Jack Cade, a rebel
George Bevis, John Holland, Dick the butcher, Smith the weaver, Michael, etc, followers of Cade
Lords, Ladies, Attendants; Petitioners, Aldermen, a Herald, a Beadle, a Sheriff, a Lieutenant, a Shipmaster, a Master's Mate, two Gentlemen (prisoners with Suffolk), Matthew Goffe, a Spirit raised by Bolingbroke, Officers, Citizens, Prentices, Falconers, Guards, Soldiers, Messengers

**THE SCENE**
England

# SYNOPSIS

Here the main theme is York's gradual rise to power; in the middle is Jack Cade's mob-law rebellion. The Quarto of 1594 puts it all in the title: "The First Part of the Contention betwixt the two famous Houses of Yorke and Lancaster, with the death of the good Duke Humphrey: And the banishment and death of the Duke of Suffolke, and the Tragicall end of the proud Cardinall of Winchester, with the notable Rebellion of Jacke Cade: And the Duke of Yorkes first claime unto the Crowne."

York (Act I), in the speech beginning "Anjou and Maine are given to the French", vows "when I spy advantage" to claim the crown. The peers have split into their factions. The Duchess of Gloucester, the Lord Protector's thrusting wife, attempts to learn the future from a "conjuror" and a witch and is arrested for treason. She is banished (Act II) to the Isle of Man after doing penance through London, barefoot and in a white sheet, and warning her honest husband of his enemies. The King, though believing the heavily assailed Gloucester to be honest, removes him from the Protectorship; he, too, is arrested (Act III) — York manages to implicate him in what is now the complete loss of France — and he is later murdered through the agency of Suffolk and of Cardinal Beaufort, who dies while confessing it.

York has gone to quell an Irish rising, leaving the ruffianly Jack Cade of Ashford (claiming to be John Mortimer, Richard II's heir) to begin a rebellion in and around London: this (Act IV) ends with a pardon to those who forsake Cade, and Cade's death in combat with Alexander Iden in a Kentish garden. Pirates, meanwhile, have murdered Suffolk who, in spite of Margaret, has been banished.

When York returns with his army (Act V) the Wars of the Roses begin in earnest: Henry, Margaret, Somerset, and old Clifford for Lancaster; Warwick and Salisbury for York and his sons. York, demanding the crown, wins the battle of St Albans where Clifford and Somerset are slain. "Sound drum and trumpets", cries Warwick, "and to London all;/And more such days as these to us befall!"

# IN PERFORMANCE

*Henry VI, Part 2*, the best of the plays, was rather more fortunate than Part 1 — not that this says much, as the adaptations and compressions were so mutilated. Edmund Kean (1817) had one of his less acclaimed nights as York in a version of the trilogy resting heavily on Part 2, entitled *Richard, Duke of York; or, The Contentions of York and Lancaster*, and obviously a frightful mess. Frank Benson did the play by itself at Stratford (1899, 1901, and — as part of the trilogy — in 1906). W.B. Yeats, writing about the so-called Stratford "Week of Kings" in 1901, called the chronicles (including Part 2) "a strange procession of kings and queens, of warring nobles, of insurgent crowds, of courtiers, and of people of the gutter." The mingling of the second half of Part 2 with Part 3 in the Barton trilogy was labelled *Edward IV*. (For other major productions, see Part 1, "In Performance".)

# CHIEF CHARACTERS

**Henry VI** Mature by now but better fitted to be a monk than to rule what Hazlitt described as "the bear-garden in uproar" of his England.

**Queen Margaret** The tigress testing her claws for the years ahead. Her line, "I stood upon the hatches in the storm" (III.2), might be an epigraph for the trilogy.

**Richard Plantagenet, Duke of York** The longest part in the play (380 lines): "Dogged York that reaches at the moon."

**Humphrey, Duke of Gloucester** Fourth son of Henry IV, the dismissed Lord Protector, the King's true friend.

**Earl of Salisbury** York says of him after St Albans: "That winter lion, who in rage forgets/Aged contusions and all brush of time" (V.3).

**Earl of Warwick** Richard Neville, a great landowner known to history as "Warwick the Kingmaker". Son of the Earl of Salisbury and husband of Anne Beauchamp, daughter of Richard Beauchamp, Earl of Warwick, to whose title he succeeded.

**Duke of Suffolk** A study in relentless arrogance.

**Cardinal Beaufort** "As stout and proud as if he were lord of all", but he has a frenzied death scene (III.3).

**Jack Cade of Ashford** Brutal Kentish rebel of an attempted civil war. "There shall be in England seven halfpenny loaves sold for a penny; the three-hoop'd pot shall have ten hoops, and I will make it felony to drink small beer" (IV.2).

# Henry VI, Part 3
## 1590–1

⚜ **THE CHARACTERS**

| | |
|---|---|
| King Henry VI | Lord Hastings |
| Queen Margaret | Lord Stafford |
| Edward, Prince of Wales | Sir John Mortimer and Sir Hugh |
| Louis XI, King of France |    Mortimer, uncles to the Duke of York |
| Duke of Somerset | Henry, Earl of Richmond, a youth |
| Duke of Exeter | Lady Grey, later Queen to Edward IV |
| Earl of Oxford | Lord Rivers, brother to Lady Grey |
| Earl of Northumberland | Sir William Stanley |
| Earl of Westmoreland | Sir John Montgomery |
| Lord Clifford | Sir John Somerville |
| Richard Plantagenet, Duke of York | Bona, sister to the French Queen |
| Edward, Earl of March, afterwards | A Son that has killed his father |
|    Edward IV | A Father that has killed his son |
| Edmund, Earl of Rutland | Tutor (to Rutland), Mayor of York, |
| George, later Duke of Clarence |    Lieutenant of the Tower, |
| Richard, later, Duke of Gloucester (the |    a Nobleman, Keepers, |
|    four sons to Richard Plantagenet) |    a Huntsman, Soldiers, |
| Duke of Norfolk |    Attendants, Messengers, |
| Marquess of Montague |    Watchmen, etc. |
| Earl of Warwick | |
| Earl of Pembroke | ⚜ **THE SCENE** |
| | England and, briefly, France |

# SYNOPSIS

Early in this masque of kings, Henry makes York his heir if he himself is allowed to reign undisturbed during his life, a hopeless provision. Queen Margaret, aided by young Lord Clifford, continues to fight on behalf of her son, Edward, Prince of Wales. At the Battle of Wakefield, Clifford kills York's youngest son, Rutland; York is taken prisoner, humiliated, and stabbed to death by Clifford and the devilishly mocking Margaret. Avenging him, his three other sons defeat the Lancastrians at Towton (Act III) where Clifford dies. King Henry, away from the battle and soliloquizing about the peace of country life as a shepherd ("O God, methinks it were a happy life/To be no better than a homely swain"), listens to the terrors of civil war symbolized in the laments of a son who has killed his father and a father who has killed his son (II.5).

The King escapes to the North; Edward, having ennobled his brothers as the Dukes of Clarence and Gloucester, makes for London and the crown. Henry is captured (Act

III) and sent to the Tower; Warwick, angered by Edward's decision to marry Lady Grey, joins Margaret, and (Act IV) releases and reinstates Henry and captures Edward. Promptly Edward escapes in his turn and Henry is sent back to imprisonment. Ultimately (Act V), Warwick is defeated and killed at Barnet; and Margaret, who has brought reinforcements from France ("Great lords, wise men ne'er sit and wail their loss") is taken at Tewkesbury, where York's sons stab the Prince of Wales to death. Richard, on his sanguinary way to the throne, kills Henry in the Tower ("He's sudden if a thing comes in his head," says Edward). Margaret is banished to France, and Edward IV has the last words. The child Henry, Earl of Richmond, who appears for a moment (IV.6) in a non-speaking part, is the future Henry VII who will conquer Richard at Bosworth Field.

# IN PERFORMANCE

This is the whole fury of civil war, a record of revenge. Part 3 (see *Henry VI, Part 1* "In performance") had full recognition only in the 20th century; the productions have shown how unwise it is to discount a play because it may not flash in the study. The Irish dramatist, Sean O'Casey, described the trilogy as "Battles, castles, and marching armies; kings, queens, knights, and esquires in robes today and in armour tomorrow, shouting their soldiers to the attack, or saying a last lone word before poor life gave out; of mighty men of valour joining this king and ravaging that one; of a king gaining a crown and a king losing it; of kings and knights rushing on their foes and of kings and captains flying from them."

"Here, I hope, begins our lasting joy" are Edward's last words. As they ceased in the Birmingham Repertory production of 1952, the sardonic Richard of Gloucester swept into the first soliloquy of *Richard III*, "Now is the winter of our discontent/ Made glorious summer by this sun of York." He had spoken barely half a dozen lines when the offstage noises of bells and cheering blurred his words, the lights dimmed, and the curtain fell. Exceptionally, Part 3 was given a stand-alone production as *Henry VI: The Battle for the Throne*, directed by Katie Mitchell, for the RSC in its studio theatre, The Other Place, in 1994. Sombre and earnest, it reflected contemporary struggles in its exploration of the evils of Civil War; ironically, the "throne" was a small wooden chair.

# CHIEF CHARACTERS

**Henry VI** A wise man in the wrong place. Harried across his realm during the alarums of the war, he is finally killed by Richard in the Tower ("O, God forgive my sins and pardon thee!").

**Queen Margaret** The brave but pitiless woman for whom York, in his extremity (I.4), cannot find curses enough. "She-wolf of France, but worse than wolves of France", he cries to her. And again: "O tiger's heart wrapp'd in a woman's hide", a phrase that the dramatist Robert Greene, who attacked Shakespeare (1592) in a work written on his deathbed, parodied as "Tiger's heart wrapt in a Player's hide".

**Richard, Duke of York** Captured at last at Wakefield and stabbed to death after being reviled by Margaret, who gives him a cloth dipped in his young son's blood.

**Edward IV** York's eldest son, the former Earl of March. "The wanton Edward", says Margaret (I.4).

**Richard** York's son, who becomes Duke of Gloucester and will soon be King Richard III. A hunchback with a withered arm, who declares himself able to "set the murderous Machiavel to school".

**Earl of Warwick** Margaret calls him "proud setter up and puller down of kings" (III.3). The longest part, 443 lines.

**Lord Clifford** The "Young Clifford" of Part 2. He kills York's son, Rutland (I.3), "Thy father slew my father; therefore, die"; mocks and stabs the helpless York, crowned by Margaret with paper (I.4); and dies at Towton (II.6), "Here burns my candle out; ay, here it dies,/Which, whiles it lasted, gave King Henry light".

# Richard III
## 1592–3

 **THE CHARACTERS**

King Edward IV

Edward, Prince of Wales, son to the King, afterwards

Edward V

Richard, Duke of York, son to the King

George, Duke of Clarence, brother to the King

Richard, Duke of Gloucester, brother to the King, afterwards Richard III

Elizabeth, Queen to Edward IV

Duchess of York, mother to Edward IV, Clarence and Gloucester

Lady Anne, widow of Edward, Prince of Wales (son to Henry VI), afterwards married to Duke of Gloucester

A young son of Clarence (Edward, Earl of Warwick)

A young daughter of Clarence (Margaret Plantagenet, Countess of Salisbury)

Margaret, widow of Henry VI

Henry, Earl of Richmond, afterwards Henry VII

Cardinal Bourchier, Archbishop of Canterbury

Thomas Rotherham, Archbishop of York

John Morton, Bishop of Ely

Duke of Buckingham

Duke of Norfolk

Earl of Surrey, his son

Earl of Oxford

Anthony Woodville, Earl Rivers, brother to Edward's Queen Elizabeth

Marquis of Dorset and Lord Grey, the Queen's sons

William, Lord Hastings

Lord Stanley, called also Earl of Derby

Lord Lovel

Sir Thomas Vaughan

Sir Richard Ratcliff

Sir William Catesby

Sir James Tyrrel

Sir James Blount

Sir Walter Herbert

Sir Robert Brakenbury, Lieutenant of the Tower

Sir William Brandon

Christopher Urswick, a priest

Lord Mayor of London

Sheriff of Wiltshire

Hastings, a pursuivant

Tressel and Berkeley, gentlemen attending on Lady Anne

Ghosts of Richard's victims; Lords, Gentlemen, and Attendants; Priest, Scrivener, Page, Bishops, Aldermen, Citizens, Soldiers, Messengers, Murderers, Keeper

 **THE SCENE**

England

# SYNOPSIS

The First Quarto (1597) summarizes the play: "The Tragedy of King Richard the Third, Containing, His treacherous Plots against his brother Clarence: the pittiefull murther of his innocent nephewes: his tyrannical usurpation: with the whole course of his detested life, and most deserved death."

Shakespeare has no more dramatic opening than that of "Richard Duke of Gloucester, *solus"*. Today, a society exists to clear Richard's name and to prove that historians (especially Sir Thomas More in a section of Halle's chronicle) vilified him in the Tudor cause. Still, little can soften the impact of Shakespeare's blazing melodrama, and the first scene when Richard limps downstage to reveal himself in a soliloquy that begins, "Now is the winter of our discontent/Made glorious summer by this sun of York", and goes on to an unflinching resolve, "I am determined to prove a villain/And hate the idle pleasures of these days." Richard has to dispose of the six people between him and the throne when his dying brother, Edward IV, has gone. When he takes the crown, he has removed only one of them: the others he will deal with later.

First comes the dissimulation with his elder brother, the Duke of Clarence. By playing on Edward's fears he has Clarence sent to the Tower. Having seen this done and affected great concern ("I will deliver you"), he meets the bearers of the coffin of Henry VI (the King he murdered), followed by Henry's daughter-in-law, Lady Anne, whose husband he and his brothers had killed at Tewkesbury. Out of mischief or masochism, or both, he woos her over the coffin. She yields, and Richard gloats: Next, he stirs trouble at court while the former Queen Margaret — who, unhistorically, still prowls about — releases some of her fiercest invective: "Thou elvish-mark'd, abortive, rooting hog", "That bottled spider", "This poisonous hunchback'd toad." Clarence, by Richard's order (and despite a royal pardon), is murdered in the Tower and his corpse pushed into a butt of malmsey (sweet wine).

Overwhelmed by Clarence's death, King Edward dies (Act II); the young Prince of Wales is to be brought from Ludlow. By then Richard and his associates, notably Buckingham, have begun to direct affairs as they wish. When the Prince arrives (Act III) he and his younger brother, the Duke of York, are "lodged" in the Tower, presumably until the coronation. Various men of the Queen's party, dangerous to Richard, are executed, among them at a few minutes' notice the rash Lord Hastings. Buckingham, primed, gets the Lord Mayor and citizens of London to urge an apparently unwilling Richard to accept the throne. Once crowned (Act IV), Richard does all he can to safeguard himself, such as inciting Tyrrel to procure the death of the Princes in the Tower; forsaking his wife whose end is merely suggested ("Anne, my wife, hath bid this world good night"); and proposing, though this does not take place, to wed his niece, Edward IV's daughter Elizabeth. Buckingham revolts against him, raising an army; Henry, Earl of Richmond, lands from France. Richard, environed by enemies, must fight to keep the throne.

He goes to battle (Act V) when he meets the invader at Bosworth Field near Leicester.

Buckingham has been captured and executed; but Richmond is the first danger. After a night during which Richmond has fair dreams and Richard is harassed by the ghosts of his victims — conscience is a dominant theme in the play — he fights desperately ("A horse! A horse! My kingdom for a horse!") only to be defeated and killed. All ends with Richmond's decision to marry Elizabeth: "We will unite the white rose and the red,/ Smile heaven upon this fair conjunction."

# IN PERFORMANCE

John Dover Wilson called *Richard III* "a melodrama of genius". Where *Henry VI* has too little stage history, this play, completing the tetralogy, and a tremendous advance on its forerunners, has almost too much. The first edition (1597) was anonymous, but the next five were attributed to Shakespeare. The First Folio appeared in 1623. Since Burbage created Richard in Shakespeare's lifetime, hundreds of actors have been in thrall to one of the most theatrical parts ever written. True, too often these men would offer the mask without the mind, a grotesque strutting Crookback snatched from a child's history book. Shakespeare's *Richard III* may move to melodrama incarnadined; but its blood is the blood royal. The Red King is not simply an animated oleograph.

Curiously, between 1700 and 1850 the approved acting version was not Shakespeare's but a mosaic devised by the actor-dramatist Colley Cibber for production at Drury Lane. He was not much good himself; indeed, his performance was remembered, critically, as "the distorted Heavings of an unjointed Caterpillar". His text lived on; a few traces of Cibber survive, e.g. in the Olivier film (1955). He wrote himself into the records with his notorious accretions — such a "claptrap" as "Off with his head! — so much for Buckingham!" An astute, coarse melodramatist, his composite version, with scraps from other histories and a great many additions of his own, could hold a theatre, though a few purists regretted the loss of (for example) Margaret and the wailing women, Clarence and his dream, and Stanley.

Among English Richards, David Garrick (from 1741, date of his anonymous London début at Goodman's Fields) was always a Cibber man: something to be remembered when we see the Hogarth picture of Richard waking after the phantoms ("Despair and die!") have encircled him on the night before Bosworth. Garrick was splendidly relaxed, sardonic, and menacing: "He dwindles neither into the buffoon nor the brute", wrote a contemporary. It is said his performance was so powerful that women shrieked when he died. George Frederick Cooke (Covent Garden, 1800) displeased Charles Lamb, who spoke of him in a letter: "The lofty imagery and high sentiments and high passions of *Poetry* come black and prose-smoked from his prose Lips."

John Philip Kemble's main performances (1783, 1811) had a far more refined villainy, and that "little, keenly-visaged man", Edmund Kean (Drury Lane, 1814) a *diablerie* that terrified. Hazlitt, to whom we owe so much of what we know of Kean as an artist — it has been said, cynically perhaps, that the critic invented the actor — reported the final combat in which Kean "fought like one drunk with wounds". William Charles Macready, who played the Cibber version at Covent Garden (1819) with a sharp theatrical intelligence and unexpected lightness, came nearer to Shakespeare in 1821 with a text that contained not more than 200 Cibber lines; the production failed. Though he often acted Richard later, Macready was unhappy about it. (A frequently unnoticed line in his journal, 23 December, 1838, when managing Covent Garden, reads: "Looked through the unused plays of Shakespeare for *cementing* lines for Richard III.") Samuel Phelps, restoring the original text at Sadler's Wells (1845) — he would later go back to Cibber — was "careful and judicious". Charles Kean, equally careful, and anxiously spectacular, had no luck with Cibber (Princess's, 1854), though he called the text more "striking and spirit-stirring" than Shakespeare's. At the Lyceum (1877) Henry Irving reverted to Shakespeare, very badly cut; in his short-lived revival, 1896, he played (said Henry James) "on the chord dominant of the sinister-sardonic, flowered over... with the elegant-grotesque".

In the 20th century, Robert Atkins, during various Vic seasons (1915, 1921, and 1923), had what James Agate called a "quiet ferocity": he diminished the man by acting him as an upstart instead of a princely usurper. A finer portrait was Baliol Holloway's pictorial, grimly royal devil (Old Vic, 1925; New, 1930). Donald Wolfit (Strand, 1941) offered a study in scarlet, never entirely melodrama, though he could verge on it.

Laurence Olivier's performance for the Old Vic company at the New Theatre (1944) was one of the major classical occasions of the century. Outwardly a limping panther, there was no lameness in his mind. Pale, lankly black-haired, evilly debonair, he preserved Richard's pride; he had a glittering irony, a frightening rage. History records the outflung gesture at "Set the murderous Machiavel to school", one of the lines (*Henry VI, Part 3*, III.2) inserted in the first soliloquy of the Old Vic text, the malice of the "giving vein", the swoop back to the throne at "Is the chair empty?", the strangled sobbing at "There is no creature loves me" and the doom in the distorted face on the lost field at Bosworth. Shaw had said (1896), when criticizing Irving: "The attempt to make a stage combat look as imposing as Hazlitt's description of the death of Edmund

Kean reads, is hopeless. If Kean were to return to life and do the combat for us, we should very likely find it as absurd as his habit of lying down on a sofa when too tired or too drunk to keep his feet during the final scenes." But when he wrote this Shaw was nearly half a century too soon for Olivier's combat at the New in 1944.

Ian Holm (*The Wars of the Roses*, Stratford/Aldwych, 1963–4), played a not particularly demonic Richard playing the "power game". Alan Howard was Richard III and Richard II on alternate nights at Stratford (1980). Antony Sher's grotesque villain (Stratford/Barbican, 1984–5) has thrilled audiences; the South African actor kept a diary of the role, published later as *The Year of the King*. Anton Lesser was Richard in the RSC's *The Plantagenets* (Stratford/Barbican 1988–9), directed by Adrian Noble. Richard Eyre directed Ian McKellen at the National Theatre (1990). More recently, Simon Russell Beale's triumphant Richard, directed by Sam Mendes, was darkly comic (Stratford, 1992).

The United States, where Cibber was long popular, has had several eminent Richards. Edwin Booth, son of the English-born Junius Brutus Booth, made his name with a potent performance (1852). He developed his Richard over the years and restored Shakespeare's text to New York in 1876. As late as 1889 (in London; later in the United States) the American tragedian, Richard Mansfield, was remembering Cibber, beginning in *Henry VI, Part 3* and omitting Margaret: the portrait had a closely graduated malignancy shadowed by rising fear.

Robert Mantell (1904) kept to Cibber; John Barrymore (1920), using the Mansfield text, was a man spiritually warped, but of searching intellect; Walter Hampden (1934) retained "Off with his head! — So much for Buckingham!" and Hume Cronyn (Minneapolis, 1965) gave an almost "black-comedy" treatment for Tyrone Guthrie. In July 1953, also for Guthrie, Alec Guinness — at the opening festival in Stratford, Ontario — was a dagger in the heart from his first appearance. The press called it "the most exciting night in the history of Canadian theatre".

## IN OTHER TERMS

Laurence Olivier's film performance (1955), dominating though it was in a production with a steady insistence on betrayal, could not match his Richard in the theatre. Margaret had been cut, but a silent personage, not in Shakespeare's cast list, was Jane Shore, Edward IV's mistress, whom the extrovert Hastings annexes. John Burrell had her on stage — "decorative but dumb" said *Punch* — in his production for Olivier (1944). Jane Shore has arrived on other occasions, notably Stratford (1970). 1996 was a good year for the play. Al Pacino's film *Looking for Richard* documented his personal fascination with it. Richard Loncraine collaborated with Ian McKellen, a Hitlerish Richard, in a brilliantly inventive, heavily politicized film indebted to Richard Eyre's National Theatre production which suggested many parallels with modern times. And at the RSC, David Troughton played Richard as a psychotic jester in Steven Pimlott's production.

# CHIEF CHARACTERS

**Richard, Duke of Gloucester (King Richard III)** Misshapen in body as in mind, but facially handsome and sinister. After Hamlet, the longest part in Shakespeare (1,164 lines).

**Lady Anne** Daughter-in-law of Henry VI; married to Richard after the wooing over the coffin (I.2). She vanishes from the play after she has been crowned Queen, though her end is mentioned meaningly and there is a salient passage (IV.2) when Richard says to Catesby: "Give out/That Anne, my Queen, is sick and like to die." In one post-war production at Oxford University, Richard said this in Anne's hearing.

**Queen Margaret** "Foul, wrinkled witch" (Richard, I.3); "Remember, Margaret was a prophetess" (Buckingham, V.I). Still at court, she acts as a dark chorus, especially in I.3 and IV.4 ("Here in these confines slily have I lurk'd/To watch the waning of mine enemies"). Cut from the Cibber version.

**Duke of Buckingham** "The deep-revolving, witty Buckingham" (IV.2) who helps Richard to the throne, who is warned by the malice of the "giving vein" speech, and who is captured and executed just too early for his revenge. The second-longest part: 361 lines.

**George, Duke of Clarence** Cut from the Cibber text. Valued for his narrative of the dream in the Tower when the dead Prince of Wales — this is a haunted play — cries to him: "Clarence is come — false, fleeting, perjur'd Clarence,/That stabb'd me in the field by Tewkesbury." William, Lord Hastings Incautious extrovert Lord Chamberlain, whose support of Edward's "heirs in true descent" leads to his sudden death.

**Sir James Tyrrel** The "discontented gentleman" who obtains the murder of the Princes. He speaks the soliloquy (IV.3), quoting one of the murderers who described the children as they lay in each other's arms: "Their lips were four red roses on a stalk,/ Which in their summer beauty kiss'd each other." In Richard Mansfield's revival there was a suggestion that after reporting to Richard, Tyrrel had been murdered: a commotion (off) and a horrified, smothered cry.

**Henry, Earl of Richmond** (afterwards King Henry VII). Richmond fulfills Henry's prophecy in *Henry VI, Part 3*, IV.6; he is the Tudor equivalent of St George destroying the dragon. In the Old Vic/New Theatre programme for the Olivier first night, a collector's piece now, Richmond was described, remarkably, as "later King Edward VII".

**Ghosts** In his tortured dream on the night before Bosworth they urge Richard to "despair and die" and Richmond, in his quiet sleep, to "live and flourish".

---

# Titus Andronicus
## 1593–4

⚜ **THE CHARACTERS**
Saturninus, son to the late Emperor of Rome, afterwards Emperor
Bassianus, his brother
Titus Andronicus, a noble Roman
Lavinia, daughter to Titus Andronicus
Lucius, Quintus, Martius and Mutius, sons to Titus
Marcus Andronicus, Tribune of the People and brother to Titus
Young Lucius, a boy, son to Lucius
Publius, son to Marcus Andronicus
Sempronius, Caius, Valentine, kinsmen to Titus

Aemilius, a noble Roman
Tamora, Queen of the Goths
Alarbus, Demetrius, Chiron, sons to Tamora
Aaron, a Moor beloved of Tamora
A Nurse, a Black Child, a Captain, a Messenger, a Clown (simple peasant), Romans, Goths, Senators, Tribunes, Officers, Soldiers, Attendants

⚜ **THE SCENE**
Rome and the neighbourhood

---

## SYNOPSIS

Two sons of the late Roman Emperor, Saturninus (the elder) and Bassianus, strive to succeed him, but Titus Andronicus, veteran general triumphant against the Goths, is chosen. He has just returned with his prisoners: Tamora, Queen of the Goths, her sons, and Aaron, her Moorish paramour. Heedless of entreaty, Titus orders her eldest son, Alarbus, to be sacrificed to appease the spirits of his own dead sons. He refuses the crown, urging the choice of Saturninus, to whom he gives his daughter Lavinia and yields his Gothic prisoners. Bassianus, secretly pledged to Lavinia, runs off with her; Saturninus, to curb the influence of Titus, announces that he will marry Tamora, who tells him to remain silent while she plans revenge upon the Andronici.

In a rush of events (Act II), Tamora's sons, Demetrius and Chiron, kill Bassianus during a hunt in the forest. They rape Lavinia, cut off her hands and cut out her tongue. Meanwhile, Aaron manages to implicate the sons of Titus in the murder of Bassianus. They are sentenced to death (Act III), and another son, Lucius, is banished. Titus, already overcome by the plight of Lavinia, is tricked into losing his hand as fruitless ransom for his sons.

While Lucius is raising a revenging army among the Goths, the mutilated Lavinia (Act IV), by the manipulation of a staff in the sand, accuses Chiron and Demetrius. Titus behaves like a madman ("Is not this a heavy case?" asks Marcus), despatching messages to the gods to redress his wrongs.

Tamora has had a black child by Aaron, who removes it for safety; captured by the Gothic army on its way, under Lucius, to attack Rome, he tells the whole story (Act V). Tamora, seeking to persuade Titus — whom she regards merely as crazed — to recall Lucius, has come to him dressed as Revenge, with her two sons as Murder and Rape. Having promised to invite "the Empress and her sons" and Saturninus, with Lucius, to a feast, Titus — who has seen through the charade — later kills Chiron and Demetrius and at the banquet serves their flesh baked in a pie. The end is a frenzy in which Lavinia, Tamora, Titus and Saturninus all die. Lucius becomes Emperor and after sentencing Aaron to be buried breast-deep and starved to death, resolves — not too soon — "to order well the state."

# IN PERFORMANCE

When London's Royal Court Theatre revived *The London Cuckolds*, a Restoration farce by Edward Ravenscroft, in 1979, no one remarked on another part of Ravenscroft's record. A barrister-dramatist, competent in the cuckoldry-based jests of the period's uninhibited theatre, he succumbed to the prevailing vice of adapting Shakespeare. The play he chose (acted in 1678) was one of the least-regarded, the tragedy of *Titus Andronicus*, which he claimed to have constructed from "rather a heap of Rubbish than a Structure".

Shakespeare's tragedy was much admired in its day, though in 1614 Ben Jonson observed that anyone who swore *Jeronimo (The Spanish Tragedy)* or *Andronicus* were the best plays yet must be a man "whose judgement has stood still these five and twenty, or thirty, years". *Titus Andronicus* may have been suggested by the Roman Seneca's *Thyestes* and *Troades*, Ovid's *Metamorphoses*, and a chapbook (discovered in 1936) of which only an 18th-century version exists. For a long time scholars, who have disagreed about dates and details, refused to think that Shakespeare could have written so horrific a play, an exercise in the sensational (more than a dozen violent deaths) that resembled the Senecan "tragedies of blood". Today there is little reason to believe that the drama is not Shakespeare's own, though George Peele, especially for Act I, has his supporters.

The play is to be acted rather than read. Even so, various secondary productions have failed to burnish a text that at Stratford (1955) needed the combined gifts of Peter Brook (director) and Laurence Olivier. A great actor is an alchemist; few — Betterton during the Restoration could have been one — have yet attempted Titus. Ravenscroft's version, which until its last frightful scene did not deviate as much from Shakespeare as the adaptor promised, was done now and then during the first quarter of the 18th century (James Quin often an applauded Aaron). Afterwards, silence until a black actor, Ira Aldridge, "the African Roscius", appeared in 1852 and 1857 at the Britannia Theatre, Hoxton, a flaring old melodrama house in East London. In what was mainly Aldridge's own highly emasculated text, Aaron — reasonably in the circumstances — became "a noble and lofty character." Certainly Aldridge did not use Ravenscroft's ferocious climax where the Moor is racked, the heads and hands of Tamora's sons hang on the wall and their bodies put "in chairs in bloody linen", Tamora stabs her black child ("Give me the child, I'll eat it," cries Aaron), Saturninus expires in horror, and Aaron is put to death on stage by racking and burning.

Shakespeare's text, directed by Robert Atkins, returned in 1923 (Old Vic; tercentenary of the First Folio) with such expert players as Wilfrid Walter, George Hayes, Ion Swinley and Florence Saunders: a gallant experiment remembered for Hayes as Aaron, his diabolism and the sudden moment of tenderness for his infant son. He and Walter had the same parts on BBC radio (1953), a period when everything for *Titus Andronicus* began to happen at once; there was a Marlowe Society revival at Cambridge, one that tried to show how humanity and retribution balanced sadism and terror; and in the summer of 1955, on the Stratford stage at last, the play re-entered the professional repertory. Peter Brook had organized the text, and its final succession of murders (V.3), so that his company could let drive without being deflected by derisive laughter. The grimness remained: at the same time Brook imposed a formalized dignity on these strong, uncomplicated emotions. Just as Lear was identified with the storm in his mind, Titus was identified with the sea, his constant image: "I *am* the sea; look, how her sighs do flow." The actor reached a meridian none could have divined from the printed word. Brook's *musique concrète* intensified the atmosphere. His production, which toured Europe during 1957 — *"un spectacle stupéfiant"* they called it in Paris — was revived that year in the vast cavern of the now vanished Stoll Theatre, London.

No further attempt approached this, though Barbara Jefford was a powerful Tamora (Old Vic, 1957), Derek Jacobi a consistent Aaron (Birmingham Repertory, 1963), and John Wood's vicious Saturninus fortified a Stratford/Aldwych revival, 1972–3. A misguided effort to perform the tragedy on a staircase-set (Round House, London, 1971) had an inadequate cast.

*Titus Andronicus* has twice been part of a double bill: in the 1960s it was paired disastrously with *The Comedy of Errors* at the Old Vic, and, also unsuccessfully, with *The Two Gentlemen of Verona* — both heavily cut and sharing the same cast (Stratford, 1981). Even more revelatory than Brook with Olivier was Deborah Warner's Swan Theatre production (1987) which showed that the complete text can be brilliantly successful, and utterly harrowing, when directed with full awareness of its complex ironies. Brian Cox was a fully-rounded Titus, and Donald Sumpter showed that Marcus Andronicus's long speech (omitted by Brook) reacting to the sight of the raped and mutilated Lavinia (Sonia Ritter) can be profoundly moving when spoken with full appreciation of its stylized eloquence. Bill Alexander directed the play at Stratford in 2003 with David Bradley as a lean and hungry Titus.

In the United States a version by N.H. Bannister (1839), "altered into a beautiful play" said a local critic, ran four nights in Philadelphia. It has twice been produced as part of the New York Shakespeare Festival: Joseph Papp presented it in 1967, and the Riverside Shakespeare Company performed it in 1988. Julie Taynor's off-Broadway production for Theatre for a New Audience (1994) developed into her splendid film.

## IN OTHER TERMS

The only picture we have of an Elizabethan play in its own setting is in a manuscript at Longleat, Wiltshire, home of the Marquess of Bath. It is a pen-and-ink drawing of Tamora apparently pleading before Titus; the chief characters are in Roman dress, the minor ones in contemporary Elizabethan costume.

The BBC Shakespeare film was notable. Sensitively directed by Jane Howell in 1985, the play brought the BBC television series to a notable conclusion; the action was seen through the eyes of Young Lucius, a device also used in Julie Taymor's astonishing film of 2000 (astonishing both in technique and in having been made at all) which, starring Anthony Hopkins and Jessica Lange (Tamora), introduced the play to previously undreamt-of audiences with brilliant inventiveness as a decadent and horrifying fantasy.

# CHIEF CHARACTERS

**Titus Andronicus** Laurence Olivier turned the "sea" speech (III.1) into a great moment of the modern repertory. Elsewhere there are fine phrases among the fustian: "What fool hath added water to the sea,/Or brought a faggot to bright-burning Troy?" (III.1) The longest part: 715 lines.

**Saturninus** An almost Neronic voluptuary.

**Marcus Andronicus** The play is full of classical allusion. No doubt the Elizabethans, who did not think it odd to watch bear-baiting on the South Bank while lute music drifted over the Thames, would have seen nothing strange when Lavinia's uncle addressed the lopped and ravished girl in a stream of classical conceits instead of hurrying a surgeon to her.

**Tamora** The evil queen and empress, whom Aaron calls "this goddess, this Semiramis, this nymph", has one unexpectedly evocative speech in the forest, "The birds chant melody on every bush" (II.3). She is an involuntary cannibal in the final feast.

**Aaron Tamora's Moorish lover** ("your swarth Cimmerian") is a full-scale villain, with a passage of true affection for his black child. He could be a forerunner of Iago: "If one good deed in all my life I did,/I do repent it from my very soul" (V.3).

Lavinia Brook merely hinted at her mutilation. Thus she appeared (II.4) holding up her arms from which long ribbons of brilliant red velvet fell and wavered.

# The Comedy of Errors
## 1594 (or earlier)

 **THE CHARACTERS**
Solinus, Duke of Ephesus
Aegeon, a merchant of Syracuse
Aemilia, wife to Aegeon, and Abbess at
   Ephesus
Antipholus of Ephesus, Antipholus
   of Syracuse, twin brothers, sons of
   Aegeon and Aemilia
Dromio of Ephesus, Dromio of
   Syracuse, twin brothers and
   attendants on the Antipholus twins
Adriana, wife to Antipholus
   of Ephesus
Luciana, her sister

Luce, kitchenmaid to Adriana (also
   called Nell)
Angelo, a goldsmith
Balthazar, a merchant
A Courtesan
Pinch, a schoolmaster
First Merchant, friend to Antipholus of
   Syracuse
Second Merchant, to whom Angelo is
   a debtor
Gaoler, Officers, Headsman, Attendants

 **THE SCENE**
Ephesus

# SYNOPSIS

Aegeon, a veteran merchant of Syracuse, is in distress in Ephesus, his town's implacable enemy. Any Syracusian seen in Ephesus will be executed unless he can pay a ransom of a thousand marks. Aegeon's goods, at the highest rate, cannot reach a hundred marks. Then why has he risked the penalty? He explains to the Duke (sympathetic, but unable to break the law), that long before, at Epidamnum, where he had gone on business, his wife had borne him "two goodly sons,/And, which was strange, the one so like the other/As could not be distinguished but by names." Strangely, at that same hour and in the same inn, a peasant woman had given birth to indistinguishable twins whom Aegeon had bought so that they could attend as slaves upon his sons. But on the way home their vessel was shipwrecked; he was separated from his wife, one of his twins and one of the peasant boys, and heard no more of them. When the other twins were eighteen they asked to go in search of their lost brothers. They did not return, and Aegeon, alone, had spent five years looking for them, coming at last to Ephesus and his apparent fate unless, at the day's end, he could make up the ransom.

The second scene introduces the wanderers who happen to have arrived, unknown to him, at the same time as Aegeon. Very soon, Antipholus and Dromio of Syracuse are involved in a furious sequence of misunderstandings and false identifications with Antipholus and Dromio of Ephesus. (Oddly, four people but only two names.) Throughout the piece — which observes the unities of action, time and place — A is always being mistaken for B and C for D. Shakespeare keeps it up with fantastic ingenuity until (in Act V.1) when the plot seems impossible to disentangle, an abbess emerges from the priory in mid-Ephesus and reunites Aegeon and Aemilia. Within a short scene everything is more or less explained; and the Abbess invites the baffled Duke, "To go with us into the abbey here,/And hear at large discoursed all our fortunes."

# IN PERFORMANCE

This is both the shortest of the plays (1,777 lines) and the most crowded. Shakespeare probably wrote the play before 1594, taking much of his plot from the *Menaechmi* by the Roman dramatist Plautus and a little from the *Amphitruo*. To complicate things he doubled slaves as well as masters. The play is necessarily farcical in plot, but it should not be underrated in the scamped and scurrying treatment it has often had. Few audiences will be patient enough to look beneath the surface; in performance, alas, *The Comedy of Errors* is always likely to be a director's punch-ball.

The earliest recorded production is one during a Christmas revel, a night of chaos at Gray's Inn on 28 December, 1594; maybe the play was commissioned for this occasion. It is set in Ephesus because the city was deemed to be the home of sorcerers and cheaters ("This town is full of cozenage", I.2); because it was the centre of the cult of Diana, goddess of childbirth; and because (some propose, though this is arguable) it is relevant to remember Paul in the *Epistle to the Ephesians*: "Wives, submit yourselves unto your own husbands, as to the Lord." (Shakespeare would later have something to add to this in *The Taming of the Shrew*.)

Not many have made even such a unity of the piece as Komisarjevsky did during an otherwise poor season at Stratford in 1938. His method was broad enough, operatic and balletic, the men in plumed pink bowler hats, the women in farthingales and carrying modern handbags. But with a large clock, its hands racing, always prominently in sight, Komisarjevsky did insist upon the passage of time that is here so important.

There were 18th-century adaptations. Later, the incorrigible Frederick Reynolds (1819) treated it as an operatic exercise; Samuel Phelps (Sadler's Wells, 1855) brought back Shakespeare; the Irish brothers, Charles and Henry Webb, were peas-in-the-pod Dromios (Princess's, 1864, and tercentenary revival at Stratford); and at Gray's Inn (1895) William Poel put it on, barebones fashion, with his amateurs of the Elizabethan Stage Society ("Huge and quite unnecessary cuts in the last act," said the critic, William Archer).

Not much emerged from a cluster of 20th-century revivals: played straight, as at the Old Vic (1914); heavily cut, as a curtain-raiser to *The Bells*, in Henry Baynton's provincial productions (and Savoy, 1924), with the Dromios in black-face; scampered through (Open Air, 1949) in a double bill with *The Two Gentlemen of Verona*; in Edwardian dress (Court, 1952); shortened to an hour and put on before *Titus Andronicus* (Old Vic, 1957). Clifford Williams directed an elegant production in *Commedia dell'arte* style (Stratford, 1962 etc, also televized) which paid the play the compliment of treating it as the romantic comedy that it is. Alec McCowen and Ian Richardson played the twin masters with immaculate timing. Trevor Nunn reverted to the comic opera tradition in a song-and-dance version (Stratford/Aldwych, 1976–7, music by Guy Woolfenden), starring Judi Dench as an imperious Adriana, which won the Society of West End Theatre Managers' award for the best musical of 1976. It has circulated widely on video, mistitled *A Comedy of Errors*. Ian Judge ingeniously directed Desmond Barrit and Graham Turner, each playing a pair of twins, at Stratford (1991–2). Tim Supple was more respectful of the play's complexities in a sensitive production at The Other Place (1996).

The United States had popular 19th-century Dromios in the brothers Henry and Thomas Placide and (from 1878) William Henry Crane and Stuart Robson. The New York Shakespeare Festival staged the play in 1967. In 1987 it was presented by the Flying Karamazov Brothers and Avner the Eccentric in New York.

## IN OTHER TERMS

A light opera version by Julian Slade (composer of *The Boy Friend*) was televized in 1956 and staged two years later. A bouncing musical, *The Boys from Syracuse*, by Rodgers, Hart, and Abbott, ran in New York (1938–9, 1963–4), but failed in London at Drury Lane, 1963. Judi Dench's production in Regents Park, with Louise Gold and Jenny Galloway, won the Laurence Olivier Award for Outstanding Musical Revival of the Year (1991).

## CHIEF CHARACTERS

**Brothers Antipholus** The twin from Syracuse ties for the longest part with his brother's wife, Adriana (each has 264 lines). A fussily bland young man, he finds himself, as he thinks, in an extraordinary world of illusion. Antipholus of Ephesus is, reasonably, the more worried of the brothers, with his home life in confusion.

**Brothers Dromio** These quibbling slaves, like their masters, have — remarkably — the same names. Dromio of Syracuse (263 lines) has been the more popular figure, probably because of his close geographical description of Nell, the kitchenmaid

(III.2)): "She is spherical, like a globe; I could find out countries in her."

**Aegeon** His first-act exposition can be affecting if it is left alone, but any long speech of this kind, especially in a reputed farce, is a temptation to directors. He can be played desperately, and is not helped by the Duke's interruptions.

**Solinus** He can be acted (old style) as a kind of stern Theseus, or more usually today, with a baffled gravity: "Why, what an intricate impeach is this?" (V.1).

**Adriana** The jealous Ephesian wife, about whom the Abbess (V.1) says everything.

Luciana Her gentler sister.

**Aemilia** The redoubtable Abbess has lines that can be difficult before a modern audience: "Whoever bound him, I will loose his bonds,/And gain a husband by his liberty". The story of Aegeon and Aemilia, "nautically considered", is improbable, said John Masefield, poet and critic, who had been a sailor.

**A courtesan** Only 32 lines (IV.3)

**Luce** (also called **Nell**) Adriana's kitchenmaid. "Spherical, like a globe" (III.2).

**Pinch** The "conjuring" schoolmaster, "a needy, hollow-eyed, sharp-looking wretch,/A living dead man" (V.1). A part that has invited disastrous overplaying.

---

# The Taming of the Shrew
## 1593–4

 **INDUCTION**
Christopher Sly, a drunken tinker
A Hostess
A Lord
Page, Huntsmen, Players, Servants

 **THE CHARACTERS**
Baptista Minola, a wealthy citizen of
  Padua
Katharina (Kate), the Shrew; daughter to
  Baptista
Petruchio, a gentleman of
  Verona, a suitor to Katharina
Grumio, Curtis, servants to Petruchio

Bianca, sister to Katharina
Gremio, Hortensio, gentlemen of Padua,
  suitors to Bianca, Tranio, Biondello,
  servants to Lucentio
Vincentio, a merchant of Pisa
Lucentio, son to Vincentio, in love with
  Bianca
A Pedant
A widow; wife to Hortensio
Tailor, Haberdasher, Servants

 **THE SCENE**
Padua and Petruchio's country house

# SYNOPSIS

This is a play within another play that peters out after the Induction. There a nobleman and his hunting party discover a drunken tinker, Christopher Sly. They establish him in transient luxury, tell him that he is a lord who has been dreaming for fifteen years, and bring in a group of strolling players — "pomping folk", as they used to be known in one part of England — to entertain him. The comedy they present might take as its epigraph a line spoken to Sly by the young page disguised as his wife: "I am your wife in all obedience."

The scene here could be Warwickshire, but the play proper has an Italian setting. It is about the marriage and consequent taming of the shrewish Katharina, elder daughter of a wealthy Paduan, Baptista. No one wants her, but everyone wants her sister Bianca, who cannot be given in marriage until Kate is off her father's hands. Hence the excitement when a swaggering adventurer, Petruchio, appears, seeking a rich wife.

The contest for Bianca involves a battery of impersonations; the Petruchio/Kate story goes straight on, beginning (Act II) with a first meeting, angry on Kate's side, determined on her suitor's, and reaching a wedding day (Act III) when Petruchio, dressed with deliberate absurdity, carries off an unwilling bride to his country house near Verona. Here (Act IV) Petruchio contrives to keep Kate hungry, sleepless, and frustrated until she agrees to anything he says — and all "done in reverend care of her". Though Kate's agreement is severely tested on the homeward journey to Padua, the plot is resolved (Act V) when at a wedding feast for Bianca and her Lucentio — who have been married secretly — Kate lectures Bianca and another new bride on the whole duty of a wife.

# IN PERFORMANCE

Another play, *The Taming of a Shrew* (published 1594), may be either the source of Shakespeare's broad comedy or — and this is more probable — an imitation of the original text. In any event, modern directors, except those who do not use the Induction, usually tag on to the recognized play the last scene of *A Shrew* in which Sly, himself again, wakes outside the tavern and plans an experiment on his own wife: "I know now how to tame a shrew… I'll to my wife presently, and tame her, too, an if she anger me." The piece, which takes some hints (the Bianca plot) from the translation of an Italian comedy, has prospered down the years, though for a long time only in adaptations. One (1667) by a low comedian, John Lacy, vulgarized and called *Sauny the Scot*, had Grumio (Sauny) as the principal character. Samuel Pepys wrote in his diary (9 April 1667): "To the King's house, and there saw 'The Tameing of a Shrew', which hath some very good pieces in it, but generally is but a mean play." (Pepys could not follow Lacy's dialect.) David Garrick's three-act abbreviation, *Catherine and Petruchio* (1754), which cut the Induction and Bianca's wooing, had a longer life.

In fact, possibly the first return to Shakespeare's text was in 1844, when Benjamin Webster and J.R. Planché did the play at the Haymarket in neo-Elizabethan fashion, at that period astonishing. More than 40 years later (1888), the American Ada Rehan, the Kate of all time, came from New York to London's Gaiety Theatre in Augustin Daly's production (in 1893 this also opened the new Daly's Theatre). Ada Rehan's portrait, by Eliot Gregory, now hangs in the Picture Gallery at Stratford-upon-Avon; the Shrew, wearing a rose-coloured gown, stands with upflung head and folded arms, her eyes sparkling defiance. It was said of her after a Stratford appearance (1888): "Here is a girl with a fiery and unbridled temper… wrought to this pitch by uncongenial surroundings. She is a woman well worth taming."

Thenceforward the comedy was acted again and again in London and at Stratford. Oscar Asche, a massive Old Bensonian, doubled Petruchio with Sly (Benson himself had a trick of lopping the Induction) at the Adelphi (1904). Martin Harvey (Prince of Wales's, 1913), in a production that had been influenced by the German director, Max Reinhardt, established Sly permanently in the conductor's place — though here it was a carved stone seat — above the orchestra well, with his back to the audience. Laurence Olivier swooped through Kate while still a 14-year-old choirboy from All Saints, Margaret Street (1922). Edith Evans (Old Vic, 1925) was a tornado, far better than she would be in a West End revival (New, 1937) when the part was dissipated in mannerism. Inevitably, the play reached modern dress. During Barry Jackson's Court Theatre season (1928), Frank Pettingell played Sly as a vagabond who watched all night from a stage-box, with Laurence Oliver as the Lord in attendance; Petruchio (Ralph Richardson) addressed "Come on, in God's name!" to the starting-handle of a battered Ford. At Stratford (1939), in his last production there and by no means his best, Komisarjevsky relied on polychromatic artificiality. The stage was carnation and blue and citron and apple-green, the costumes were *Commedia dell'arte*-cum-Restoration, and Komisarjevsky provided a patchwork-quilt text with interpolated nonsense-songs.

Other performances include a rough-house, Crazy-Gang treatment at Stratford (1948); Peggy Ashcroft and Peter O'Toole (Stratford, 1960) in a romantic production (John Barton's) that, according to Robert Speaight, traced its pedigree from Chaucer and Langland; and Jonathan Miller's muted Chichester revival (1972), which seemed to study the power-structure in family life. As early as 1897 Bernard Shaw had said of Kate's last long speech "No man with any decency of feeling can sit it out in the company of a woman without being extremely ashamed of the lord-of-creation moral implied in the wager and the speech put into the woman's own mouth." And, since the 1960s, directors have been acutely aware of feminist issues, often brutalizing Petruchio, as in Charles Marowitz's adaptation *The Shrew*, in which he sodomized Kate, and in Michael Bogdanov's 1978 RSC production, in which Sly emerged from the audience, pushing aside a supposed usherette and smashed the picturesquely old-fashioned scenery to pieces before the play began. He was played by Jonathan Pryce, who later became a loutish Petruchio, but squirmed with embarrassment during Kate's speech of submission. Fiona Shaw was an initially neurotic Kate with Brian Cox as a virile Petruchio in a Stratford production in 1987. Vanessa Redgrave, who had taken over from Peggy Ashcroft in a revival of John Barton's production, returned to the role with Timothy Dalton at Theatr Clwyd, Mold (1988), in a production which transferred to London's Haymarket Theatre. In a full-blown return to romanticism, Gregory Doran directed Alexander Gilbreath and Jasper Britton in a brilliant Stratford production (2003, also seen in London and America) interestingly paired in the Swan with a no less enjoyable production of John Fletcher's *The Tamer Tamed*.

In North America, *Catherine and Petruchio* was staged in Philadelphia in 1766. Daly's Shakespearian text, with the Induction and Ada Rehan, first appeared in the United States, in New York, in 1887; in her time as Kate, Ada Rehan acted her unmatched Kate with many Petruchios, among them John Drew and George Clarke. Ellen Terry said in her diary that she had never seen the part done better by anyone except Ada Rehan. Later revivals included E.H. Sothern and Julia Marlowe's (1907, no Induction, Kate "a lovely fish-wife"); and the century's richest (Guild, New York, 1935), which had Alfred Lunt and Lynn Fontanne in relishing swirl, directed by Harry Wagstaff Gribble. More recently, a 1993 production by the Orange Coast Theatre, Los Angeles, billed as a cross between Le Cirque de Soleil and the Marx Brothers, was a gymnastic romp in a *Commedia dell'arte* style.

## IN OTHER TERMS

*Kiss Me, Kate* opened in New York in 1948, and in London in 1951. With score and lyrics by Cole Porter, it is a musical with Shakespearian echoes. Its best numbers include "Wunderbar", "Too Darned Hot", and the immortal "Brush up your Shakespeare".

Numerous revivals include one directed by Adrian Noble for the RSC (1987). The BBC television production (which regrettably omits the Induction) was soberly directed by Jonathan Miller with John Cleese as a subdued Petruchio. A silent film of *The Taming of the Shrew* was directed by D.W. Griffith as early as 1908. Mary Pickford and Douglas Fairbanks starred in a flamboyant film "with additional dialogue by Sam Taylor" which was issued in both silent and audible form. Franco Zeffirelli directed a picturesque free-for-all harking back to Garrick with Elizabeth Taylor and Richard Burton (1966).

# CHIEF CHARACTERS

**Christopher Sly** The drunken tinker of the Induction, "old Sly's son" from Barton-on-the-Heath ("Burton-heath" in the text), out to the south of Stratford, where Shakespeare had an uncle and aunt. Directors, often unsure what to do with Sly, sometimes cut the Induction altogether. In the text he vanishes after I.1, but today Sly often gets involved in the action; at the New (1937) Arthur Sinclair doubled him with the Pedant. Occasionally he has been doubled with Petruchio.

**Katharina** "The curst", the shrew, who is soon (in the modern theatre) in love with her tempestuous tamer, though she has to endure a good deal before the last speech (V.2), "Fie, fie, unknit that threatening, unkind brow", which today is often gently tongue-in-cheek.

**Petruchio** The flamboyant young man from Verona announces himself in the Paduan marriage market (I.2): "Wealth is burden of my wooing dance." He tells Baptista that he "woos not like a babe", and throughout he is the rulèr. His bullying and whip-cracking have lessened in recent years. Much the longest part (585 lines).

**Grumio** Petruchio's man, a comic servitor with a mind — and tongue — of his own.

**Biondello** Lucentio's second servant — the first is Tranio — has one show-piece, the headlong description (III.2) of Petruchio's arrival for the mad wedding, something spoken in as few breaths as possible.

**Gremio** Bianca's veteran suitor, a pantaloon-figure who is out of luck, has two good acting scenes — the bidding for Bianca with the disguised Tranio (II.1) and the description of the wedding ceremony (III.2).

**Tranio** The servant disguised as his master Lucentio, he produces a fine flourish in the contest with Gremio for Bianca (II.1).

**Bianca** Kate's apparently insipid younger sister who may be a shrew in embryo.

**A lord** He has, in the Induction, some of the most pictorial verse in the play, but he needs a sympathetic director to allow him to speak it.

For the rest, we can get some idea of the confusion from a stage direction (II.1) in a modern text: "Enter Gremio, with Lucentio, disguised as Cambio, in the habit of a mean man; Petruchio, with Hortensio disguised as Licio; and Tranio, disguised as Lucentio, with his boy Biondello bearing a lute and books."

# The Two Gentlemen of Verona
## 1594

**THE CHARACTERS**

Valentine and Proteus, the two Gentlemen of Verona
Speed, a clownish servant to Valentine
Julia, a lady of Verona loved by Proteus
Lucetta, Julia's waiting-woman
Antonio, father to Proteus
Panthino, servant to Antonio
Silvia, the Duke's daughter, loved by Valentine
Launce, a clownish servant to Proteus
Thurio, a foolish rival to Valentine
Duke of Milan, father to Silvia
Host of Julia in Milan
Sir Eglamour, agent for Silvia in her escape
Outlaws, Servants, Musicians

**THE SCENE**

Verona, Milan, a forest between Milan and Mantua

## SYNOPSIS

Valentine, seeking to be "tutor'd in the world", goes with his servant Speed from Verona to Milan, saying goodbye to his friend Proteus ("Cease to persuade, my loving Proteus;/Home-keeping youth have ever homely wits"). Presently, Proteus, enamoured of Julia (as she is of him), is also ordered by his father to leave for Milan. There (Act II) Valentine falls in love with the Duke's daughter, Silvia; when Proteus arrives they tell him that because the Duke prefers a wealthier suitor, Thurio, they propose to elope.

Proteus, himself infatuated with Silvia, informs the Duke, who (Act III) finds a rope ladder under Valentine's cloak and banishes him. He becomes (Act IV) leader of a highly selective band of outlaws. Julia, who has followed Proteus disguised as a boy, hears Thurio's musicians serenading Silvia with "Who is Silvia? What is she,/That all our swains commend her?" Proteus is listening and after Thurio has gone, he proclaims his love, which Silvia scorns, asking Sir Eglamour to conduct her to Valentine. Proteus, taking the disguised Julia ("Sebastian") as his page, sends a message to Silvia who again rejects him.

The Duke (Act V) pursues his escaping daughter and is captured by outlaws while she is rescued by Proteus. The watching Valentine attacks his treachery, then for a moment becomes all too magnanimous by giving up Silvia to him. Julia/Sebastian, swooning, reveals herself, the outlaws bring in the Duke who pardons them, and there is a correct pairing-off. Last line: "One feast, one house, one mutual happiness."

# IN PERFORMANCE

*The Two Gentlemen of Verona* is based, maybe indirectly, on *Diana*, a chivalrous and pastoral romance written in Spanish by a Portuguese (Jorge de Montemayor); this was the theme of a lost Elizabethan play. It is enough that the comedy of friendship and treachery, as we have it, is a Shakespearian notebook foreshadowing much to come. Herbert Farjeon, the critic, said rightly (1925) that we find in it hints for half a dozen later plays and the substance of some of the Sonnets. Apprentice-work, careless in its facts but undervalued, it can have a lyrical gaiety.

Apart from an "improvement" (Drury Lane, 1762), the first recorded revival was in 1784 at Covent Garden. The notorious Frederick Reynolds as usual puffed it out operatically (1821). William Charles Macready played Valentine — "imperfectly", he said — when he managed Drury Lane (1841). Ada Rehan "moved and spoke with imposing rhythmic grace" (Shaw) in a poor production by Augustin Daly (Daly's Theatre, 1895). Next, in April 1904, the young Granville-Barker (not hyphenated then) directed it at the Royal Court and even appeared as Speed, an arrangement made for the sake of what might, and did, follow — his famous sequence (1904–07) of mainly new plays by Shaw and others. The florid Beerbohm Tree invited William Poel, austere neo-Elizabethan zealot, to direct a few performances at His Majesty's in 1910; they came off well, for all Poel's oddities. Since then it has seldom been staged. Eric Porter's gusty idea of the Duke is now the most potent memory of a revival directed by Peter Hall (1960) at Stratford where ten years later Robin Phillips established the play in modern dress by a campus swimming-pool, a conception he repeated at Stratford, Ontario (1975). A double bill with *Titus Andronicus* (Stratford, 1981) — both heavily cut and with the same cast — was unsuccessful. David Thacker directed an intelligent version for the RSC in the Swan (1994) using costumes of the 1930s, with songs of the period by Cole Porter and others interpolated between the scenes. Edward Hall similarly showed that the play can work well in the intimate surroundings of the Swan in 1998.

Although the play has been little performed in North America, a version directed by Deborah Nitzberg opened the 1993 Los Angeles Shakespeare Festival.

# IN OTHER TERMS

A musical based on *The Two Gentlemen of Verona* and borrowing its name ran in New York in various versions (1971 — at first there was a character called Sir Brilliantine — and 1973); also Phoenix, London (1973), for a moderate run.

# CHIEF CHARACTERS

**Valentine** The more magnanimous of the two gentlemen, who in a sudden access of generosity yields Silvia to his rival, though not for long: "And that my love may appear plain and free,/All that was mine in Silvia I give thee" (V.4).

**Proteus** Certainly a better theatrical chance than Valentine, besides being the longest part (448 lines). His name is symbolic, yet (II.4) Valentine believes in him resolutely: "His years but young, but his experience old;/His head unmellowed, but his judgement ripe." Launce Servant to Proteus, is usually the night's favourite person because of his low-comedy monologues with his dog Crab.

**Speed** Valentine's servant. A part bristling with word-play. Acted, for business reasons, by the young Granville-Barker (see "In Performance").

**Thurio** Like Cloten in *Cymbeline* 15 or so years later, a foolish suitor who orders a song for his lady. Cloten's is an aubade, Thurio's a serenade, "Who is Silvia?" (IV.3), a lyric he would never have had the wit to write.

**Julia** The first Shakespearian heroine to be disguised as a page (Sebastian) — no trouble in an Elizabethan company. In her first scene, as herself and with her confidante Lucetta, she might be an early draft for Portia discussing the suitors with Nerissa. In II.7 she has the lyric passage, "The current that with gentle murmur glides".

**Silvia** "What light is light, if Silvia be not seen?/What joy is joy, if Silvia be not by?" (Valentine, III.1).

**Sir Eglamour** "Valiant, wise, remorseful, well accomplish'd" (IV.3). The knight, who helps Silvia to escape, is generally caricatured in the modern theatre because of one unhappy line (V.3), the Second Outlaw's observation, "Being nimble-footed, he hath outrun us." At Stratford in 1970 he was a scoutmaster.

**Outlaws** The outlaws in the forest scenes — "the frontiers of Mantua" — are sheer comic-opera.

# Love's Labour's Lost
## 1594–5

❀ **THE CHARACTERS**
Ferdinand, King of Navarre
Berowne, Longaville, Dumain, Lords
   attending on the King
Don Adriano de Armado, a fantastical
   Spaniard
Moth, Armado's page
Holofernes, a schoolmaster
Sir Nathaniel, a curate
Dull, a constable
Costard, a clown (peasant)

Jaquenetta, a country wench
A Forester
The Princess of France
Rosaline, Maria, Katharine, Ladies
   attending on the Princess
Boyet, Marcade, Lords attending on the
   Princess of France
Lords, Villagers, Attendants

❀ **THE SCENE**
Navarre

# SYNOPSIS

Ferdinand, King of Navarre, and three of his lords, have sworn to study for three years during which no woman shall come within a mile of them. They are swayed almost at once by the arrival (Act II) of the Princess of France, with three of her ladies, to discuss her father's debts to the King.

Costard, the clown, told (Act III) to deliver two letters, muddles them so that (Act IV) a letter from Armado, a courtier, to the village wench, Jaquenetta, is read to the Princess and her ladies, and a love sonnet from Berowne to Rosaline is read (for Jaquenetta) by Sir Nathaniel, the curate. Holofernes, the schoolmaster, tells the girl to show it to Ferdinand. She does so just when, in succession, the young men have caught each other reciting love-rhymes. Berowne, in an irresistible lyrical speech, claims that love belongs to study, that women's eyes are "the books, the arts, the academes,/That show, contain, and nourish all the world."

Presently (Act V) they meet the ladies — who have taken pains to trick them — in an unsuccessful mock-Russian entertainment. At length they are all settled, watching the masque of the Nine Worthies, arranged by Armado and Holofernes, when Marcade brings news to the Princess that her father has died. She and her ladies prepare to leave, having put their lovers on probation, with tasks for a year and a day before they can come together. But before departing they listen in the twilight to the villagers' songs of spring ("When daisies pied and violets blue") and winter ("When icicles hang by the wall") — the cuckoo and the owl.

# IN PERFORMANCE

*Love's Labour's Lost* (the plot is Shakespeare's own, probably based on a report of a French diplomatic mission to Aquitaine) comes to us as a young and zestful lyric comedy, reborn in the 20th century. It might be described in two lines from Berowne's famous outburst: "Subtle as Sphinx; as sweet and musical/As bright Apollo's lute, strung with his hair." Its narrative is negligible. We know that the four young men who have sworn to flout love will be immediately forsworn; besides the flashing raillery of the lovers we have the "singular and choice epitaphs" of the pedants and the fantastic Armado. A German writer called the play "excessively jocular"; it has never suited the Holofernes type of critic, who is content to search for lost topicalities. Again, in a snatch from the play, we can think of it as, in the language of Armado: "Some delightful ostentation, or show, or pageant, or antic, or firework" (V.1).

The play was acted before Queen Elizabeth at Christmas 1596 or 1597, and at the Earl of Southampton's house at Christmas 1605. There were apparently no revivals until the 19th century. Then (1839) Madame Vestris, who also played Rosaline, did an elaborate production at Covent Garden. Little else counted except a Sadler's Wells revival (1857) with Samuel Phelps as Armado, until Ion Swinley and George Hayes acted Berowne and Armado at the Old Vic in 1923; James Agate called it "a Watteau … of that significance in ordered beauty which unity alone can give".

From 1920 onwards, *Love's Labour's Lost*, "so picked, so spruce, so peregrinate" (as Holofernes more or less describes Armado, V.1), suddenly found its directors and its audiences. W. Bridges-Adams, a sustained admirer, did it at Stratford (1925), where there had been only two previous productions, and again (1934), now at the new Memorial Theatre before an immense oak tree, a permanent set for the park of Navarre. Tyrone Guthrie put it on at the Westminster (1932); and in another of his revivals (1936), Ernest Milton was a marvellous peacock of an Armado. Open Air Theatre audiences appreciated it under Robert Atkins; but it was not until 1946 that the comedy, destined for a happy efflorescence on any stage, had one of its three major revivals of the century.

This was at Stratford-upon-Avon, where no one argued about a production by Peter Brook, then 20 years old. That spring in Paris he had seen the first French *Love's Labour's Lost* for 30 years, a translation that seemed to anticipate Molière, Marivaux and Musset, with certain scenes changed and rewritten. By this time Brook had fixed on his own treatment. Like Agate (whom he had not read) he thought of Watteau: his production, pictorial, witty and rhythmical, never cast out the verse, and though some harlequinade-comedy was unexpected, the revival as a whole came as a valuable gift to Shakespearian theatre. Armado (Paul Scofield) was particularly fine — meditatively detached, with generations of grandees speaking in his resolute, fragile tones. Brook had a long and daring pause when, conceits and silken terms at an end, the messenger in Act V brought with his tidings of death the realities of life.

It seemed impossible to match this revival but Hugh Hunt (for the Old Vic at the New, 1949) achieved it in a production of great visual beauty, with a lakeside setting and costume designs (Berkeley Sutcliffe) inspired by the miniatures of Nicholas Hilliard and Isaac Oliver. Michael Redgrave's Berowne was in full flood, and Miles Malleson (Nathaniel) and Mark Dignam (Holofernes) were the most beguiling of their period, straight — one would have said — from Stratford-atte-Navarre. A third memorable production, John Barton's (Stratford/ Aldwych, 1978–9) had the benefit of an exquisite screen of autumnal trees by Ralph Koltai and Ruby Wax played a memorable Jaquenetta. Another very pretty production was Barry Kyle's for the RSC (1984–5) in which Kenneth Branagh played the King. Terry Hands directed the play for the RSC in 1990, with Ralph Fiennes as Berowne and Simon Russell Beale as the King. Ian Judge's four-men-in-a-boat production for the RSC (1993) set the play in an Oxbridge college on the eve of the First World War. Trevor Nunn brought similar resonances somewhat heavy-handedly to his beautifully designed National Theatre production (2003) starring Joseph Fiennes, in which the men sang the poems addressed to their ladies.

Stratford, Ontario, presented the comedy in 1961 and 1974. Oddly, the play was adapted in French as an alternative libretto for Mozart's opera *Cosi fan Tutte* in the 19th century. No less oddly, considering its obsession with language, there were five silent film versions. The BBC television version directed by Elijah Moshinsky (1984) set it in the 18th century. Kenneth Branagh's feature film (2000) is notable mainly for its enjoyable song-and-dance routines set to music by Cole Porter and others.

# CHIEF CHARACTERS

**Ferdinand** The graceful, mildly academic King of Navarre, who has a totally unworkable idea. "Necessity," says Berowne, "will make us all forsworn."

**Berowne** Most eloquent of the lords: the longest part (597 lines). Rosaline's description of him (II.1) might be Shakespeare's self-portrait: "A merrier man,/Within the limit of becoming mirth,/I never spent an hour's talk withal."

**Longaville** In love with Maria. His name and those of Berowne and Dumain are from commanders in the French civil war, 1589–93. The Ducs de Longueville and de Biron supported Henry of Navarre; the Duc de Mayenne opposed him.

**Dumain** In love with Katharine.

**Don Adriano de Armado** A "fantastical Spaniard" at court. His name echoes the Armada, still fresh in English minds. A difficult part, especially in the opening scene with Moth, the page. Hunters have suggested many Elizabethan originals for the part but these identifications are needless. Armado's language, his "mint of phrases", is in key with the affected "Euphuism" made fashionable by the dramatist, John Lyly (c1554–1606).

**Holofernes** The bristling village schoolmaster, all pedant, a man who cannot talk without unpeeling a Latin tag or pulling some curious word from the basket.

**Sir Nathaniel** Unforgettably acted by Miles Malleson (New, 1949), whose curate, a milky mouse with only a score of speeches, was one of the richest Shakespeare-comedy creations of the period.

**Dull** The village constable who will expand one day into Dogberry of *Much Ado*. "Thou hast spoken no word all this while," says Holofernes to him (V.1), and Dull replies: "Nor understood none neither, sir."

**Costard** Mildest of country youths. Pompey the Great in the masque. "If your ladyship would say, 'Thanks, Pompey,' I had done."

**Jaquenetta** The village hoyden.

**The Princess of France** Witty and responsible, she will be a distinguished Queen. Brook (1946) gave to her the final speech, "The words of Mercury are harsh after the songs of Apollo. You that way — we this way." In the text it is attributed to Armado, who generally delivers it, though it has also been given to Boyet.

**Rosaline** The "whitely wanton with a velvet brow" (III.1), possibly another projection of the Dark Lady of the Sonnets.

**Maria** The youngest of the Princess's ladies.

**Katharine** Has a passing moment of sadness (V.2).

**Boyet** Middle-aged and "honey-tongued" diplomatist.

**Marcade** The usually black-clad figure who brings the news of the King's death to the Princess of France. Three lines only, but a profoundly impressive entrance, often heightened — and especially in Brook's 1946 production — by a long pause before he speaks.

# Edward III
## 1594–6

**THE CHARACTERS**
**The English:**
King Edward III
Queen Philippa, his wife
Edward, Prince of Wales, their eldest son
The Earl of Salisbury
The Countess of Salisbury, his wife
The Earl of Warwick, the Countess's
   father
Sir William de Montague, Salisbury's
   nephew
The Earl of Derby
Sir James Audley
Henry, Lord Percy
John Copland, an esquire, later knighted
Lodowick, King Edward's secretary
Two Squires
A herald to King Edward from the
   Prince of Wales
Four heralds who bear the Prince
   of Wales' armour

**Allied with the English:**
Robert, Comte d'Artois and Earl of
   Richmond
Jean, Comte de Montfort and, later, Duc
   de Bretagne
Gobin de Grâce, a French Prisoner

**The French:**
Jean II, King of France

Prince Charles, Jean's eldest son, Duc de
   Normandie, the Dauphin
Prince Philippe, Jean's fourth son
The Duc de Lorraine
Villiers, a prisoner sent as an envoy by
   the Earl of Salisbury to the Dauphin
The Captain of Calais
Another French Captain
A mariner
Three heralds to the Prince of Wales
   from the King of France, the Dauphin
   and Prince Philippe
Six poor men, residents of Calais
Six supplicants, wealthy merchants and
   citizens of Calais
Five other Frenchmen
A Frenchwoman with two children

**Allied with the French:**
The King of Bohemia
A Polish captain
Polish and Muscovite soldiers

David II, King of Scotland
Sir William Douglas
Two Scottish messengers

**THE SCENE**
England and France

# SYNOPSIS

Based on Lord Berners's translation of Froissart's *Chronicles*, *The Reign of Edward III* dramatizes the opening of the Hundred Years' War, mingling them with a romance from Painter's *Palace of Pleasure*. King Edward sends his son, Prince Edward, to raise troops against France while himself seeking to subdue the rebellious Scots and to liberate the imprisoned Countess of Salisbury. Falling in love with her, he gets his servant Lodowick to write a love letter on his behalf (Act II). When she rejects him he commands her father, Warwick, to plead on his behalf. But she not only rejects the

King's advances but shows him the error of his ways. The over-confident French King and his sons (Act III) hear that the invading English have won a great naval battle and established themselves at Crécy. After much speechifying Prince Edward confronts the French. The King, hearing that his son is captured, insists that he must fend for himself; when the Prince enters in triumph his father knights him. Besieging Calais (Act IV) the King hears that King David of Scotland has been captured. Edward will sack the city unless six of its most prominent burghers humiliate themselves before him. They do so (Act V) and although Edward is reluctant to forgive them, his Queen, Philippa, successfully intercedes with him on their behalf. Prince Edward presents his father with the conquered French king's crown, and pays homage to his father.

# IN PERFORMANCE

Entered in the Stationers' Register in 1595, the play appeared in print anonymously the following year "as it hath been sundry times played about the City of London". From the 18th century onwards scholars have suspected that parts of it may have been written by Shakespeare. The most Shakespearian scenes have been thought to be those involving the Countess of Salisbury. The play is stronger on rhetoric than on either character or action, but along with much bombast there are fine passages of verse and tantalizing parallels with Shakespeare, most notably the occurrence of the last line of Sonnet 94, "Lilies that fester smell far worse than weeds." Towards the end of the 20th century, with the increasing recognition that Shakespeare collaborated at the beginning and end of his career, *Edward III* has been included in editions and occasionally performed. Among productions in America, Germany, and England, the most conspicuous has been by the RSC in their "Jacobethan" season (The Swan, 2002), with strong performances by David Rintoul and Jamie Glover as the King and Prince.

# King John
## 1594–6

### THE CHARACTERS

King John, of England

Prince Henry, his son; afterwards Henry III

Queen Elinor, widow of Henry II of England and mother of King John

Arthur, Duke of Bretagne, son of Geoffrey, late Duke of Bretagne, elder brother of King John

Constance, mother of Arthur

Earl of Pembroke

Earl of Essex

Earl of Salisbury

Lord Bigot

Hubert de Burgh

Lady Faulconbridge, Sir Robert Faulconbridge's widow

Robert Faulconbridge, son of Sir Robert Faulconbridge

Philip the Bastard, his half-brother, illegitimate son of King Richard Coeur-de-Lion (Richard I of England)

James Gurney, servant to Lady Faulconbridge

Peter of Pomfret, a prophet

King Philip, of France

Blanch of Spain, daughter of the King of Castile and niece of King John

Lewis, the Dauphin

Lymoges, Archduke of Austria

Cardinal Pandulph, the Pope's legate

Melun, a French lord

Chatillon, Ambassador from France to King John

Lords, Citizens of Angiers, Sheriff, Heralds, Officers, Soldiers, Executioners, Messengers, Attendants

### THE SCENE

England and France at the beginning of the 13th century (John reigned from 1199 to 1216)

## SYNOPSIS

Chatillon, an ambassador from King Philip of France, demands King John's crown for Arthur, young son of John's dead elder brother, Geoffrey, whereupon John declares war. He is followed to France by Philip the Bastard, who becomes Sir Richard Plantagenet on the revelation that he is the illegitimate son of King Richard I.

Before Angiers (200 miles southwest of Paris) the English and French armies meet (Act II). When the citizens declare that they will recognize only the rightful King of England ("he that proves the King,/To him will we prove loyal"), the two armies temporarily unite to assault the town. Peace of a sort is made after the citizens have suggested that Lewis, Dauphin of France, should marry John's niece, Blanch of Spain; Arthur is to become Duke of Bretagne (Brittany).

Constance, the boy's mother, assails King Philip and his ally, the Duke of Austria (Act III) for his treacherous bargain. The new-patched peace is brief; Cardinal Pandulph, the papal legate, arrives to excommunicate John for disobedience to the Pope; and because King Philip is also to be excommunicated unless he breaks his pact with John, the battle begins afresh. The Bastard kills the Duke of Austria; Arthur is taken prisoner and sent to England, Constance mourning for him; and John secretly orders Hubert de Burgh to dispose of the boy.

Hubert (Act IV), receiving a royal command to blind Arthur, resolves instead to hide the boy and to announce his death, false news that takes from John the support of Lords Salisbury and Pembroke. All troubles press on him at once; the Dauphin is ready to invade England; John learns that his mother, Elinor, has died — so, too, has Constance — and now the barons fall away from him. Though he learns from Hubert that Arthur is alive, the boy has actually been killed in an attempt to escape from Northampton Castle.

John yields to the Pope (Act V), but the Dauphin refuses to obey Pandulph's order to return to France, and supported by the English barons, fights with John's army. Retiring to Swinstead Abbey in Lincolnshire, the King is joined again by Salisbury and Pembroke who have heard that the Dauphin intended to kill them. At Swinstead, John — poisoned, it is believed, by a monk — dies in the orchard; Lewis by then has withdrawn his army, leaving Pandulph to arrange terms for peace, and the Bastard acknowledges the young Prince Henry as Henry III.

## IN PERFORMANCE

*The Life and Death of King John* was probably based upon an anonymous play in two parts. *The Troublesome Raigne of King John*. Shakespeare's chronicle is sometimes dismissed as a Little Arthur's History, simply because of the brief but affecting scene (IV.1) between the young Prince Arthur, in prison, and Hubert de Burgh whom he persuades not to blind him. The play is far from being a reliable historical document; it does not even mention the principal domestic event in John's reign, the signing at Runnymede in 1215 of Magna Carta, the charter of rights which the barons forced the King to accept. In his London production (1899) Herbert Beerbohm Tree introduced this, typically, as a tableau which permitted John, according to legend, to gnaw the rushes in his rage. A dominant figure in *King John* is the no-nonsense Bastard, illegitimate son of Richard I, who has the final patriotic outburst.

The play, better in performance than in the text, had the usual troubles in the theatre. After nearly a century and a half it was revived at Covent Garden (1737), and in 1745 there were two productions: Garrick's at Drury Lane (he played John) was the Shakespearian one, and the other was Colley Cibber's version called *Papal Tyranny in the Reign of King John*, which speaks for itself.

Sarah Siddons, who came to Constance at Drury Lane in 1783 (her brother John Philip Kemble was the King), gave an emotional performance. Another Kemble, Charles (as the Bastard), produced the play at Covent Garden (1823), everyone appearing "in the precise Habit of the Period, the whole of the Dresses and Decorations being executed from indisputable Authorities such as Monumental Effigies, Seals, Illuminated MSS, etc." The public approved. Macready revived the chronicle with magnificence at Drury Lane (1842), playing John himself.

So to the archaeological Charles Kean (Princess's, 1852); Tree's revival, with tableau (Her Majesty's, 1899); a number of Old Vic and Stratford productions. At the Birmingham Repertory (1945) the young Paul Scofield, already with extraordinary personal magnetism, acted the Bastard in Peter Brook's first Shakespearian production. Beginning with a bacchanal instead of the usual court tableau, Brook never let the play drift into a monotony of booming barons. In the Bastard's "commodity" speech (II.1) he inserted an early defining phrase ("That smooth-fac'd gentleman, *expediency, or, as they say*, tickling commodity,/Commodity, the bias of the world... "), and no scholar grumbled.

There have been various more-or-less routine productions (George Devine's at the Old Vic, 1953, with Richard Burton as the Bastard); but the only one that caused any real alarm was John Barton's (Stratford, 1974), in effect a new and superfluous play based on *The Troublesome Raigne*, the earlier interlude of *Kynge John* by a Protestant apologist, John Bale, and *King John* itself. It had, at least, Richard Pasco as the Bastard. Deborah Warner directed Nicholas Woodeson as the King for the RSC at The Other Place (1988) in a characteristically intelligent production notable not least for the number of ladders used on the set. Gregory Doran's Swan Theatre version (2001) had Guy Henry (as tall as Woodeson is short) as an affectingly eccentric King.

The New York Shakespeare Festival has presented *King John* twice — in 1967 and again in 1988, directed by Stuart Vaughan at the Delacorte Theatre. Frank Rich called the latter "a cautionary tale of undercutting and overreaching".

It was staged at Stratford, Ontario in 1961, and again in 1974, then with Edward Atienza as John.

## IN OTHER TERMS

The first-ever Shakespeare film is a few brief extracts from *King John*. The only one to survive, lasting no more than one minute, shows Beerbohm Tree conscientiously illustrating the text in his death throes. The BBC television film (1984) starring

Leonard Rossiter courageously acknowledges the play's sardonic aspects.

# CHIEF CHARACTERS

**King John** A foxy monarch, one of the butts of English history, though at some time, as Holinshed says, he might have had "a princelie heart in him".

**Philip the Bastard** (becomes Sir Richard Plantagenet). The longest part (511 lines). An honest, impatient, realistic soldier, Coeur-de-Lion's illegitimate son by Lady Faulconbridge, he goes undeviatingly to the point at all times and has the last patriotic brag.

**Arthur** The scene with Hubert (IV.1), not just a popular showpiece, an Arthurian legend, can move all but the determinedly cynical. Arthur needs a good boy actor, though there is an actress tradition.

**Constance** Arthur's betrayed mother whom the stage knew as "crying Constance". Her part is a mixture of overburdened lines and such famous speeches as "I will instruct my sorrows to be proud" (III.1).

**Hubert de Burgh** Arthur's warden; some editors believe he was also the First Citizen of Angiers (II.1).

**Archduke of Austria** The pompous braggart whom the Bastard kills at Angiers. Direction in III.2: "Enter the Bastard with Austria's head." Usually it is enough to come on with the lion-skin. One theatrical variation has been "Austria's *hide*, lie there."

**Lord Salisbury** In Act IV.2, after John's second coronation, he has one of the most misquoted phrases in English literature, "To gild refinèd gold, to paint the lily."

**King Philip of France** Among the more vacillating monarchs ("I am perplex'd and know not what to say"). He says too much in one of the less fortunate speeches (III.4) when observing that a tear has fallen on the distraught Constance's unbound hair: "Even to that drop ten thousand wiry friends/Do glue themselves in sociable grief."

**Blanch of Spain** "Whoever wins, on that side shall I lose:/Assurèd loss before the match be play'd" (III.1). A small part but haunting.

**Prince Henry** The youth, who will be Henry III, speaks the lines too often either ignored or ill-delivered (V.7, before John's death in the Swinstead orchard):
'Tis strange that death should sing.
I am the cygnet to this pale faint swan
Who chants a doleful hymn to his own death,
And from the organ-pipe of frailty sings
His soul and body to their lasting rest.

**Cardinal Pandulph** "I, Pandulph, of fair Milan cardinal." Casuistical legate of the Pope, whose shadow, that of the Church Militant, falls across the play like the shadow of the great cross that in some productions is borne before him. He has been played as a massively arrogant prelate or as frail and silver-haired.

**Lewis the Dauphin** Heir to the French throne. His sudden willingness to love Blanch for politic reasons, but expressed hyperbolically (II.3), rouses the Bastard's sardonic contempt. Historically, the marriage is said to have been idyllic.

**Queen Elinor** John's mother; with little to say, she is far more than a cipher. Her son's evil inspiration, for ever at his ear: "An Até stirring him to blood and strife."

---

# Richard II
## 1595

Historically, Richard II reigned from 1377 to 1399. Born at Bordeaux in 1367 — he was the same age as his cousin, Henry Bolingbroke, later Henry IV — he succeeded Edward III in 1377, when only a child. Bolingbroke deposed him in 1399 and he died early in 1400 while imprisoned at Pontefract (Pomfret) Castle.

**THE CHARACTERS**
King Richard II
Isabel, his Queen
John of Gaunt, Duke of Lancaster, the King's uncle, and brother of the Duke of York and the late Thomas of Woodstock, Duke of Gloucester
Henry Bolingbroke, Duke of Hereford, son of John of Gaunt and afterwards Henry IV
Thomas Mowbray, Duke of Norfolk
Edmund of Langley, Duke of York; uncle of the King
The Duchess of York
Duke of Aumerle, son of the Duke of York
The Duchess of Gloucester, Thomas of Woodstock's widow
Henry Percy, Earl of Northumberland
Harry Percy, Hotspur, son of the Earl of Northumberland
Sir Henry Green
Sir John Bushy
Sir John Bagot
Lord Ross
Lord Willoughby
Lord Berkeley
Earl of Salisbury
Bishop of Carlisle
Sir Stephen Scroop
Lord Fitzwater
Duke of Surrey
Abbot of Westminster
Sir Pierce of Exton
Lord Marshal
A Welsh captain
Two gardeners
A groom of the stable to the King
Keeper of the prison at Pomfret
A Lord, Heralds, Ladies, Attendant upon Queen Isabel, Guards, Soldiers, Servants

**THE SCENE**
England and Wales

# SYNOPSIS

The play opens with Henry Bolingbroke, the King's cousin, accusing Thomas Mowbray, Duke of Norfolk, of the murder of the King's uncle, Thomas of Woodstock, Duke of Gloucester (a crime actually committed at the King's command). Richard orders Bolingbroke and Mowbray to a trial by combat at Coventry; there, as the fight is about to begin, he forbids it, sentencing Mowbray to exile for life and Bolingbroke for ten years, presently reduced to six.

Soon (Act II) Bolingbroke's father, John of Gaunt, Duke of Lancaster, dies after a noble panegyric on England ("This royal throne of kings"). At once, Richard, against the protests of his uncle York and the powerful nobleman Northumberland, seizes Gaunt's estates to pay for his coming Irish campaign. While he is in Ireland, Bolingbroke lands at Ravenspurgh in Yorkshire and, joined by Northumberland, marches to Berkeley Castle, where the vacillating York, as regent, is obliged to receive them. Bolingbroke (Act III) executes two of Richard's favourites, "the caterpillars of the commonwealth", Bushy and Green. The country rises in his favour. When Richard lands in Wales he hears only a tale of woe; Bolingbroke takes him prisoner at Flint Castle where he has gone with York's son, Aumerle.

In London, at Westminster Hall (Act IV), Richard yields the crown to Bolingbroke (who becomes King Henry IV); he is sent to Pomfret Castle and his Queen to France. Aumerle and the Bishop of Carlisle join in a plot against the King, but Aumerle's part is discovered by his father (Act V). His mother pleads for his pardon, which Henry grants. Richard is murdered by Sir Pierce of Exton at Pomfret, a crime at once mourned by the King who had prompted it. "From your own mouth, my lord, did I this deed," says Exton; and Henry answers, "They love not poison that do poison need."

# IN PERFORMANCE

*Richard II*, with Holinshed's *Chronicles* as a main source, has become conspicuous in the theatre because so many expert speakers have responded to Richard's lyrical verse in a play predominantly melodious and frequently rhymed. There are two methods of presenting Richard — as a man, luxuriating in his imagination, who is entranced by word and image and makes shivering music of his grief, or as a man who suffers profoundly with each new fall. In the theatre it can be often difficult to separate the two, but the play must always be a rare experience, given the right kind of unfussed production — one by Bridges-Adams at Stratford in the 1920s was sovereign — and a sensitive speaker who can present the King, moving from haughty insolence to contemplative artist, without blurring the arias. The night falters — and this happens seldom — only when a Richard cannot find the harmonies.

Opposed to him is the strong man, the usurping and verbally unimaginative Henry Bolingbroke, "silent king" of the Westminster Hall scenes. Richard aside, the noblest passage (II.1) and possibly the most familiar, is John of Gaunt's inspired apostrophe to England, "This royal throne of kings" (II.1). Theatrically, the trickiest scene is the "Aumerle conspiracy" (V.2 and 3) which is worked uneasily into the pattern and used regularly to be cut: a pity because we must always miss the Duke of York's memory of Richard's entrance into London behind the conquering Bolingbroke. (Various directors, e.g. Charles Kean and Beerbohm Tree, tried superfluously to illustrate this.)

We know that Queen Elizabeth — who had her influential favourites as Richard had — was angry when she was compared with him. Presumably for political reasons the abdication scene was omitted from printed editions during the Queen's reign, but restored after her death. One of her favourites, the foolhardy Earl of Essex, rose against her in 1601, the day after supporters of Essex paid the sum of 40 shillings for a special performance of *Richard II* at the Globe, complete with deposition. The revolt was suppressed and Essex was executed. The next recorded performance of the chronicle was, remarkably, in the East India Company's ship, *Dragon* (commanded by John Keeling) off the coast of Sierra Leone in the autumn of 1607. The *Dragon* was in company with the *Hector*, under Captain William Hawkins, and Keeling's log has the note: "Sept. 30. Captain Hawkins dined with me, where my companions acted King Richard the Second." (The same versatile ship's company, it seems, would also play *Hamlet*.)

After the Restoration, Nahum Tate tried a short-lived adaptation (*The Sicilian Usurper*, 1680). Lewis Theobald put together a rather luckier one (1719); and Shakespeare's own text ran at Covent Garden in 1738. Among 19th-century Richards were Edmund Kean, who used an adapted text; Macready; and Charles Kean, whose much-cut version, surrounded by all imaginable pomp, had 85 performances (Princess's, 1857).

The 19th century's only other important Richard was Frank Benson (Stratford, 1896); it was a performance, inescapably poignant, of a haunted artist and lost, spoilt child, surrendering his life with his crown. In 1899 Benson, who could be a far better actor than the too easily accepted legends suggest, played Richard in Manchester and at Flint Castle, Clwyd, on the 500th anniversary of Richard's surrender; he received from Charles Edward Montague of the Manchester *Guardian* the famous theatre essay describing how Benson expressed "that half of the character which criticism seems always to have taken pains to hide — the capable and faithful artist in the same skin as the incapable and faithless king."

Benson acted Richard in London (Lyceum, 1900) and frequently thereafter at Stratford.

Except for Tree's mannered and touching portrait (His Majesty's, 1903) in a much-decorated revival (real horses), there was no major Richard until that of George Hayes at the Old Vic (1925), which he repeated at Stratford (1929), the year when John Gielgud at the Old Vic first proved his mastery of a part he would make his own. Hayes created much excitement in Boston late in 1929 on the Stratford company's tour. The chronicle was then barely known in the American theatre (though Edwin Booth had done it in the 1870s), but it startled New York (St James's, 1937) when the English actor, Maurice Evans — who had been in an Old Vic revival of 1934 — appeared under Margaret Webster's direction. The play was unfamiliar and the Evans-Webster première is still remembered. "At the end of the 'death of kings' speech," the director said, "an outburst of applause stopped the action for almost a minute. I had never heard such a thing in the theatre before."

In the 20th century Alec Guinness' Richard (Old Vic at the New, 1946) was a proud weakling using irony as his defence. Ian Richardson and Richard Pasco alternated the King and Bolingbroke (Stratford, 1973). The record of Richards reads like a catalogue but all added something to the mosaic and all could sustain the great speeches, "Of comfort no man speak" (III.2), "We are amazed" (III.3), and the metaphysical "I have been studying" at Pomfret (V.5). Bernard Hepton (St George's, Islington, 1979) analysed the man with affecting clarity. Alan Howard played Richard III and Richard II on alternate nights at Stratford in 1980. Jeremy Irons played Richard in Barry Kyle's picturesque, book-of-hours production for the RSC (1986) while Derek Jacobi gave the play, along with *Richard III*, at the Phoenix Theatre, London, in 1989–9. Deborah Warner's National Theatre production, with Fiona Shaw as the King (1995), was also shown on television. Steven Pimlott unusually chose modern dress for the RSC's "This England" production (2000), with Samuel West as a sharply vulnerable King opposed by David Troughton's uncompromising, if troubled, Bolingbroke. Mark Rylance's audience-pleasing Richard was seen to best advantage in the splendid setting of the Middle Temple (2003) before the all-male, allegedly original-practices production homed in on the Globe.

Zoë Caldwell directed the play at Stratford, Ontario (1979), using three Richards during the run.

# IN OTHER TERMS

Derek Jacobi, sympathetic and intelligent, appeared on BBC television (1978), a production otherwise routine except for Gielgud's John of Gaunt. Gielgud's name is inseparable from the play.

# CHIEF CHARACTERS

**Richard II** Standing to the last for the divine right of kingship. John Gielgud said of the part that "the actor's vocal effects must be contrived within the framework of the verse... Too many pauses and striking variations of tempo will tend to hold up the action disastrously" and so ruin the text's symmetry and pattern.

**Henry Bolingbroke** John of Gaunt's son, who takes the throne as Henry IV. A long part (411 lines against Richard's 756), yet its strength can be in its silences. Pronounced "Bullingbrook"; the title "Hereford" is "Herford".

**John of Gaunt** "Old John of Gaunt, time-honoured Lancaster", though when the play opens (1398) he is only 58. One of the great Shakespearian elders, he has the salute to England, "This royal throne of kings".

**Thomas Mowbray, Duke of Norfolk** Vanishes from the play after his exile (I.3). In the theatre often doubled with the Bishop of Carlisle who (IV.1) reports Mowbray's death in Venice.

**Queen to King Richard** Historically she was Isabella of Valois, daughter of Charles VI of France. In the Duke of York's garden at Langley (III.4) she overhears the symbolic talk of the two Gardeners (who must never be teased into comedy): "He that hath suffered this disordered spring/Hath now himself met with the fall of leaf."

**Edmund, Duke of York** The King's uncle, and regent during Richard's absence in Ireland. Vacillating, bemused and kindly. Difficult lines not to be played for laughter.

**Duchess of York** Historically, Aumerle was only her stepson.

**Duke of Aumerle** York's son, involved in the disastrous conspiracy (Act V). He is at the centre of the quarrel in which so many gages are thrown down — difficult in the theatre, unless judiciously cut.

**Duchess of Gloucester** Her scene with Gaunt (I.2) is not easy to understand without knowledge of her husband's murder.

**Earl of Northumberland** Richard's implacable enemy.

**Henry (Harry) Percy** Northumberland's son: the Hotspur of *Henry IV, Part I* though one might never guess this from *Richard II*. Actually he was two years older than Bolingbroke himself.

**Earl of Salisbury** He has the famous line (III.2), "O, call back yesterday, bid time return", which has been varied so often in other plays down the years.

**Captain of a band of Welshmen** Briefly met (II.4), this superstitious Welshman can be reasonably identified with Owen Glendower, though some critics consider that he is a purely choric figure.

**Groom** He comes to the prisoner at Pomfret (V.5), telling him how Bolingbroke had ridden on Richard's favourite horse, roan Barbary. The part, at Stratford (1973–4), was represented capriciously as the disguised Bolingbroke.

# Romeo and Juliet
## 1595–6

 CHORUS
Escalus, Prince of Verona
Mercutio, the Prince's kinsman and
    Romeo's friend
Paris, a young nobleman, the Prince's
    kinsman
Montague head of a Veronese family at
    feud with the Capulets
Lady Montague, wife to Montague
Romeo, Montague's son
Benvolio, Montague's nephew and
    Romeo's friend
Abraham, Montague's servant
Balthasar, Romeo's servant
Capulet head of a Veronese family
    at feud with the Montagues
Lady Capulet, wife to Capulet

Juliet, Capulet's daughter
Tybalt, Lady Capulet's nephew
An Old Man, of the Capulet family
Nurse, to Juliet
Peter, servant to Juliet's Nurse
Sampson, Gregory, Capulet's servants
Friar Lawrence, a Franciscan
Friar John, of the same Order
An Apothecary, Three Musicians, Page
    to Paris, another Page, an Officer,
    Citizens of Verona, Kinsfolk of
    both Houses, Masquers, Guards,
    Watchmen, and Attendants

 THE SCENE
Verona, Mantua

# SYNOPSIS

After a brawl between the rival families of Montague and Capulet ("Two households both alike in dignity"), the Prince threatens with death anyone who "disturbs our streets again". Romeo, Montague's heir, masked at a Capulet dance, becomes infatuated with Capulet's daughter, Juliet. From the garden (Act II) he overhears her avowal ("Take all myself") as she stands on her balcony and their love scene follows (II.2). Next afternoon Friar Lawrence marries them in secret.

When (Act III) Romeo refuses to fight with Tybalt, a passionate Capulet (who is now his cousin by marriage), the gallant Mercutio takes the challenge himself. He is killed by mischance, and Romeo, enraged, kills Tybalt. In his absence the Prince banishes him; the Friar tells him to stay the night with Juliet and then wait in Mantua until recall is possible (III.3). When Juliet's father insists that she shall marry a young nobleman, Paris, and she gets no aid from either her mother or her nurse, the Friar (Act IV) gives her an opiate (to take on the following night) that will put her in a death-like trance for "two-and-forty hours". She will be laid in the Capulet vault; when she wakes, Romeo will be there.

Juliet is duly placed in the vault as dead, but the Friar's messenger to Mantua miscarries; hearing only of Juliet's "death" ("Then I defy you, stars!", Act V), Romeo hastens to the tomb at night and is surprised by Paris whom he kills; in the vault he drinks poison he has bought from a Mantuan apothecary, and dies by Juliet's side. She wakes as the desperate Friar enters, and on seeing Romeo dead, stabs herself. The Prince and the heads of the families are roused; over the bodies of their children Capulet and Montague are reconciled, and the Prince closes the play: "For never was a story of more woe/Than this of Juliet and her Romeo."

# IN PERFORMANCE

"A tragedy of youth as youth sees it," wrote Harley Granville-Barker. Set in a Veronese high summer, it is both the tale of "star-crossed lovers" and the healing of their parents' feud: Shakespeare's principal source was a poem by Arthur Brooke (1562), a version of a story long popular. The play is what Bernard Shaw, unassailable for once, called "an irresistibly impetuous march of music", though the "two hours' traffic of our stage" (a phrase from the Prologue) cannot be taken literally.

Few plays have been acted so often; but it had much ado to find itself. Thomas Otway (1679) provided a travesty, *The History and Fall of Caius Marius*; Theophilus Cibber's version (1744), less distorted, also supplied what was (for the taste of the period) an obligatory farewell dialogue in the tomb; David Garrick (1748), in a text enormously successful, was also far too self-indulgent. "Bless me," said the waking Juliet. "How cold it is! Who's there?" Whereupon Romeo replied: "Thy husband. 'Tis thy Romeo, raised from despair to joy unutterable." Joy was brief; the apothecary's poison worked: "My powers are blasted./'Twixt death and life I am torn, I am distracted." Listeners were not; indeed, the alterations were in use well into the 19th century. Through many mid-18th-century seasons London's two principal theatres competed in performances of the tragedy; Garrick himself played Romeo for 11 years from 1750.

The sequence of revivals continued. Charles Kemble (Romeo first in 1803) became Mercutio in 1829. Eliza O'Neill (1814), 19-year-old Fanny Kemble (1829) and Helen Faucit (1836) were historic Juliets. The American Charlotte Cushman, as Romeo to her sister Susan (Haymarket, 1845), omitted the interpolated dialogue in death; Adelaide Neilson was Juliet for 15 years (in England and the United States) from 1865; and the realistic Lyceum décor (1882) meant more than the playing of Henry Irving and Ellen Terry. In spite of a procession of distinguished names there would be no memorable excitement until the veteran Ellen Terry (as the Nurse) had her last triumph (Lyric 1919). Eric Portman and Jean Forbes-Robertson (Old Vic, 1928) caused the author and artist, Graham Robertson, to say: "The two very young lovers made the whole thing so poignant and real that you longed to wait for them at the stage door with a double perambulator to wheel them home to bed."

Seven years later, the century's most exciting revival brought the John Gielgud-Laurence Olivier alternation of Romeo and Mercutio (New, 1935), with Peggy Ashcroft's Juliet magically right, and Edith Evans as the Nurse described definitively by W.A. Darlington: "Earthy as a potato, slow as a cart-horse, cunning as a badger."

Peter Brook's Stratford production (1947, on the note of "The mad blood stirring") is recalled for Paul Scofield's Mercutio. There were Old Vic performances by John Stride and the impulsively young Judi Dench (1960); Franco Zeffirelli, who directed, chopped the Mab speech into untidy little cubes and opened the Mantuan scene at "Then I defy you, stars!". Peter Hall's Stratford production of 1961 had Dorothy Tutin as an intense Juliet, and Edith Evans in a reprise of her classic performance as the Nurse. Terry Hands's RSC versions of 1973 and 1987 (Swan) sought a homoerotic subtext in the relationship between Romeo and Mercutio. In 1976 Ian McKellen and Francesca Annis were the lovers in Trevor Nunn's neo-Elizabethan production in which the audience extended round the playing area. Ten years later, Michael Bogdanov's RSC production came to be known as the *Alfa Romeo and Juliet* because of the presence on stage of a large red sports car. Erratically brilliant, it was (like Brook's) severely cut, especially in the closing scene which became a media event, the lovers posing in golden robes as their own statues. Sean Bean and Niamh Cusack were the lovers. Adrian Noble's RSC production of 1996 had Julian Glover as an outstanding Friar. Michael Attenborough directed Ray Fearon and Zoe Waites as the lovers in a demoticized, sun-baked production in the Swan (1997) and on tour. In 2000 at the RSC Michael Boyd directed a tough-minded production with David Tennant and Alexandra Gilbreath in which the ghosts of Tybalt and Mercutio returned to oversee the later stages of the action.

There is a record of American productions since the mid-18th-century. In the 19th century Charlotte Cushman's Romeo and the Juliets of Adelaide Neilson and Mary Anderson (New York, 1885, with Forbes-Robertson as Romeo) were all applauded. Julia Marlowe (1904) was ardent and heroic. Rollo Peters and Jane Cowl had more than 150 performances at the Henry Miller Theatre (1928); and of other players — e.g. Eva Le Gallienne and Donald Cameron (1930), and Olivia de Havilland and Douglas Watson (1951) — probably the most satisfying was Katharine Cornell (1934, Basil Rathbone as Romeo, Edith Evans as the Nurse; 1935, Maurice Evans as Romeo). Bill Alexander directed for the Theatre for a New Audience, New York (1991) and in the same year Robert Lepage directed a bilingual Canadian production, the Capulets speaking French, the Montagues English. Michael Arabian's imaginative 1993 production on a CBS backlot in Studio City, Los Angeles, used swastikas and Stars of David to suggest wider, racial questions.

# IN OTHER TERMS

The play has been prolific in offspring. A Hollywood film of 1936 had Norma Shearer and Leslie Howard (on a "wedding-cake balcony") as the not-so-young lovers and John Barrymore as Mercutio. A colourful film by Renato Castellani (1954) was notable rather for picturesque realism than for drama. The genuinely young lovers (Olivia Hussey and Leonard Whiting) in Franco Zeffirelli's stunningly beautiful and often exciting film (1968) illustrated the paradox that actors rarely have the technique to play these roles while looking young enough to be convincing. The disappointing BBC television film (1978) was similarly flawed. Baz Lurhmann's *William Shakespeare's Romeo + Juliet* (1996) did for young people of the 1990s what Zeffirelli's film had done for those of the 1960s. Violent, witty, sexy, superimposing contemporary images on a shortened version of the original text, and featuring young, beautiful, popular stars — Leonardo di Caprio and Claire Danes — it adapts the play brilliantly into modern cinematic terms.

The story of Romeo and Juliet, rather than the play, lies behind many fine musical works including the operas *I Capuletti ed I Montecchi* (Vincenzio Bellini, 1830), in which Romeo is sung by a woman, *Roméo et Juliette* (Charles Gounod, 1867) and *A Village Romeo and Juliet* (Frederick Delius, 1901). Hector Berlioz, whose private life was much involved with the play, wrote a magnificent dramatic symphony (1839) for soloists and chorus with a sublime, purely orchestral, love scene. Tchaikovsky's popular orchestral fantasy overture (1880) comes closer to the structure of Shakespeare's play, and has been used for a ballet. Serge Prokofiev's full-length ballet (1936) has become a staple of the repertoire, and Leonard Bernstein's popular musical *West Side Story* is less directly related to Shakespeare.

# CHIEF CHARACTERS

**Romeo** Juliet's passionate lover, and no part for a timid actor: Romeo is a youth who, in grief, must not fear to "fall upon the ground as I do now,/Taking the measure of an unmade grave" (III.3).

**Juliet** "O, she doth teach the torches to burn bright." She is 13; she would have been 14 on Lammas Eve, soon after her death. In performance she must come from the right latitude — no hint of northern skies — and she needs far more than a child's experience: experiments with very young actresses have usually failed. Few Victorian players spoke the lines "Lovers can see to do their amorous rites/By their own beauties" (III.2) because they were deemed immodest.

**Mercutio** Romeo's friend, a kinsman of the Prince. Mercurial (hence his name), gallant (he jests to the end), imaginative (the Queen Mab speech), and doomed: Tybalt strikes him under Romeo's arm.

**Tybalt** "Talk of peace! I hate the word/As I hate hell, all Montagues, and thee" (I.1). He goes on from there.

**Benvolio** Romeo and Mercutio's friend, vanishes from the play after his description of the duel (III.1).

**Paris** Kinsman of both the Prince and Mercutio. An amiable young man and unlucky.

**Escalus** Prince of Verona. Three times the voice of much-troubled authority (I.1, III.1, V.3).

**Capulet** Juliet's father; much older than his wife. Proud, hospitable, unimaginative and honest in his grief.

**Friar Lawrence** "Ghostly confessor" (II.6). Happier as a botanist than a conspirator; full of helpful maxims.

**Lady Capulet** Juliet's mother; a thankless part. She is, we gather, not yet 30 but speaks of "my old age" (V.3).

**Nurse** There is no need for the Nurse, garrulous, bawdy and fickle, to be an ancient. She could be 50 though we are used to the type of bulky, voluble peasant played by Edith Evans (New, 1935).

**Apothecary** Romeo describes him in detail. "Meagre were his looks./Sharp misery had worn him to the bones" (V.1). It is a dangerous invitation to a young actor; but Alec

Guinness (New, 1935) was perfectly credible and did not carry about the dram of poison as if he were expecting a customer.

**Rosaline** Does not appear (though much talked about, and some directors have brought her to Capulet's ball); Romeo's first love and Juliet's cousin. Mercutio calls her a "pale, hard-hearted wench" (II.4).

---

# A Midsummer Night's Dream
## 1595–6

 **THE CHARACTERS**
Theseus, Duke of Athens
Hippolyta, Queen of the Amazons,
    betrothed to Theseus
Egeus, father of Hermia
Hermia, daughter of Egeus, in love with
    Lysander
Lysander and Demetrius, each in love
    with Hermia
Helena, in love with Demetrius
Philostrate, master of the revels to
    Theseus
Oberon, King of the Fairies
Titania, Queen of the Fairies
Puck, or Robin Goodfellow
A Fairy

Peaseblossom, Cobweb, Moth,
    Mustardseed, fairy attendants on
    Titania
Quince, a carpenter
Snug, a joiner
Bottom, a weaver
Flute, a bellows-mender
Snout, a tinker
Starveling, a tailor
Attendants on Theseus and Hippolyta;
    other fairies attending the King and
    Queen

 **THE SCENE**
Athens, and a wood near it

---

# SYNOPSIS

While Theseus, Duke of Athens, and the Amazon Queen Hippolyta, whom he has defeated in battle, are contemplating their marriage, Theseus has to judge a matrimonial dispute. Egeus wishes his daughter Hermia to wed Demetrius when her heart is set upon Lysander. Though warned of the consequences if she disobeys, Hermia resolves to elope and on the next night to meet Lysander in a wood close to Athens. They tell Helena who is herself in love with Demetrius and who promptly reveals the plan to him.

In the wood (Act II) the pixie or hobgoblin Puck (more properly Robin Goodfellow) and one of the Fairy Queen's train talk of the quarrel between Oberon and Titania over the changeling boy she has adopted and his desires for a henchman. She refuses to yield, whereupon Oberon orders Puck to fetch a flower whose juice, squeezed on Titania's sleeping eyelids, will cause her on awakening to love the first live creature that she sees. Helena has followed Demetrius to the wood; Oberon, invisible and sympathetic, orders Puck to squeeze the flower on the lids of the "Athenian youth", while he himself anoints Titania. But Puck, mistaking, chooses Lysander, who when he wakes immediately pursues Helena.

Puck (Act III) mischievously gives an ass's head to Bottom, the weaver, one of a group of "mechanicals" rehearsing a play for the wedding of Theseus. Titania, waking, falls in love with Bottom. Presently confusion is worse than ever because Demetrius (who has now been anointed) and Lysander fight over Helena, to Hermia's distress. The only thing to do is to get the lovers to sleep and to restore Lysander's sight before he wakes.

Oberon (Act IV) releases Titania; Puck removes the ass's head, and one quarrel is settled as Fairy King and Queen leave before dawn. Theseus and Hippolyta, hunting early, rouse the lovers who, back as they were, are assured by Theseus that they shall be wedded that day. Bottom, baffled by his apparent dream, goes off to find his fellows.

In Act V they perform, in all sincerity, their interlude of Pyramus and Thisby before the amused court audience. Midnight sounds. When all have retired the fairies return to give their blessing to the house and lovers, and Puck says the final word.

## IN PERFORMANCE

The legend that the magical play of *A Midsummer Night's Dream*, with some of Shakespeare's loveliest lyric verse, was written for a wedding has no hard evidence to support it. Its tripartite narrative of Romantics, Immortals and Mechanicals is an enchanted fantasy possessed by moonlight, though one or two modern critics perversely reduce it to an erotic nightmare. So much has happened to it through the centuries that we are often surprised now to find a straight performance.

Samuel Pepys (1662) called it "the most insipid, ridiculous play that I ever saw in my life." It was the core of a Restoration operatic version, *The Fairy Queen*, with Purcell's music and a last act choked by a near-demented efflorescence of spectacle, a dance of six monkeys, and a chorus of "Chineses" in a Chinese garden. *A Midsummer Night's Dream* returned to the stage, almost as itself — after various song-crowded versions in the 18th century — when Madame Vestris and her husband, Charles Mathews, put it on at Covent Garden (1840). Samuel Phelps (who played Bottom) did it beautifully at Sadler's Wells in 1853, a production more Shakespearian than Charles Kean's desperately archaeological effort at the Princess's (1856); there a nine-year-old Ellen

Terry was Puck, belted and garlanded with flowers. For a long time any revival involved a proliferation of needless accessories (e.g. Tree's rabbits and bluebell thickets at Her Majesty's, 1900). Nothing much counted until Harley Granville-Barker (Savoy, 1914) rejected Mendelssohn and muslin ballet skirts, peopling the wood with gold-and-bronze Cambodian-idol fairies. The Mechanicals were charmingly earnest, working against fate without any sequence of venerable gags.

Later, there were dozens of revivals: at the Old Vic; in central London (Basil Dean's Drury Lane production, 1924, was one of the last predominantly spectacular); at the Open Air Theatre in Regent's Park; and in Stratford. The most evocative performances in those years were the Jacobean-masque treatment (Old Vic, 1929), with the young Gielgud as Oberon and Leslie French as Puck ("I go, I go; *look* how I go"); and the patrician courtliness, under Bridges-Adams, at Stratford's new theatre (1932). There a critic described the Norman Wilkinson sets as "a nocturne in blue and silver, Elizabethan figures in alabaster stepping through some fold of time".

At Christmas 1937 Tyrone Guthrie delighted most people with his Old Vic album of Victoriana, flying fairies and tarlatan skirts, and Vivien Leigh's Titania like an engraving of the ballerina Taglioni. Gielgud and Peggy Ashcroft were Oberon and Titania at the Haymarket (1945). Peter Hall tried various Stratford/Aldwych versions, the last in 1963; and at length in 1970 Peter Brook's Stratford production invited us to consider the play as though it were entirely new. The setting, a white cube, became a wood when coils and tendrils of helical steel wire were released; Oberon and Puck were on trapezes; Titania and Oberon doubled with Hippolyta and Theseus, their other selves released in dream and night; the interlude was not a repository for the myriad accretions of the years; and in general the company spoke the verse better than one had ever known it.

Bill Bryden directed Paul Scofield in a promenade production (Cottesloe, 1982). A notable Cheek by Jowl production won two Olivier awards — for Best Comedy and Best Director (Declan Donnellan) (touring 1985–6). Bill Alexander's 1986 production for the RSC, with Janet McTeer as Titania and Hippolyta, was described as "Victorian fantasy". John Caird's popular updated version had fairies in Dr Martens (Stratford/Barbican, 1989–90), but Robert Lepage's production in mud (National Theatre, 1992) had the audience more worried about slipping actors than entranced by the play.

Ever seeking new approaches to a comedy whose popularity with audiences creates a constant demand for new productions, directors have often either reacted against the Victorian pictorial tradition or deconstructed it, exploring — perhaps sometimes creating — a dark side to the play's exploration of marital relationships, of the dramatist's relation to the natural world and to animality, and to its concerns with individual identity. Ron Daniels (RSC, 1981) consciously and beautifully evoked the Victorian age and played with images of theatricality — the fairies were puppets manipulated by visible operators. Bill Alexander's 1986 RSC production doubled Hippolyta and Titania but not Theseus and Oberon, creating an eerie forest which dwarfed its inhabitants. Hippolyta clearly found Oberon more attractive than Theseus. John Caird's RSC production (1989) irreverently, wittily, and unsentimentally mocked tradition while creating a magic of its own. Adrian Noble's production (RSC, 1994, later filmed), like Brook's (and possibly like Shakespeare's) doubled the mechanicals with the fairies. Michael Boyd (RSC, 1999) offered a joyously sexualized approach. Bottom, one of the richest roles in the comic repertoire, became Mrs Bottom in a West End production (2001) starring the television entertainer Dawn French. Edward Hall's all-male Watermill, Newbury (2003) production toured widely in England and overseas.

A short version of the play, *Bottom the Weaver*, was performed by London apprentices as early as 1661, and the original is a favourite with amateur and school groups.

The United States had its first performance in New York (1826); Charlotte Cushman played Oberon (Park Theatre, 1841), and Laure Keene, Puck (at her own theatre, 1859, a production scenically adventurous). Later, Augustin Daly put on three revivals between 1873 and 1890; he brought the last to Daly's, London (1895), with Ada Rehan's Helena, an occasion when Bernard Shaw wrote rudely that the panoramic illusion of Theseus' barge on its way to Athens seemed "more absurd than anything that occurs in the tragedy of Pyramus and Thisby." Granville-Barker's Savoy production, as contentious as in London, reached Broadway in 1915.

Numerous later revivals included Max Reinhardt's spectacle (Century, 1927), acted in German, with Alexander Moissi's Oberon; and Joseph Papp's for the New York Shakespeare Festival, 1961. Douglas Campbell directed the comedy at Stratford, Ontario (1961), and Maggie Smith doubled Titania and Hippolyta for Robin Phillips (1977). Kenneth Branagh took his Renaissance Theatre Company to the United States, with Emma Thompson as Puck, whose "mucky, primevil wriggling" failed to please Robert Koehler of the *LA Times* (Mark Taper Forum, NY/Group Repertory Theater, LA, 1990).

## IN OTHER TERMS

Max Reinhardt's 1935 Hollywood film, grandiose, fantastic, with an all-star cast including Mickey Rooney as Puck and James Cagney as Bottom, has become a cult classic that demands, and deserves, to be taken on its own terms. Peter Hall used the house and gardens of Compton Verney, in Warwickshire, for a rarely seen film (1969) based on his own Stratford production and starring Judi Dench and Ian Richardson, two of the finest-ever exponents of Titania and Bottom. The BBC television film (1980) was directed by Elijah Moshinsky. Michael Hoffman's film (1999) transposed the action to 19th-century Italy, gave the opera-singing Bottom (Kevin Kline) a long-suffering wife, and cast Michelle Pfeiffer as Titania. The play's appeal for young people is reflected in Christine Edzard's film, *The Children's Midsummer Night's Dream* (2001), disarmingly performed by London schoolchildren.

The celebrated overture (1826) by the 17-year-old Felix Mendelssohn and the incidental music — including the inescapable wedding march — which he wrote later for a production (1843) by Ludwig Tieck were regularly used until Granville-Barker substituted English folk tunes in his Savoy Theatre production (1914). In New York, Louis Armstrong and Benny Goodman produced *Swingin' the Dream* in 1939 with a predominantly black cast. The setting was New Orleans in the late 19th century, and Armstrong played Bottom. The profoundest translation of the play into another art form is Benjamin Britten's masterly and magical opera (1960), for which he and Peter Pears created a libretto using about half of Shakespeare's lines. The play has also had great appeal for visual artists, especially the fairy painters of the 1840s, who anticipated later explorations of the play's sexual subtext.

## CHIEF CHARACTERS

**Theseus** Legendary Duke of Athens. He will reappear in *The Two Noble Kinsmen*. Unexpectedly the second longest part.

**Hippolyta** Queen of the Amazons, conquered by Theseus before the play opens and later wedded to him. Surprisingly, at the Old Vic (1960) appeared at curtain-rise in manacles.

**Egeus** Hermia's heavy father. Brook (1970) doubled the part with Quince; each is an example of paternalism.

**Hermia** Smallest of the lovers; probably acted by the boy who would play Maria in *Twelfth Night*. "You bead, you acorn", says the bemused Lysander (III.1).

**Lysander** He and Demetrius are practically interchangeable; Lysander has a "widow aunt, a dowager of great revenue" (I.1).

**Demetrius** Lysander calls him rudely a "spotted and inconstant man".

**Helena** Taller of the two girls.

**Quince** Peter Quince, the carpenter (the name is from "quines", or blocks of wood) is the Mechanicals' producer. Usually a benevolent martinet, thoroughly nervous when he speaks the prologue to "Pyramus and Thisby" instead of playing Thisby's mother.

**Snug** The joiner (hence his name, "close-fitting"). Frequently plays "the lion's part" with a mild purr.

**Bottom** Nick Bottom, the weaver, whose name is from the "bottom" or core of the skein upon which the weaver's yarn was wound. He has the longest part which is only right.

**Flute** Francis Flute, the bellows-mender. Cast as Thisby, with an intermittent tendency to become gruff and masculine.

**Snout** Tom Snout, the tinker. Originally the father of Pyramus. Ends as a rather sulky Wall.

**Starveling** Robin Starveling, the tailor, was possibly created by John Sincklo, who in Shakespeare's company was noted for parts requiring a thin man (e.g. Apothecary in *Romeo and Juliet*). Starveling was cast as Thisby's mother; finally a deaf, garrulous Moonshine with lantern, dog and bush of thorns.

**Oberon** King of the Fairies, with much of the finest verse ("Well, go thy way" and "I know a bank where the wild thyme blows" — both II.1 — and "We are spirits of another sort", III.2). There have been various Oberon fashions; at one period he was an actress who would sing "I know a bank"; today he can have sinister overtones, but he is a figure of great dignity and power.

**Titania** Queen of the Fairies, who has the key speech, though it can be unwisely clipped, "These are the forgeries of jealousy" (II.1). Shakespeare omitted a last-act song for the visiting fairies (" …will we sing and bless this place", V.1), so we often get "Roses, their sharp spines being gone" from *The Two Noble Kinsmen*.

**Puck** or Robin Goodfellow, Oberon's attendant and messenger. Unless discreetly acted, he can be trying.

# The Merchant of Venice
## 1596–7

 **THE CHARACTERS**
Duke of Venice
Portia, a rich heiress of Belmont
Nerissa, her gentlewoman
Princes of Morocco and Arragon, suitors
   to Portia
Antonio, a merchant of Venice
Bassanio, his friend, suitor to Portia
Solanio, Salerio, Gratiano, friends to
   Antonio and Bassanio
Lorenzo, in love with Jessica
Shylock, a rich Jew
Tubal, a Jew, his friend

Jessica, daughter to Shylock
Launcelot Gobbo, Shylock's servant,
   later servant to Bassanio
Old Gobbo, his father
Leonardo, servant to Bassanio
Balthasar, Stephano, servants to Portia
Magnificoes of Venice, Officers of the
   Court of Justice, Gaolers, Servants,
   Other Attendants

**THE SCENE**
Venice, and Portia's house near Belmont

## SYNOPSIS

Bassanio, needing money to woo Portia, heiress of Belmont, asks his friend Antonio, a Venetian merchant, for 3,000 ducats. Having no money by him, and with all his ships at sea, Antonio goes to a Jewish moneylender, Shylock, who hates him for his loathing of usury. Shylock proposes what he calls a "merry bond" by which, if the money is not repaid within three months, he may take a pound of Antonio's flesh; foolishly Antonio agrees.

Portia at Belmont (Act II) receives the Prince of Morocco, come to make his choice as suitor under the will of Portia's father. All suitors must choose from three caskets (gold, silver and lead) the one that contains her portrait; those who fail can never contemplate marriage again. Morocco fails with the golden casket, and the Prince of Arragon with the silver. Meanwhile, Bassanio and his friend Gratiano are on their way to Belmont; and Jessica, Shylock's daughter, in the disguise of a boy, has eloped with Lorenzo, taking rings and ducats with her.

Shylock (Act III) is furious about his losses. But Bassanio, choosing the correct (leaden) casket, prepares to wed Portia; her gentlewoman Nerissa and Gratiano also plan to marry. Then Salerio, Lorenzo, and Jessica bring news that Shylock is demanding his due and that Antonio's ships have "all miscarried". There must be a trial; Portia arranges to be present at the court as a young lawyer (Balthasar), Nerissa as "his" clerk. There (Act IV.1), admitting that the bond is flawless, she begs mercy from Shylock, who refuses and rejects all offers of money. He is about to take his pound of flesh when Portia turns on him: "Tarry a little; there is something else." She warns him that according to the bond, he is not entitled to "one jot of blood". Baffled, he will take his 3,000 ducats — only to be told that as an alien who has conspired against a Venetian's life, his own life is forfeit. However, he is pardoned and allowed half his fortune on the pledge that he will become a Christian and bequeath the money to Lorenzo and Jessica at his death.

When he has left the court the play is practically over except (Act V) for the tranquil coda (it used often to be cut) in the moonlight at Belmont, some comedy with rings, and tidings that Antonio's "argosies" (ships) have safely come to port.

# IN PERFORMANCE

Once more the full title of a Quarto text, that of 1600, gives a useful simplified summary: "The most excellent Historie of the Merchant of Venice. With the extreame crueltie of Shylocke the Jewe towards the sayd Merchant, in cutting a just pound of his flesh; and the obtayning of Portia by the choyse of three chests." Shakespeare — as so often — took suggestions from various sources, Italian and English, for the pound-of-flesh and casket stories which he amalgamated and transmuted. Marlowe's *The Jew of Malta* might have given some hints; the RSC valuably staged this at Stratford (1965) in the same season as a revival of *The Merchant of Venice*, Eric Porter playing both Shylock and the monstrous Barabas.

However often it is heard, Portia's "Tarry a little; there is something else" at the climax of the trial can remain startlingly dramatic. Shylock, of the alien minority in Venice, is the governing figure: in spite of the title of the play, Antonio is secondary to both his enemy and his saviour.

Between 1605 and 1741 there was no recorded performance of Shakespeare's text. A silly version by George Granville, afterwards Lord Lansdowne, held the stage for some years from 1701; it began with Shakespeare and Dryden rising laurel-crowned. There was also a masque of Peleus and Thetis, besides a banquet with a comic Shylock drinking a toast to money. Charles Macklin (Drury Lane, 1741) brought back what was hailed as "the Jew that Shakespeare drew", a ferocious, revengeful, redwigged figure that Macklin acted (as "the Nestor of the stage") until he was nearly 90. John Philip Kemble played Shylock for many years at Drury Lane from 1786, with Sarah Siddons as Portia; George Frederick Cooke played him like a depraved demon.

The most astonishing was Edmund Kean (Drury Lane, 1814) who, in black beard and wig, changed Shylock from a malignant fiend to a man of racial pride, plausibly resentful ("Hath not a Jew eyes?", III.1), an avenger through force of circumstance. Macready (Covent Garden, 1823) added touches of nobility to his harshness. More than half a century later Henry Irving's Shylock (a long Lyceum run, 1879, with Ellen Terry's radiant Portia) was intensely proud, gently menacing, the type of a persecuted race.

The 20th century brought many versions: hysterical, extravagantly theatrical (Tree, His Majesty's, 1908); repulsively realistic (Maurice Moscovitch, Royal Court, 1919, his first part in English); dignified and implacable in the Irving manner (Ernest Milton, St James's, 1932); and so on, through performances by such players as Gielgud (in the manner of Granville-Barker's "sordid little outsider, passionate, resentful"), Donald Wolfit and Michael Redgrave, to Laurence Olivier's prosperous private banker (for the National company, Cambridge Theatre, London, 1970). His dance of triumph on hearing of Antonio's ill-fortune lingers in memory, with the offstage cry of anguish after Shylock had left the court (Jonathan Miller directed). Actor managers such as Henry Irving, Beerbohm Tree, and Donald Wolfit tended to treat the play as a star vehicle and to interpret Shylock as a near-tragic role. Notoriously, Irving occasionally omitted the entire last act. Modern directors often seek to redress the balance of roles, restoring passages that were previously cut and casting strongly in the subsidiary roles. In a post-Holocaust age-racial issues have become particularly sensitive. And a homoerotic subtext has often been discerned and projected in the relationship between Antonio and Bassanio, a procedure which can enrich the overall interpretation. In a searching production by John Barton at Stratford's Other Place (1978), Patrick Stewart, far from seeking tragic effect on his final exit, cringed in humiliated obeisance before his persecutors. Bill Alexander's racially charged Stratford production of 1987 had Antony Sher as a powerful, intensely Hebraic Shylock who was mocked by spitting Christians. At "You have among you many a purchased slave", he pulled forward a trembling black boy from among the onlookers. Peter Hall's Phoenix Theatre production (1989) with Dustin Hoffman trod a more neutral path, and in David Thacker's modern-dress RSC version (1993) David Calder's Shylock was a cultivated music lover who played Mahler on his CD player, cherished a photograph of his late wife, and recoiled from a world dominated by the mechanistic techniques of the computerized stock exchange. Trevor Nunn's National Theatre production (1999) with Henry Goodman as Shylock set the play in Central Europe shortly before the Nazi era.

The most capricious production, Terence Gray's at Cambridge aside (Gray was bored by the play and showed it), was Komisarjevsky's (Stratford, 1932), a wild fantastication in which Randle Ayrton's unyielding Jew seemed out of key. Alec Guinness was Shylock at Chichester (1984); Antony Sher took the part for the RSC (Stratford, 1987). Dustin Hoffman appeared in Peter Hall's West End production (Phoenix, 1989–90); Geraldine James was Portia. The ESC toured a notable production (Lyric, 1991 and tour).

There have been productions in the United States since 1752. George Frederick Cooke came to New York from London in 1810; Edmund Kean, Charles Kemble, Charles Kean and Henry Irving were other 19th-century English visitors. Prominent American players were Edwin Booth (1867, grim and self-centred); Richard Mansfield, at first (1893) highly sympathetic, but growing into extreme malevolence in later years; and John Drew (with Ada Rehan, 1898) in a revival of Augustin Daly opulence. Walter Hampden was probably the Shylock of his day (New York, 1925, with Ethel Barrymore as Portia), a lonely, dominating, vindictive man. Most succeeding actors, George Arliss (1928) among them, were fairly colourless until Boris Tumarin (Gate Theatre) and George C. Scott (New York Shakespeare Festival), both in 1962, reanimated Shylock, Scott especially in a sardonic and obsessive performance. The play has been done at Stratford, Ontario (e.g. Frederick Valk, 1955) and Stratford, Connecticut (1957; with Morris Carnovsky and Katharine Hepburn in the main parts).

Reinhardt had an spectacular production in the Campo San Trovaso, Venice (1934).

## IN OTHER TERMS

A ten-minute silent film of 1910 published by the British Film Institute gives a fascinating glimpse of a comic Shylock played on location in Venice. Jonathan Miller directed Warren Mitchell for the BBC television film series (1980) and memorably adapted for television his National Theatre production with Olivier as a patriarchal Shylock (1969). Michael Radford's 2004 film, picturesquely filmed in Venice, has distinguished performances from Al Pacino (Shylock), Jeremy Irons (Antonio), and Ralph Fiennes (Bassanio).

St John Ervine, the critic and playwright, wrote a sequel, *The Lady of Belmont* (1923), set ten years after the trial, with Shylock now a Venetian senator and the Doge's friend. Gabriel Fauré wrote incidental music published as *Shylock* (1889) for a play based on Shakespeare's. Ralph Vaughan Williams's beautiful *Serenade to Music* (1938) sets lines from the opening of Act V for sixteen solo singers and orchestra.

## CHIEF CHARACTERS

**Shylock** Second longest part (359 lines), probably created by Richard Burbage. Outraged father, avenging creditor and usurer — the name is a transliteration of the Hebrew word for "cormorant" — the precise emphasis must vary with the actor, and also with the changing responses to Jewry across the centuries. Shylock is both villain and victim.

**Antonio** The unselfish, serious, patient merchant, who in the theatre must have personality enough not to be a cipher before the obliterating Shylock. He is not just a distillation of melancholy.

**Bassanio** "A Venetian, a scholar, and a soldier"; nobly spoken; deeply remorseful at the news of Antonio's misfortune. Though critics have abused him, he is more than a fortune-hunter.

**Gratiano** "Let me play the fool./With mirth and laughter let old wrinkles come" (I.1). Overplayed, he can be tedious, and he needs great tact in performance, especially in his interruption to the trial scene.

**Portia** The great lady of Belmont, patrician, witty, adventurous, is at the heart of the fantasy.

**Nerissa** Portia's gentlewoman (a first draft was Lucetta in *The Two Gentlemen of Verona*). She is "echoing merriment; not much more", said Granville-Barker. We can agree; but she has to be a capable lawyer's clerk.

**Duke of Venice** A purely functional character; but he should be imposing enough to distract us from the bizarre workings of the so-called "strict court".

**Prince of Morocco** The sonorously rhetorical suitor ("a tawny Moor all in white") who chooses the gold casket.

**Prince of Arragon** This affected Spanish suitor (man of the silver casket) used frequently to be cut, but his scene can take the theatre, if kept within bounds.

**Launcelot Gobbo** One of Shakespeare's dreariest clowns, especially in the scene (II.2) with his father, Old Gobbo. Still, Jessica calls him a "merry devil".

**Balthasar** Portia's servant, whose name is shared, carelessly, with the young "lawyer". He depends in the theatre on one line, "Madam, I go with all convenient speed" (III.4), which means a snail's pace.

**Jessica** The eloping daughter exists less when she is on the stage than in Shylock's passion when she is absent.

**Lorenzo** Jessica's lover lives almost entirely on his praise of music in the Belmont epilogue (V.1).

**Solanio** and **Salerio** In theatre jargon these gentlemen of Venice are "the Sals" or "the Salads".

# Henry IV, Part 1
## 1596–7

Historically, the period of the action is the summer of 1402 to the summer of 1403. When the play opens, Henry IV (Henry Bolingbroke), who reigned from 1399 to 1413, has been on the throne for three years. Hotspur was 23 years older than Prince Hal; but Shakespeare, for his own purposes, treats them as contemporaries.

## THE CHARACTERS

King Henry IV
Henry, Prince of Wales and Prince John of Lancaster (his sons)
Earl of Westmoreland and Sir Walter Blunt, friends of the King
Thomas Percy, Earl of Worcester
Henry Percy, Earl of Northumberland
Henry Percy, surnamed Hotspur, his son Edmund Mortimer, Earl of March
Archibald, Earl of Douglas
Owen Glendower
Sir Richard Vernon
Scroop, Archbishop of York
Sir Michael, friend of the Archbishop
Sir John Falstaff, Poins, Bardolph, Peto, Gadshill, irregular humorists
Francis, a drawer (potboy)
Lady Percy, wife of Hotspur and sister of Mortimer
Lady Mortimer, Mortimer's wife and daughter of Glendower
Hostess Quickly, of the Boar's Head, Eastcheap
Lords, Officers, Attendants, Sheriff, Vintner, Chamberlain, Drawers, Carriers, Travellers

## THE SCENE
England

# SYNOPSIS

King Henry IV ("So shaken as we are, so wan with care") is deeply troubled by affairs national and domestic. Nationally, he has to meet a rebellion raised by the Welshman, Glendower, who is joined by the fiery Harry Percy (Hotspur), and Hotspur's uncle (Worcester) and father (Northumberland). Domestically, the King mourns the behaviour of his son, the Prince of Wales (Prince Hal), who is always in the most dubious company, the fat knight Sir John Falstaff and his associates. Hal, in a soliloquy at the end of Act I, promises to redeem himself when the need comes.

The companions (Act II) join in a robbery, after which Hal and Poins, disguised, scare away Falstaff and Bardolph, though Falstaff at the Boar's Head boasts of his enterprise before Hal exposes him. During a long tavern charade Falstaff and Hal in turn impersonate the King, and Hal speaks with uncomfortable candour. In Wales (Act III) the rebels are assembled: Glendower, his former prisoner Mortimer, Hotspur's brother-in-law (now married to Glendower's daughter), Hotspur himself, and Worcester. Between them they plan how to divide the kingdom when victory is won. Meanwhile in London the King admonishes his son, comparing his behaviour with the splendour of Hotspur ("Mars in swathling clothes"). Hal promises him that there will be a change, and before leaving with his father to fight the rebels, offers to Falstaff a command of foot soldiers.

The rebels find that their forces are depleted (Act IV), but Hotspur urges battle. Though (Act V) the King offers pardon if the rebels disband, Worcester distrustfully keeps the news from Hotspur. In the battle of Shrewsbury Hal kills Hotspur in a single fight (Falstaff, who earlier in V.1 has had his famous cynical soliloquy on honour, claims that he is responsible). After the royal army has won and two of the rebels have been sent for execution, Hal and his brother Prince John set off on various punitive expeditions.

# IN PERFORMANCE

*Henry IV* is Falstaff's play, the record of the fat knight who was not only witty in himself, but the cause of wit in other men: "the voice of spontaneous anarchy," said Robert Speaight, "opposed to calculating order". He and his irregular humorists supply only a secondary plot in the great twin brethren of the chronicle plays; but Falstaff stands — not by sheer bulk alone — at stage centre, something that in Part 1 can be a little unfair to the captains and the kings, the Prince of Wales and Hotspur, both grand theatrical parts. The fusion of high dramatic verse and robust comedy is almost unmatched in the Shakespeare Folio.

Part 1 has always been first in two senses. It has had more productions than its even finer sequel; and only in recent years have we found them played together in consecutive performances. The sources here are Holinshed and a play which was the first half of the surviving and anonymous *Famous Victories of Henry V* (1598). In the earliest performance Falstaff was named Oldcastle. The change came about as the result of protests from Oldcastle's descendant Lord Cobham, who was Queen Elizabeth's Lord Chamberlain at around the time the play was first performed. We cannot say for certain who were the first Prince and Falstaff (in 1596 or 1597) — Burbage, perhaps, and Kemp, but this is speculation. In 1682 Betterton was Hotspur and in 1700 Falstaff, "hitting the humour better than any that have aimed at it before", said a playgoer. James Quin (first half of the 18th century) was praised as a Falstaff of intellect and breeding; John Henderson, always laughing, was the best of a later plethora.

Stephen Kemble, John Philip's brother, arrived early in the 19th century with an apparently unimaginative portrait much liked — as other Falstaffs had been — because he could play without padding. Macready, Hotspur at first, became a majestic King in Part 2. Phelps, as Falstaff, put on Part 1 often at Sadler's Wells. Tree ("he will never be even moderately good," said Shaw) was Falstaff at the Haymarket (1896). Matheson Lang, Hotspur for Tree at His Majesty's (1914), probably began the tradition of stammering. The only warrant for this is Lady Percy's line (Part 2, II.3), "Speaking thick/Which nature made his blemish", something that means merely "thick and fast", pelting speech. Tree/ Lang's notion remained fashionable for some decades.

Stratford audiences loved Roy Byford's convulsively laughing Falstaff — like Stephen Kemble, free from padding — on several "festival" occasions for Bridges-Adams in the 1920s and 1930s. Two acclaimed revivals were Robert Atkins's (His Majesty's, 1935), with the comedian George Robey in a sack-and-sugar performance inevitably overpraised at the time; and a marvellous 1945 production (Old Vic company at the New Theatre under John Burrell), with Richardson's Falstaff and Olivier's Hotspur. No one had driven more surely than Richardson into the knight's wise, agile mind or examined the rich prose with a livelier zest. Laurence Olivier, who played Hotspur with stabbing, darting fire, chose to stammer on the letter "w" so that he died with his last word struggling for utterance: "Thou art dust/And food for —" To which the Prince replies: "For worms, brave Percy. Fare thee well, great heart." Michael Redgrave chose a thick Northumbrian accent (Stratford, 1951). Michael Bogdanov directed the inaugural ESC production of *Henry IV*, with Michael Pennington as Henry and John Woodvine as a pinstriped Falstaff (Old Vic, 1986–7). Robert Stephens was Falstaff in Adrian Noble's RSC production of Parts 1 and 2 (1991–2). Michael Attenborough's fine production (Swan, 2000), part of the RSC's "This England" sequence, had Desmond Barrit as a memorable Falstaff.

Part 1 appeared at the Chapel Street Theatre, New York, in December 1761. William Warren and Thomas Abthorpe Cooper (Philadelphia, 1796) were a famous pair as Falstaff and Hotspur. But probably the most accomplished American Falstaff was James Henry Hackett, between 1828 and 1871. Not everyone liked him (he held that Falstaff had neither refinement, intellect nor breeding) but mere length of service would have kept him in the records. Maurice Evans was Falstaff in Philadelphia (1937) and New York (1939). Part 1 was staged at Stratford, Ontario in 1958, 1965 and 1979.

John Goodman played Falstaff in Central Park for the New York Shakespeare Festival (1981).

# IN OTHER TERMS

American television screened a two-hour adaptation in 1960. The BBC television series (1979) had Anthony Quayle as Falstaff. In 1995 John Caird directed a BBC television adaptation. Part of Gus Van Sant's 1991 idiosyncratic film *My Own Private Idaho* includes a modern, gay adaptation of *Henry IV, Part 1*, portraying the young boy hustlers' mentor as a Falstaffian character. Gustav Holst's one-act opera *At the Boar's Head* (1925) adapts the tavern scenes, movingly counterpointing them with two of Shakespeare's sonnets on time sung by Hal.

# CHIEF CHARACTERS

**Henry IV** Historically, he is 37 years old, but in the play he seems nearly twice that age, though there is no reason to present him as a glum neurotic. He speaks nobly in the scene with the Prince (III.2), "I know not whether God will have it so/For some displeasing service I have done."

**Henry, Prince of Wales** Determined, as it has been said, to be a prince for all seasons. Actors emphasize his "I do, I will" in reply to Falstaff's charade-speech (II.4).

**Henry Percy (Hotspur)** Not a mere romantic blazon, but a man hurtling and passionate. He has the great cry (I.3), "By heaven, methinks it were an easy leap/To pluck bright honour from the pale-fac'd moon."

**Sir John Falstaff** In comedy, Shakespeare's fullest creation and a prodigious coiner of phrases.

**Sir Richard Vernon** Remembered for the speech (IV.1), describing the Prince, "I saw young Harry, with his beaver on."

**Bardolph** Falstaff's follower, whose red-purple face inspires his master to a prose aria (III.3), "I never see thy face but I think upon hell-fire."

**Owen Glendower** "That great magician, damn'd Glendower." We must assume that someone in Shakespeare's company had a gift for Welsh character.

**Earl of Worcester** Hotspur's uncle ("Your presence is too bold and peremptory," says the King, I.3).

**Earl of Northumberland** Hotspur's father; he disappears after the first act. Formerly the tyrant of *Richard II*, he speaks now (I.3) of "the unhappy king."

**Lady Percy** Hotspur's wife, with two very brief but — especially the first — rewarding scenes.

**Hostess** Quickly Angry, infatuated, voluble.

**Lady Mortimer** Edmund Mortimer's Welsh-speaking wife, Glendower's daughter.

Her song (III.1), in a passage that was formerly too often cut, is a wistful moment in a twilit scene miraculously evoked by Bridges-Adams (Stratford, 1930, 1932).

---

# Henry IV, Part 2
## 1598

Historically, Henry IV died in 1413. Shakespeare presents him (IV.5) as urging his son "to busy giddy minds/ With foreign quarrels, that action, hence borne out,/May waste the memory of the former days."

**THE CHARACTERS**
**Rumour, the Presenter**
King Henry IV
Henry, Prince of Wales, afterwards
  Henry V
Prince John of Lancaster, Prince
  Humphrey of Gloucester and Thomas,
  Duke of Clarence, his brothers

**Opposing the King:**
Earl of Northumberland
Scroop, Archbishop of York
Lord Mowbray
Lord Hastings
Lord Bardolph
Sir John Colville
Travers and Morton, Northumberland's
  retainers

**For the King:**
Earl of Warwick

Earl of Westmoreland
Earl of Surrey, Earl of Kent, Sir John
  Blunt, do not speak
Gower
Harcourt
The Lord Chief Justice

Sir John Falstaff, Edward Poins,
  Bardolph, Pistol, Peto, Falstaff's Page,
  irregular humorists
Robert Shallow, Silence, Gloucestershire
  country justices
Davy, Shallow's servant
Ralph Mouldy, Simon Shadow, Thomas
  Wart, Francis Feeble, Peter Bullcalf,
  countrymen
Fang and Snare, Sheriff's officers
Francis, a drawer (potboy)
Lady Northumberland
Lady Percy, Hotspur's widow
Hostess Quickly, of the Boar's Head,
  Eastcheap
Doll Tearsheet, a whore
Lords, Attendants, Porters, Drawers,
  Beadles, Grooms, Servants

**THE SCENE**
England

---

# SYNOPSIS

In his castle at Warkworth the Earl of Northumberland learns, after previous false tidings, that Hotspur has been killed and that royal troops, commanded by Prince John of Lancaster and the Earl of Westmoreland, are advancing on him. In London the Lord Chief Justice rebukes Falstaff and reminds him that he is to join Prince John's forces. Falstaff (Act II) persuades Hostess Quickly of the Boar's Head Tavern to lend him still more money; the old man, at supper with Doll Tearsheet, speaks unguardedly of Prince Hal and Poins who, disguised as potmen, overhear it all.

The King (Act III) is told of Owen Glendower's death; and Falstaff, recruiting in the Cotswolds, meets an old friend, Justice Robert Shallow (and another country justice, Silence). The northern rebels, without Northumberland, are tricked (Act IV) into surrendering to Prince John's army. The King is ill at Westminster: Hal, finding him asleep and believing him to be dead, takes the crown from the pillow. Later, deeply moved, he is rebuked by the awakened King. They are reconciled (IV.5): "God put it in thy mind to take it hence,/ That thou mightst win the more thy father's love."

Down in Gloucestershire (V.3), Falstaff (who has returned that way to visit Shallow) hears from Pistol that the King is dead and Hal has succeeded him. Certain of fortune, Falstaff sets out for London with his followers (and Shallow); but when he calls to the new King, Henry V, coming from the coronation, he is rejected and sent with his party to the Fleet prison until "their conversations/Appear more wise and modest to the world."

# IN PERFORMANCE

The sixth longest of the plays, with nearly twice as many characters as Part 1, *Henry IV, Part 2*, relatively autumnal, has lagged behind its partner. Falstaff, if a little quieter, is no whit diminished (the Cotswold scenes are incomparable comedy); and Prince Hal's character grows with his accession as Henry V. There is, of course, no Hotspur; the northern rebellion is a sour interlude; and moralists, especially in the 19th century, were affronted by that "abandoned creature, Doll Tearsheet", with (said *The Athenaeum* in 1853) "certain freedoms not exactly in accordance with the prevailing taste in modern stage manners". Probably the play was not performed between the pre-Civil War period and early in the 18th century, when a distorted version reached Drury Lane. Later, Part 2, though never as popular as Part 1, had numerous productions (James Quin and John Henderson were sometimes its Falstaff); John Philip Kemble played the King at Covent Garden (1804); a revival there (1821) mocked George IV's coronation; Macready, a superb Hotspur in Part 1, often acted the King in Part 2 with his hypnotic grandeur; and Phelps, at Sadler's Wells, contrived to double the King and Hotspur on various occasions from 1853.

Frank Benson, who had special affection for Part 2, often staged it at Stratford with a comedian of gusto, George Weir, as Falstaff. Barry Jackson, in 1913, did what was then a rarity, a full text of Part 1 at the Birmingham Repertory; and on Shakespeare's birthday, nine years later, he put on both parts consecutively. So did Bridges-Adams in 1932, at the opening of the present theatre in Stratford-upon-Avon (Roy Byford as Falstaff, Randle Ayrton as the King beneath the throne's crimson canopy, and Gyles Isham as Hal). In later years, when possible, the two parts would be acted in conjunction at the Old Vic and Stratford. Memorable productions were the Vic company's performance at the New (1945), with Ralph Richardson as Falstaff and Laurence Olivier as Shallow in Part 2; and at Stratford (1964), a production by Peter Hall, John Barton and Clifford Williams (Falstaff, Hugh Griffith). The Cotswold scenes were especially affecting in Michael Attenborough's 2000 Stratford production of Parts 1 and 2 (see *Henry IV, Part 1*).

Tony van Bridge played Falstaff at Stratford, Ontario, in 1965; and the chronicles were revived there in 1979.

# IN OTHER TERMS

Orson Welles's film *Chimes at Midnight* (1966; *Falstaff* in USA) is a conflation; technically flawed, it has John Gielgud as a superb Henry IV. Sir Edward Elgar's great symphonic study *Falstaff* (1913) programmatically portrays the fat knight's fortunes in a manner reminiscent of a Richard Strauss symphonic poem.

# CHIEF CHARACTERS

**Henry IV** Macready used to glorify the part. With its apostrophe to sleep (III.1) and its rebuke to Hal (IV.5) it can be darkly impressive; midway there is such a sudden leap in the mind as "O Westmoreland, thou art a summer bird,/Which ever in the haunch of winter sings/The lifting up of day" (IV.4).

**Henry, Prince of Wales** After one relapse into the old mood, he is a graver figure, finding maturity with the succession to the throne. In the circumstances, the rejection of Falstaff (V.5) is inevitable.

**Prince John of Lancaster** The unlikeable prince ("this same young sober-blooded boy") who quells the northern rebellion (Act IV).

**Lord Chief Justice** Early in the play he is coping with Falstaff; at the end he is the new King's adviser ("You shall be as a father to my youth").

**Sir John Falstaff** A trifle quieter than in Part 1, but still sovereign. We think of him when he suddenly turns aside at the Boar's Head with "Peace, good Doll!... Do not bid me remember mine end" (II.4).

**Bardolph** Now with Falstaff in the wars and in Gloucestershire. Shakespeare is as careless as ever with names. The cast includes an inconsiderable Lord Bardolph, who comes from Shrewsbury to Warkworth.

**Pistol** A "swaggering rascal", whose Marlovian histrionics are in the *Tamburlaine* manner: "Packhorses/And hollow pamper'd jades of Asia,/Which cannot go but thirty miles a day" (II.4), "Under which King, Bezonian! speak, or die" (V.3).

**Robert Shallow** The husk of a man who remembers, in his Cotswold orchard, the mad days he knew when he and all the world were young and Jack Falstaff was "a crack not thus high" and page to Thomas Mowbray, Duke of Norfolk. Shallow lives for ever in our first sight of him ("And is old Double dead?" III.2), and in that warm silver night-piece with Silence jetting into song, and Falstaff sitting by, contemplative (V.3).

**Silence** The other Gloucestershire justice, "Cousin Silence", who is in more or less unquenchable song throughout the orchard scene. "Now comes in the sweet o'th'night" (V.3).

**Feeble** The women's tailor, chosen as a recruit in the first Cotswold scene (III.2): "I will do my good will, sir; you can have no more." His natural courage is opposed to the cowardice of the roaring "Peter Bullcalf o'th'green".

**Lady Percy** Her single scene (II.3) used regularly to be cut, a sad loss, for the widowed Kate uses the unforgettable phrase about dead Hotspur, "By his light/Did all the chivalry of England move".

**Hostess Quickly** Talkative to the bitter end, which has to be bitter indeed (V.4). Hers is the line, "He hath eaten me out of house and home" (II.1).

**Doll Tearsheet** The boisterous Boar's Head whore endeared to us for her moments of affection for Falstaff. But we have to leave her (V.4) near the whipping-post.

**Rumour** The Prologue or Presenter, "painted full of tongues". A surging pictorial speech, it has often been cut; once, too, split capriciously among a whole corps of players.

# The Merry Wives of Windsor
## 1597–8

### ❀ THE CHARACTERS
Sir John Falstaff
Mistress Alice Ford
Mistress Margaret Page
Anne Page, her daughter
Fenton, a young gentleman
Robert Shallow, a country justice
Abraham Slender, Shallow's cousin
Frank Ford and George Page, citizens of
   Windsor
William Page, a boy; Page's son
Sir Hugh Evans, a Welsh parson

Doctor Caius, a French physician
Host of the Garter Inn
Bardolph, Nym, Pistol, Falstaff's
   followers
Robin, a page to Falstaff
Simple, Slender's servant
John Rugby, servant to Dr Caius
Mistress Quickly, servant to Caius
Servants to Page, Ford, etc.

### ❀ THE SCENE
Windsor and the neighbourhood

# SYNOPSIS

Sir John Falstaff, in Windsor and short of money, decides to woo both Mistress Ford and Mistress Page, prosperous citizens' wives, and sends identical letters to them. Two of Falstaff's discharged followers, Pistol and Nym, reveal this (Act II) to the husbands, though only the jealous Ford takes real notice. Going to the Garter Inn, disguised as a "Master Brook", he asks Falstaff to woo Mistress Ford on his behalf and learns that the knight already has an assignation. The wives prepare to trick Falstaff. At the same time other complex love-matters are in progress. The French physician, Caius, in love with Anne Page, has challenged Parson Hugh Evans to a duel, simply because Evans has asked the doctor's housekeeper, Quickly, to help the foolish Abraham Slender to Anne's hand. Actually, Anne — as we have seen in Act I — is in love with Master Fenton who has already enlisted the versatile Quickly as an ally. Caius and Evans (Act III) are reconciled by the Host of the Garter who has neatly prevented the duel.

In III.3 Falstaff is carried from Ford's house (just as Ford arrives to search it) in a laundry-basket of dirty linen; later, as "Brook", Ford discovers what has happened and hears of a new assignation between Falstaff and Mistress Ford (III.5). This time (IV.2) Falstaff escapes in the clothes of a maid's aunt whom Ford, still unknowing, beats unmercifully as a witch. At length, the jest revealed to their husbands, the wives get Falstaff, disguised as the ghost of Herne the Hunter, to meet Mistress Ford in Windsor Forest at midnight. There (Act V) all is settled when Falstaff is assailed by a group of Windsor children, disguised as fairies and hobgoblins. Caius and Slender are each tricked into running off with boy "fairies", thinking them to be Anne. Fenton and Anne appear, just married; and the end will be a journey home "to laugh this sport o'er by a country fire."

# IN PERFORMANCE

Legend says that Queen Elizabeth wished to see Falstaff in love, and this predominantly prose comedy is the result, doubtless written in a hurry (legend, again, suggests a fortnight). One idea is that it was written early in 1597 and performed for a Garter celebration at Windsor. Never a favourite with academic critics, it usually goes well in the theatre, in its repetitive method, once we have realized that some of the characters (Falstaff himself, Shallow, Pistol, Bardolph, Quickly) have the names of great originals and little else. Falstaff, so mercilessly deceived by the merry wives, is an ample acting part, though the sharpest character is Ford, who might be described as Leontes (*The Winter's Tale*) in the key of comedy, and who works himself into a glorious rage never better managed than by Ian Richardson at Stratford (1975).

The piece used to be acted in a summer setting; but many points ("sea-coal fire", "this raw rheumatic day", and so on) show that it is a winter piece influenced, no doubt, by the season when Shakespeare wrote it. The speech on the Order of the Garter (V.5), assigned to the "Fairy Queen" (often, and oddly, Mistress Quickly), is frequently cut; so, too, with more reason, though they did appear at e.g. the Mermaid (1975) and Stratford/Aldwych (1979–80), are the references (IV.3 and IV.5) to horse-stealing "Germans" which had a purely topical significance as dead now as so many topical jokes can be.

The comedy was approved in 18th-century London (James Quin and John Henderson were notable Falstaffs), and through the 19th century as well. Charles Kean, who played Ford at the Princess's (1851) was better than usual. Tree was a rather juiceless Falstaff at the Haymarket (1889) and — here with Ellen Terry and Madge Kendal as the wives — at His Majesty's (1902). Oscar Asche was brave enough to do the piece in its proper winter setting (Garrick, 1911); Bridges-Adams directed it famously (Lyric, Hammersmith, 1923, with Edith Evans and Dorothy Green as the wives, Roy Byford as Falstaff, Randle Ayrton as Ford); Theodore Komisarjevsky (Stratford, 1935) turned it into something like a Viennese operetta, though remaining — he said cheerfully — "faithful in word and gesture to Shakespeare". Other notable Old Vic and Stratford performances were in 1951 (Old Vic, Roger Livesey as Falstaff, Peggy Ashcroft as

Mistress Page), 1955 (Paul Rogers at the Old Vic, Anthony Quayle at Stratford), and 1975 (Stratford, Brewster Mason as an unusually dignified Falstaff, Ian Richardson as Ford). Bill Alexander's 1986 production updated the action with close detail to the 1950s, with Falstaff (Peter Jeffrey) as a seedy ex-officer. The wives (Lindsay Duncan and Janet Dale) played their letter scene hilariously under hair dryers. Ian Judge's Stratford production (1996) had Leslie Phillips as Falstaff and Christopher Luscombe as a sweetly gay Slender whose relief at not getting to marry Anne Page was palpable. At the Swan in 2002, Greg Hicks, under the direction of Rachel Kavanaugh, was outstanding as an obsessive Dr Caius, his repeated "By Gar"s sounding remarkably like a two-syllabled word of similar construction.

The first American production was in Philadelphia, 1770; the first in New York, 1789. James Henry Hackett, for nearly 40 years until 1871, was the definitive American Falstaff (described as "exorbitantly funny") in the comedy and in *Henry IV*. Ada Rehan was Mistress Ford for Daly (1885 and 1898; originally with Charles Fisher, later with George Clarke). Otis Skinner was Falstaff at the Knickerbocker (1928). Stratford, Ontario: Douglas Campbell, 1956; Tony van Bridge, 1967.

## IN OTHER TERMS

Frederick Reynolds made a wild musical adaptation (Drury Lane, 1824.) Otto Nicolai's delightful opera (1849) has been unfairly overshadowed by Verdi's late masterpiece *Falstaff* (1893), which imports the "honour" soliloquy from *Henry IV Part 1*. Ralph Vaughan Williams's opera *Sir John in Love* (1929), well worth reviving, uses English folk tunes and includes his well-known fantasia on "Greensleeves". After it failed on stage he made of it a cantata, "In Windsor Forest".

## CHIEF CHARACTERS

**Sir John Falstaff** The knight of the Garter Inn at Windsor is, intellectually, only a wraith of the knight of the Boar's Head in Eastcheap. The Falstaff of *Henry IV* would never have submitted to these humiliations, but the part (496 lines) is theatrically useful at the centre of a farce; the old wit can flicker.
**Mistress Alice Ford** She is the wife who three times traps Falstaff. When he first enters her house she should be asleep. His greeting, "Have I caught thee, my heavenly jewel?" is the first line of a sonnet by Philip Sidney that the Elizabethan audience would know and which goes on: "Teaching sleep most fair to be?"
**Mistress Page** The other laughing conspirator, and the longer part.

**Anne Page** "Sweet Anne", much courted, would live if only for her protest on hearing her mother's support of Caius as a husband: "I had rather be set quick i'th'earth and bowl'd to death with turnips" (III.4).

**Mistress Quickly** The third longest part, and no wonder, for she is a desperately loquacious "she-Mercury". Here she is housekeeper to Dr Caius, and the play's go-between. Nothing (except the name and the verbosity) to do with Hostess Quickly.

**Slender** A minor Sir Andrew (*Twelfth Night*), invariably in peril of burlesque.

**Shallow** Only the name connects this thin sketch with Falstaff's Cotswold host in *Henry IV, Part 2*.

**Ford** The jealous husband who — as himself and as "Master Brook" — runs a high temperature throughout.

**Page** A bluff, intelligent contrast with the hysterical Ford.

**Parson Hugh Evans** Another Welsh part for the actor in Shakespeare's company who, we must surmise, played Glendower in *Henry IV, Part 1* and Fluellen in *Henry V*.

**Caius** A parodied Frenchman represented by a series of fizzing verbal rockets.

**Host of the Garter** Heartily jovial, but too often boomed out of existence.

**Fenton** A personable blank.

**Simple** Slender's man who at least can remind his master that Alice Shortcake borrowed his copy of the Book of Riddles "upon All-Hallowmass last, a fortnight afore Michaelmas" (I.1).

**Bardolph** Becomes a tapster at the Garter Inn.

**Pistol** Still speaking inflated blank verse, he fades away feebly in Act II, though he returns as a Hobgoblin at Herne's Oak. One familiar observation: "The world's mine oyster/Which I with sword will open" (II.2).

**Nym** Makes tedious play with the fashionable word "humours", and also disappears.

# Much Ado About Nothing
## 1598–9

 **THE CHARACTERS**

Don Pedro, Prince of Arragon
Don John, his bastard brother
Claudio, a young lord of Florence
Benedick, a young lord of Padua
Leonato, Governor of Messina
Hero, Leonato's daughter
Beatrice, Leonato's niece
Antonio, his brother
Balthasar, attendant on Don Pedro
Margaret, Ursula, gentlewomen
    attending on Hero

Borachio and Conrade, followers of Don
    John
Friar Francis
Dogberry, a constable
Verges, a headborough (parish officer or
    petty constable)
A Sexton
A Boy
Messengers, Watch, Attendants

**THE SCENE**

Messina (Sicily)

# SYNOPSIS

Leonato, Governor of Messina, is host to Don Pedro, the Prince of Arragon, who has come from suppressing a rebellion by his bastard brother, Don John. With Pedro are John, now "reconciled" to him; Claudio, a young Florentine lord, of whom John is bitterly resentful; and a Paduan lord, Benedick, said to be a confirmed bachelor and engaged in a "merry war" with Leonato's niece, Beatrice, apparently a confirmed spinster. Claudio loves Leonato's daughter, Hero; Don John swears to thwart him. After a masked ball (Act II) the wedding of Claudio and Hero is planned. Borachio, Don John's follower, tells him that having seen that the Prince and Claudio are listening, he will exchange love vows by night with Hero's gentlewoman, dressed in her mistress's clothes, at Hero's bedroom window.

Pedro, Claudio and Leonato ensure that Benedick (hidden in a garden arbour) hears them discuss Beatrice's presumably passionate love for him. Hero and Ursula play a similar trick (Act III) on the listening Beatrice (here the passion is Benedick's). On the night before the wedding Don John offers to give the Prince and Claudio proof of Hero's unfaithfulness. Later, Borachio, heard boasting about his successful deceit to a drunken comrade, is arrested by the Watch and taken to Dogberry, the constable. Before Leonato can know anything, the wedding ceremony (Act IV) is due. In the church Claudio denounces Hero, who faints. The Prince and Claudio leave. Friar Francis, disbelieving the charge, proposes that Hero should be reported dead and hidden until the truth is known. Beatrice, much grieved, urges Benedick to kill

Claudio. At length (Act V) all is revealed, and the penitent Claudio promises to marry a niece of Leonato, said to be the image of "dead" Hero. She is, of course, Hero herself; Beatrice and Benedick, as expected, resolve their "merry war", and news comes that Don John has been taken prisoner.

# IN PERFORMANCE

Just as Falstaff steps out in front of the chronicle-figures in Henry IV, so Benedick and Beatrice, fighting their "merry war", rule the patrician comedy of *Much Ado About Nothing*, a comedy of eavesdropping. Based on a traditional Italian tale, the play is a work of glittering artifice that needs in performance a style sometimes absent. Directors have often sought to vary it by changing the period: it has been put into British Regency fashions, Italy in the mid-19th century (the *Risorgimento*), Sicily in 1890, Latin America, and — most daring and curiously effective of all — post-Mutiny India in some counterpart of Simla or Darjeeling, with Dogberry as a babu. A West End production had an Ulster-accented Benedick dancing masked with Beatrice at a 1920s Wild West Ball.

Nothing of this has much damaged what the critic, A.B. Walkley, writing in 1891, called a "composite picture of the multifarious, seething, fermenting life, the polychromatic phantasmagoria of the Renaissance", and what Bernard Shaw (1905) preferred to dismiss as "a hopeless story, pleasing only to lovers of the illustrated police papers." One passage has become a test of technique: the moment after the spurning of Hero when Benedick and Beatrice are left alone (IV.1). "Come," he urges, "bid me do anything for thee." She turns on him sharply with "Kill Claudio", and his spontaneous answer is "Ha! Not for the wide world." Mishandled, the exchange will bring jarring laughter. In John Gielgud's production of 1952 at the Phoenix, Beatrice (Diana Wynyard) paused in charged silence after Benedick's demand. "Kill Claudio" was almost forced from her, and Benedick's response, quick, low-toned, came as the near-incredulous exclamation of a man who had not realized how friendship must struggle with love and honour.

The other play-stealers are Dogberry, the portentous bullfrog constable, his timid lieutenant, Verges, and members of their Watch. Dogberry is a master of what, two centuries on, grew into a "malapropism" (after Sheridan's Mrs Malaprop in *The Rivals*). The misapplication of words — e.g. "For the watch to babble and to talk is most tolerable and not to be endured" (III.3) — has long been a stage cliché, but Dogberry's exercises, when spoken unselfconsciously, remain comic ("Comparisons are odorous", III.5).

*Much Ado About Nothing* was exceedingly popular in early years — it was among the plays acted at Court during the festivities for the betrothal and marriage of Princess Elizabeth and the Elector Palatine (May 1613). For all that, it vanished until 1721 and it did not really regain itself until Garrick, who had rehearsed himself for two months, played Benedick to Mrs Pritchard's Beatrice at Drury Lane (1748) and continued, off and on, until retirement in 1776. Various eminent Beatrices (such as Frances Abington and Mrs Jordan) appeared during the last two decades of the century; the major Benedick was John Philip Kemble (Drury Lane, 1788–1802), his brother Charles taking over in 1803. There was little of note until Irving's shining Lyceum revival (1882); Ellen Terry, more than any Beatrice before her, seemed to have been born under a dancing star. In the 1903 revival (Imperial) her designer son, Gordon Craig, indicated the church simply by the widening light that illuminated the colours of a huge cross.

For a while thereafter, except for intermittent Old Vic revivals, the piece belonged to Stratford-upon-Avon. There, in 1879, Barry Sullivan, with Helen Faucit (who left retirement for this performance), acted at the opening of the Memorial Theatre. Benson often did the comedy during his long management of the festivals; it was the jubilee choice of 1929; thereafter, the most complete production in a long sequence was Gielgud's (1949, Anthony Quayle, Diana Wynyard). Next year Gielgud himself and Peggy Ashcroft took over; and in 1952 Gielgud with Diana Wynyard (and Paul Scofield's Pedro) were in a London run at the Phoenix. There was a New York season (1959, Lunt-Fontanne Theatre, with Gielgud and Margaret Leighton). In the theatre the action has frequently been updated and even relocated. Michael Redgrave and Googie Withers played Beatrice and Benedick in Douglas Seale's Stratford production (1958) set in mid-19th-century Italy. John Barton directed an Anglo-Indian production at Stratford in 1976 in which Donald Sinden was a larger-than-life Benedick and Judi Dench an incomparable Beatrice. Judi Dench was to direct Kenneth Branagh and Samantha Bond with the Renaissance Theatre Company in the play (1988). A National Theatre production of 1981, directed by Peter Gill, had Michael Gambon and Penelope Wilton as Beatrice and Benedick. The play is a staple of the RSC repertoire. David Waller, an unrivalled Dogberry, played the role in Trevor Nunn's 1968 production and also in Di Trevis's 1988 production. A 1990 production by Bill Alexander had Roger Allam as Benedick and Beatrice. Gregory Doran's delightful and picturesque RSC production of 2002, with Harriet Walter and Nicholas le Prevost as Beatrice and Benedick, transferred to the Haymarket.

The New York Shakespeare Festival's 1988 production in Central Park, with Kevin Kline and Blythe Danner, was popular enough to have its run extended.

The comedy has come to Stratford, Ontario, e.g. in 1971 and (Alan Scarfe, Martha Henry) in 1977.

## IN OTHER TERMS

Hector Berlioz's opera *Béatrice et Bénédict* (1862) replaces Dogberry with a comic musician, Somarone. Berlioz wrote sparkling music for Beatrice, but the longest number in the work is a beautiful nocturne sung by Hero and Ursula. Kenneth Branagh's film (1993), shot on location in Tuscany, has a fine cast including Emma Thompson, Keanu Reeves, and Denzel Washington.

## CHIEF CHARACTERS

**Don Pedro, Prince of Arragon** A Renaissance nobleman, who believes too easily what he is told. Bridges-Adams, the Stratford director (1919–34), one of whose favourite plays this was, insisted that we should always be mindful in Shakespeare of what the dramatist called "degree": thus, "no one should touch Pedro on the arm, or sit in his presence without his gesture of assent."

**Hero** A wronged innocent.

**Don John** The bastard malcontent whose almost motiveless malice springs the main plot; his excuse is envy of Claudio, but he has a restless desire for mischief.

**Benedick** With the longest part (471 lines), he might be called a mature Berowne (*Love's Labour's Lost*). A figure of high comedy.

**Beatrice** "Dear Lady Disdain", Shakespeare's wittiest woman; born under a dancing star (II.1). John Dover Wilson described Beatrice as "the first woman in our literature… who has not only a brain but delights in its constant employment."

**Claudio** Difficult to make sympathetic; but we can feel for him in the brief elegiac scene (V.3: "Done to death by slanderous tongues/Was the Hero that here lies").

**Leonato** He has a sometimes too lightly regarded speech in the Church scene (IV.1): "Why, doth not every earthly thing/Cry shame upon her?"

**Dogberry** The massively complacent constable created in Shakespeare's company by Will Kempe. John Aubrey said in *Brief Lives* — though he got the play wrong — that Shakespeare took Dogberry's humours from a man at Grendon in Buckinghamshire "which is the road from London to Stratford".

**Verges** Dogberry's lieutenant. A wisp of a man.

**Borachio** A functional minor villain.

# As You Like It
## 1599

 **THE CHARACTERS**

Duke, living in exile
Rosalind, the banished Duke's daughter
Amiens, Jaques, lords attending
  on the banished Duke
Frederick, his brother, usurper of his
  dominions
Celia, Frederick's daughter
Le Beau, a courtier attending
  upon Frederick
Charles, wrestler to Frederick
Oliver, son to Sir Rowland de Boys
Jaques, his younger brother
Orlando, the youngest brother
Adam, Dennis, Oliver's servants
Touchstone, Frederick's court jester

Sir Oliver Martext, a vicar
Corin, Silvius, shepherds
Audrey, a country wench
William, a country fellow, in love with
  Audrey
Phebe, a shepherdess
A person representing Hymen
Lords, Pages, Foresters, and Attendants

 **THE SCENE**

Oliver's house, Frederick's court, the
Forest of Arden (which, though probably
intended for the Ardennes, is more easily
identifiable with Arden in Warwickshire
— that is, if identification is needed)

# SYNOPSIS

The late Sir Rowland de Boys had three sons: Oliver, the eldest, hates the youngest, Orlando ("It is the stubbornest young fellow of France", I.1), whom he has steadily humiliated. Orlando is matched against the usurping Duke Frederick's deadly wrestler, Charles; the fight, which the youth wins, is watched by Rosalind, the banished Duke's daughter, and her cousin, Frederick's daughter Celia. Orlando and Rosalind fall immediately in love; Frederick, jealous of her popularity, banishes her; and in the disguise of a boy (Ganymede) she leaves with Celia (as Ganymede's sister) and the jester Touchstone, to find her father in the Forest of Arden, where he lives with a company ("my co-mates and brothers in exile") that includes the melancholy courtier, Jaques.

Orlando and his faithful old Adam have also gone to Arden. The travellers (Act II) arrive severally: Rosalind and Celia overhear the shepherd Silvius declaring his love for Phebe, a scornful shepherdess. Orlando becomes a member of the Duke's court, and (Act III) hangs on the trees his love poems to Rosalind. When he meets her, unknowing, as Ganymede, she promises to cure him of infatuation "if you would but call me Rosalind, and come every day to my cote to woo me".

Meanwhile Phebe falls in love with "Ganymede", and Touchstone condescends to the country wench, Audrey. Oliver (Act IV), whom Frederick has summarily banished to find Orlando, arrives in Arden; on hearing how Orlando has rescued his brother from a lioness — and seeing a bloodstained napkin — "Ganymede" faints. Oliver and Celia (Act V) are now in love. Presently all the couples in Arden are united: Rosalind reveals herself to Orlando; and Oliver and Celia, Touchstone and Audrey, and even Silvius and Phebe, are in harmony. Frederick has decided to retire from the world into contemplation; the banished Duke is restored; and Rosalind speaks an epilogue.

# IN PERFORMANCE

*As You Like It* is thought by many to be the play which opened the Globe playhouse in 1599. A glistening comedy of love (often at first sight), it is derived principally from Thomas Lodge's novel, *Rosalynde* (1590), though Shakespeare invented such people as Jaques and Touchstone. A pastoral (and satirical) romance, it belongs first of all to its bewitching Rosalind, a deity on whom the forest airs attend and one of the great testing parts for an actress. Early in the 18th century (Drury Lane, 1723) a stupid adaptation, *Love in a Forest*, left out half a dozen characters — including Touchstone and Phebe — added a mosaic from other comedies, and brought Jaques in love with Celia.

From 1740, when the genuine text returned, until today, there has been a long splendour of Rosalinds. The American Ada Rehan (London, 1890), Athene Seyler (Stratford, 1919), Fabia Drake (Stratford, 1932), the beautiful Margaretta Scott (Open Air, 1936), Edith Evans (Old Vic and New, 1936–7) in a forest that could have been designed and peopled by Watteau, with arching boughs, vague silvery distances and ornamental water. It was the Rosalind of an uncommonly sophisticated pastoral, but every word was caressed and no other player could have so danced up and down the scale on "Alas the day! What shall I do with my doublet and hose?". Margaret Leighton was willowy and tender at Stratford in 1952, with Laurence Harvey commanding in the relatively unrewarding role of Orlando. Peggy Ashcroft, who had been sketched by Walter Sickert as Rosalind at the Old Vic in 1932, returned to it at Stratford in 1957. Glen Byam Shaw's production, wintry in setting in the opening scenes, moved through spring to summer-time fruition. Vanessa Redgrave scored her first great Shakespearian success as Rosalind in Michael Elliott's Stratford production of 1961, staged against a stylized tree on a perilously sloping green knoll. Dorothy Tutin sparkled in David Jones's Stratford production of 1967, with Michael Williams as an unusually characterful Orlando and Roy Kinnear showing that a natural comic actor can make Touchstone funny. Janet Suzman was one of numerous Celias who have later graduated to the role of Rosalind. In 1986 Susan Fleetwood was most genuinely and happily from Arden, with Sinead Cusack's Celia as companion.

Feminism made its impact on the play in a 1973 Stratford revival by Buzz Goodbody, with Eileen Atkins as a Rosalind in jeans and Richard Pasco a decadently cynical Jaques. In a symbolically set Adrian Noble production of 1985 Juliet Stevenson played a warmly feminine Rosalind to the Celia of Fiona Shaw, later an award-winning Rosalind at the Old Vic. The influence of Jan Kott's *Shakespeare our Contemporary* (1964) was discerned behind Clifford Williams's pioneering all-male production for the National Theatre at the Old Vic (1967), in the days before single-sex productions became ten a penny. Declan Donellan's 1992 all-male production with his Cheek by Jowl company had Adrian Lester as a joyful, totally uncamp Rosalind.

Of many New York Rosalinds since 1786, possibly the most memorable were Mary Anderson (1885–6), the near-classical achievement of Ada Rehan (1890, Augustin Daly's production), Katharine Hepburn (1950) — though John Mason Brown said she seemed "to have mistaken the Forest of Arden for the campus of Bryn Mawr" — and Nancy Wickwire (1958). At Stratford, Ontario: Irene Worth (1959), Carole Shelley (1972), Maggie Smith, in late 18th-century costume (1977).

Oscar Asche (His Majesty's, London, 1907) strewed the stage with moss-grown logs and leaves by the cartload from the previous autumn. Jacques Copeau (1938) staged the play in the Boboli Gardens in Florence, on the site where Reinhardt had done *A Midsummer Night's Dream*. Ronald Pickup was, bravely, Rosalind for an uninspiring all-male *As You Like It* (National at Old Vic, 1967). Patrick Garland directed Patricia Hodge and Jonathan Morris (Chicester Festival Theatre, 1983). One RSC production, with Juliet Stevenson and Fiona Shaw, was called by one critic a "violation of the Trades Descriptions Act" (Stratford, 1985). John Caird directed, with Sophie Thompson as Rosalind (Stratford, 1989). Fiona Shaw and Adam Kotz were directed by Tim Albery (Old Vic, 1990). Another, rather better all-male production, from Cheek by Jowl, won Joe Dixon the Ian Charleson Award, and Adrian Lester the Time Out Award (1992).

## IN OTHER TERMS

Paul Czinner directed a British-made film (1936), with Elisabeth Bergner as a coy Rosalind, Laurence Olivier as Orlando, and Henry Ainley as the banished Duke. The BBC television version (1978), filmed in the insect-infested grounds of Glamis Castle, has Helen Mirren as Rosalind. By contrast with its scenic opulence, Christine Edzard's low-budget 1992 film has an East End of London location and doubles Orlando with Oliver, and both of the Dukes.

# CHIEF CHARACTERS

**Banished Duke** A man of patient nobility, apt at special pleading. "Happy is your Grace," says Amiens (II.1), "That can translate the stubborness of fortune/Into so quiet and so sweet a style."

**Rosalind** The longest woman's part in Shakespeare (736 lines), obviously created by a remarkable boy "actress". Wise, rapturously in love, a woman who "by heavenly synod was devised".

**Frederick** The usurper who undergoes an unlikely but convenient spiritual conversion when meeting "an old religious man" (offstage) on the borders of the forest.

**Celia** The "gentle Aliena", Frederick's daughter, who is Rosalind's foil and who will marry Oliver.

**Jaques** "The melancholy Jaques" is the banished Duke's sardonic and misanthropic courtier with a murky past, and whose future will be spent in philosophical argument with the reformed Frederick. A part often over-praised: it includes "All the world's a stage" (II.7).

**Le Beau** Frederick's courtier who bids farewell to Orlando with "Hereafter, in a better world than this,/I shall desire more love and knowledge of you" (I.2). In a Stratford revival (1977–8) he defected to Arden.

**Charles** The "sinewy" wrestler who has the unexpected lines in which he tells Oliver that many young men flock daily to the banished Duke "and fleet the time carelessly, as they did in the golden world" (I.1).

**Oliver** The eldest de Boys brother, who passes during the night from villain to lover, and who meets in Arden a green and gilded snake and a hungry lioness.

**Jaques de Boys** Again Shakespeare does not bother about names. This Jaques is "the second son of old Sir Rowland"; here to settle everything with a last-act speech so awkward at that time of night that Frank Benson's company would give a shilling to every youth who spoke it without fault.

**Orlando** The youngest brother. An expert wrestler, a versifier and an agreeable young man who cannot recognize Rosalind when she is dressed as a boy (though one or two directors have tried to suggest that he does).

**Adam** Conscientious, teetotal veteran, who slips from the play – and sometimes, nowadays, from life – once he has safely reached Arden with Orlando. Traditionally, Shakespeare might have acted him.

**Touchstone** Arguably the least amusing of Shakespeare's jesters, a pedantic professional whose marriage to Audrey may be one of his jokes. His speech on "the degrees of the lie" (V.4) is intended presumably to give Rosalind time to change from her boy's disguise.

**Phebe** This disdainful shepherdess who scorns Silvius and loves Rosalind-Ganymede, speaks the tribute to Marlowe (III.5): "Dead shepherd, now I find thy saw of might:/'Who ever lov'd that lov'd not at first sight?' " (from *Hero and Leander*).

**Audrey** The country hoyden seized by Touchstone from her yokel William.

**Silvius** A shepherd obsessed by his love for Phebe.

**Corin** A veteran shepherd whose rural philosophy contrasts with the worldly-wise artifice of Touchstone (III.2).

**Amiens** The banished Duke's singing courtier.

# Henry V
## 1599

Historically, Henry V, who succeeded his father in 1413, died in 1422. The English won the battle of Agincourt, against the French, in 1415; Henry married Princess Katherine of France (in 1420).

**CHORUS**

King Henry V
Dukes of Gloucester and Bedford, the King's brothers
Duke of Exeter, the King's uncle
Duke of York, the King's cousin
Earl of Salisbury
Earl of Westmoreland
Earl of Warwick
Archbishop of Canterbury
Bishop of Ely
Earl of Cambridge
Lord Scroop and Sir Thomas Grey, conspirators against the King
Sir Thomas Erpingham, Gower (English), Fluellen (Welsh), Macmorris (Irish), Jamy (Scottish), captains in the King's army
Bates, Court, Williams, Nym, Bardolph, Pistol, soldiers in the King's army
Hostess of the Boar's Head, Eastcheap, formerly Mistress Nell Quickly, now Pistol's wife
Boy
A Herald
Charles VI, King of France
Isabel, Queen of France
Princess Katherine, her daughter
Lewis, the Dauphin
Duke of Burgundy
Duke of Orleans
Duke of Berri
Duke of Britaine
Duke of Bourbon
The Constable of France
Rambures, Grandpré, French lords
Governor of Harfleur
Alice, Katherine's attendant lady
Montjoy, a French herald
French Ambassadors to Henry V
Lords, Ladies, Officers, Soldiers, Messengers, Attendants

**THE SCENE**

England and France

## SYNOPSIS

Henry V hears the Archbishop of Canterbury's explanation of the "Salic Law", which justifies the royal claim to the French throne, and sends word to the Dauphin that he will fight in France. Before the army sails (Act II), Bardolph, Nym and Pistol learn of Falstaff's death from Nell Quickly, now Pistol's wife (II.3); at Southampton the King sentences three traitors to death.

Henry (Act III) takes Harfleur; Princess Katherine of France has an English lesson from her confidante, Alice; and Henry's outnumbered army prepares to fight at Agincourt. Walking among his troops, disguised, on the night before battle (Act IV) — "a little touch of Harry in the night" — the King debates with three soldiers, prays for success, and at sunrise delivers his famed rallying cry. The battle is fought and won, with great losses to the French, and "of our English dead", fewer than thirty.

Fluellen, the Welsh captain (Act V) forces the braggart Pistol to eat a leek for mocking the Welsh. At a final meeting in the palace of the French King, peace is made; Henry, with attractive gaucherie, proposes to Princess Katherine and she accepts him. Chorus, who has set the scene on five occasions, now comes out to end the play: "Small time, but, in that small, most greatly lived/This star of England."

## IN PERFORMANCE

"O, for a Muse of fire!" cries Chorus in the most resounding opening to any chronicle. Chorus might well have been Shakespeare himself (at the end (V.2) there is a reference to "our bending author"): if so, he gave himself a sequence of grand set-pieces that, apologizing for failure to show the fury of the French wars "on this unworthy scaffold... within this wooden O" (the Globe Theatre, Southwark), can fire an audience's imagination at every phrase. Derived principally from Holinshed, the play is a patriotic utterance throughout. Some modern criticism may undervalue it as an exercise in chauvinism; but as Dover Wilson said, "Heroism is the theme, and Henry the hero." In the theatre, when he is speaking on the morning of Crispin's Day before Agincourt, the piece has unerring power. So, too, that moment of quieter emotion, the reading of the casualty lists after battle. If we do not search too deeply (the speech at III.3, describing the dire threat to captured Harfleur, is an example) Henry will come to us, unfashionable though it may be, as his old adversary, Hotspur, did — "the light by which the chivalry of England moved."

Records are not particularly helpful until 1735 (there had been a botched adaptation a dozen years earlier). Thenceforward the play was always familiar on the stage — for over a century at Covent Garden and Drury Lane. The principal Henry (from 1789–1811, in a bad text) was John Philip Kemble. Macready, between 1819 and 1839, acted with sustained spirit, and in the last year (Covent Garden) added spectacular effects that fortified the words of Chorus.

After Phelps (Sadler's Wells, 1852) and Charles Kean (Princess's, 1859), with his prolific pageantry, the major performances were Frank Benson's — from 1897 usually at Stratford but in some London seasons as well — and Lewis Waller's (Lyceum, 1900, and afterwards). Benson was, without complication, the "star of England" the Elizabethan theatre might have known; but he did not slide over the night-speeches that remind us the piece is more than battle music. (Strangely, he had a habit of omitting Chorus.) Lewis

Waller, an eloquent paladin, would hurtle downstage for the Crispin crescendo. Between the wars Ralph Richardson (Old Vic, 1931) and Laurence Olivier (Old Vic, 1937, chiselling away at the dead wood of tradition), were most triumphant; Robert Atkins, valiant always, directed the play under hard white light during his experimental season (1936) at the Ring, Blackfriars; and unexpectedly (1938) Ivor Novello returned Shakespeare with sincerity to Drury Lane. After the war Alec Clunes (Old Vic, 1951, Glen Byam Shaw's production) never merely banged Henry over an assault course of rhetoric; and Alan Howard (Stratford/Aldwych, 1975-6) also thought his way into the part and regilded much that had been taken for granted. Kenneth Branagh was a popular Henry, heroic but warmly human, in Adrian Noble's RSC production (1984). Directors have often evoked parallels with modern warfare, even with specific conflicts, as in Michael Bogdanov's inaugural production for the English Shakespeare Company with his co-director, Michael Pennington, as Henry (Old Vic, etc., 1986–7). Matthew Warchus's exhilarating Stratford production, with Iain Glen as a thoughtful King, had Tony Britton on stage throughout as a be-medalled old soldier with a poppy in his buttonhole. Edward Hall's bold and witty 2000 production, part of the RSC's "This England" sequence, with William Houston as the King, was still stronger on modern parallels, with heavily proletarian English soldiers; it avoided the perennial temptation to caricature the French. At the National Theatre (2003), Nicholas Hytner's modern-dress production, with exciting battle scenes, used film and live video as instruments of propaganda. Adrian Lester's King evoked parallels with Tony Blair; Chorus was played by Penny Downie.

Christopher Plummer played Henry at Stratford, Ontario (1956; Edinburgh Festival, 1957). French parts played by French Canadians. Barry Kyle directed a memorable revival at the Theatre for a New Audience, New York (1993).

## IN OTHER TERMS

*Henry V* (1944) was the first of Laurence Olivier's three Shakespeare films (score by William Walton). He produced and directed it, and acted Henry, with a comparably valuable cast (Chorus, Leslie Banks; George Robey was seen for a few moments as the dying Falstaff). Though it suited the temper of the time, it was a lesser experience than the more uncompromising stage version at the Vic in 1937.

Chorus, in the film, was a gallant Elizabethan. Among other things down the years he has been Clio, the Muse of History, an Elizabethan youth, an actor in a duffle coat, and the semblance of Shakespeare himself.

Kenneth Branagh chose *Henry V* for his first venture into film direction, in 1989, featuring a fine array of British acting talent, including Derek Jacobi, Brian Blessed, Ian Holm, Paul Scofield and Emma Thompson. Branagh himself played Henry.

The BBC television film (1979) has David Gwillim as the King. A suite from the music composed by William Walton for Olivier's film is often performed independently, sometimes with a narration with extracts from the play.

# CHIEF CHARACTERS

**Henry V** Third longest part (1105 lines) in Shakespeare: "the war-like Henry", "the mirror of all Christian kings", "the star of England". A series of famous speeches: before Harfleur (III.1), the argument with the soldier Williams (IV.1), "Upon the King!" (IV.1), the Crispin's Day speech (IV.3) (rarely treated now as an oration), and the wooing (V.2).

**Duke of Exeter** The King's uncle, he brings English defiance to Charles VI (II.4).

**Duke of York** Two lines only: but the King's cousin, who falls when leading "the vaward", is the former Aumerle (see *Richard II*). The Duke of Exeter (IV.6) describes his death.

**Archbishop of Canterbury** His verbose and thankless genealogical verification (I.2) is frequently abridged, or the Archbishop is burlesqued to the detriment of such a line as "The singing masons building roofs of gold."

**Bishop of Ely** Often suffers as Canterbury does, which means the loss of the tribute to Henry "in the very May-morn of his youth" (I.2).

**Gower** The steady average Englishman: one of four captains (Fluellen for Wales, Jamy for Scotland, Macmorris for Ireland) who represent national characteristics.

**Fluellen** The Welsh captain, a fiery little dragon and the richest of Shakespeare's Welsh parts.

**Williams** A blunt soldier who, at the camp-fire before Agincourt, argues with the disguised Henry about the King's responsibility.

**Bardolph** Lieutenant Bardolph, with flame-red face, and Corporal Nym are hanged for looting (III.6, IV.4).

**Pistol** Last of Falstaff's "irregular humorists", the roaring coward is at length humiliated by Fluellen and proposes to return home as a bawd and cutpurse (V.1).

**Boy** Killed by the French soldiers escaping from battle (IV.7).

**Charles VI** Formerly, and quite unnecessarily, played as something of a feeble wander-wit.

**Lewis the Dauphin** Sends Henry the insulting tennis balls (I.2).

**Duke of Burgundy** Makes a fervent plea for peace (V.2).

**Mountjoy** Chivalrous and lonely French herald, often doubled with the French ambassador (I.2).

**Katherine** Bubbling French princess who in the English-lesson scene (III.4) appears already to be looking forward; and who (V.2) is clearly Henry's own.

**Alice** Katherine's gentlewoman who has been in England.

**Hostess Nell Quickly** She is now Pistol's wife. In two brief scenes (II.1 and II.3), the first only a fragment, she describes Falstaff's death in an affecting passage ("'A went away an it had been any christom child") which contains the 18th-century reading of a debated text, "a babbl'd of green fields". We hear from Pistol (V.1) that Nell herself has died.

**Chorus** He has half a dozen expository speeches, asking for his hearers' imagination to supply "the vasty fields of France", the English fleet as "a city on th'inconstant billows dancing", the armies waiting in the night before battle, the King's return in triumph to England and again to France. He ends — we like to think it is Shakespeare's voice — "Thus far, with rough and all-unable pen,/Our bending author has pursued the story."

# Julius Caesar
## 1599

 **THE CHARACTERS**

Julius Caesar
Calphurnia, wife to Caesar
Octavius Caesar, his great-nephew
Marcus Antonius and M. Aemilius
    Lepidus, triumvirs after Julius Caesar's
    death
Cicero, Publius, Popilius Lena, Senators
Marcus Brutus and Caius Cassius,
    principal conspirators against Julius
    Caesar
Portia, wife to Brutus
Casca, Trebonius, Ligarius, Decius
    Brutus, Metellus Cimber,
    Cinna, other conspirators
Flavius, Marullus, tribunes

Artemidorus, a sophist, of Cnidos
A Soothsayer
Cinna, a poet
Another poet
Lucilius, Titinius, Messala, Young Cato,
    Volumnius, friends to Brutus and
    Cassius
Varro, Clitus, Claudius, Strato, Lucius,
    Dardanius, servants to Brutus
Pindarus, servant to Cassius
Senators, Citizens, Guards, Attendants,
    etc.

 **THE SCENE**
Rome, near Sardis, near Philippi

# SYNOPSIS

A powerful faction fears the growing strength of Julius Caesar in republican Rome. As he walks to the festival games, a soothsayer warns him of the Ides of March (March 15). On a stormy night, Cassius and Casca visit Marcus Brutus, who must be won to the rebel party. He receives them and other conspirators (Act II) in his garden, and Caesar's murder is planned for the next morning. Portia, wife of Brutus, observes his unrest.

Caesar's wife, Calphurnia, seeks to prevent her husband from going to the Capitol, but he does so, and (Act III) upon the Ides of March is stabbed to death. Brutus, in the Forum, tells the mob his reasons; then Mark Antony, permitted to speak as Caesar's friend, rouses the people of Rome in a speech of searching and calculated irony and passion. Antony, Caesar's great-nephew Octavius and the feeble Lepidus form a triumvirate (Act IV) against the conspirators. Brutus and the firebrand Cassius quarrel in their camp at Sardis; the quarrel is resolved, and Cassius learns that Portia, wife of Brutus, has committed suicide in Rome. The meeting of the armies will be at Philippi; the ghost of Caesar appears to Brutus, saying that he also will be there.

Cassius (Act V), believing the final battle to be lost, orders his servants to stab him; Brutus falls on his own sword; and Antony speaks the epitaph over his foe:

This was the noblest Roman of them all.

All the conspirators, save only he

Did that they did in envy of great Caesar.

# IN PERFORMANCE

In the fifth Chorus speech of *Henry V*, London pours out her citizens, "like to the senators of th'antique Rome,/With the plebeians swarming at their heels", to "fetch their conquering Caesar in." Already Shakespeare was contemplating his next play, based on Plutarch (Sir Thomas North's translation of a French version). It proved to be a tragedy of two men, the murdered Caesar who dominates after death, and one of his murderers, the liberal patrician, Marcus Brutus ("He only in a general honest thought/And common good to all made one of them", V.5). The speaker is Mark Antony, no longer in the theatre a romantic orator but an astute and masterful tactician. This is the most direct of the tragedies, speaking (in a phrase from *Timon of Athens*) "bold, and forth on". Though Caesar dies midway, his ghost rises; modern directors keep him always in our minds, Glen Byam Shaw (Stratford, 1957) through the single star ("I am constant as the northern star") that shone at the last above Philippi.

We know that a Swiss traveller in England, Thomas Platter, a doctor of Basle, saw the tragedy at the Globe in September 1599; that the poet Leonard Digges (1640) wrote of Brutus and Cassius "at half-sword parley"; and that for more than a century from the Restoration, the play — spared by improvers — was in constant service. John Philip Kemble acted Brutus at Covent Garden between 1812 and 1817, and Charles Mayne Young, who was his Cassius, became an even finer Brutus. Macready, at various times, played Cassius and Brutus with acute understanding (his last Brutus, Haymarket, 1851); and a steady run of later performances included Tree's marmoreal spectacle in its Alma-Tadema sets (from 1898, Her Majesty's); Henry Ainley as Antony (St James's, 1920) in the downright rhetorical manner and a gleaming classical Rome; and Gielgud as Antony, Donald Wolfit as Cassius (Old Vic, 1930). At the Old Vic in 1962, Minos Volanakis, a Greek director, and his designer saw Caesar's Rome as a world of rough and rusty scaffolding, with its citizens most shabbily arrayed. A National production (1977; Olivier Theatre) was distinguished by Gielgud's Caesar, lofty without being intolerable. Bloody violence characterized Steven Pimlott's Stratford production (1991), which had Robert Stephens as an elderly Caesar. David Thacker directed a promenade production involving the audience at The Other Place in 1993. Peter Hall directed the play without a break in two and a quarter hours at Stratford in 1995, avoiding the break in tension that is liable to get the second half off to a bad start. As often the stage was dominated by a huge statue of Caesar; townspeople of Stratford swelled the crowd scenes. At the Globe in 1999, though the production was in Elizabethan costume, actors in modern dress were planted among the audience; only the final jig, wrote the critic of the *Guardian*, lifted it "above the level of a humdrum school production." Peter Hall's son Edward directed a truncated, neo-Fascist version at Stratford in 2003 with Tim Pigott-Smith as Cassius and Greg Hicks as Brutus, both strong in the quarrel scene.

  In America the tragedy first arrived (1774) at Charlestown, South Carolina and there have been frequent New York revivals since 1817. Great performers were Edwin Booth as Brutus and Laurence Barrett as Cassius (together in 1871–2). Richard Mansfield, a surprisingly fanatical Brutus, staged the play (1902), moving through the part "not like a man who is painfully making up his mind, but as one fatally predestined to assassinate his friend" (Robert Speaight). A production of Orson Welles, before blood-red walls, in modern dress and "tinged with fascism", had 157 New York performances in 1937. Welles saw Brutus as "the bewildered liberal, the man of character and principle in a world threatened by fascist destruction." More recently, the play was presented by the New York Shakespeare Festival (1988). In a collectors' piece among American productions (1864), the brothers Edwin Booth, Junius Brutus Booth, and John Wilkes Booth — later Lincoln's assassin — were, respectively, Brutus, Cassius, and Antony.

# IN OTHER TERMS

*Julius Caesar* has been filmed several times (beginning in silent days). Most valuable: the American production of 1953 (Joseph L. Mankiewicz), remembered for Marlon Brando's Antony and John Gielgud's scorching Cassius; and a lesser English film (1969, directed by Stuart Burge), with Gielgud (Caesar), Charlton Heston (Antony), Jason Robards (Brutus). The BBC television series version (1978) has Richard Pasco as an outstanding Brutus.

# CHIEF CHARACTERS

**Julius Caesar** Much must depend on the actor. The dictator's portrait is more reasonable in Shakespeare than in Plutarch; and given a John Gielgud (National, 1977), we are aware that Caesar is "mighty yet".

**Octavius Caesar** Julius Caesar's great-nephew and the coming strong man. "Within *my* tent tonight his bones shall lie" (V.5).

**Marcus Antonius** A highly theatrical part (the Forum speech: "Friends, Romans, countrymen"). But the eloquently improvising opportunist is often less exciting in today's theatre than Brutus and Cassius.

**Marcus Brutus** The liberal idealist at war with himself.

**Caius Cassius** "Such men are dangerous", said Caesar; and he was right. Passionate and jealous, Cassius — as many actors have found — can speak like the Tiber in flood.

**Calphurnia** Caesar's wife is a study in fear and anxiety.

**Portia** She is Cato's daughter, to Brutus a "true and honourable wife", proud, loving, and brave.

**Lepidus** One of the triumvirs after Caesar's death. "A slight unmeritable man," says Antony (IV.1), "meet to be sent on errands." He reappears in *Antony and Cleopatra*.

**Casca** Disappears after the murder. His opening prose scene (I.2) is bluntly persuasive; afterwards it is left to the director to heighten him.

**Cinna** The poet; innocent victim of mob vengeance in a brief and agonizing scene (III.3). It has in the past been frequently cut, a casualty of too much time being spent in scene-changing.

# Twelfth Night; or, What You Will
## 1601–2

**THE CHARACTERS**
Orsino, Duke of Illyria
Valentine, Curio, gentlemen attending on
  the Duke
Viola, sister to Sebastian
Sebastian, brother to Viola
Sea Captain, friend to Viola
Antonio a sea captain, friend to
  Sebastian
Olivia, a rich countess
Maria, Olivia's gentlewoman

Sir Toby Belch, uncle to Olivia
Sir Andrew Aguecheek, suitor to Olivia
Malvolio, Olivia's steward
Fabian, in the service of Olivia
Feste, Olivia's Fool
Lords, A Priest, Sailors, Officers,
  Musicians and Attendants

**THE SCENE**
A city in Illyria and the sea coast near it

# SYNOPSIS

Viola, "of Messaline", wrecked on the Illyrian shore and believing wrongly that her twin brother Sebastian has been drowned, becomes (in the male disguise of Cesario) a page to Orsino, the Duke. She bears his reiterated and scorned love message to the young countess Olivia, who is mourning affectedly for a dead brother. Olivia falls in love with Viola/Cesario. Meanwhile (Act II) Olivia's parasitic uncle Sir Toby, her gullible suitor Sir Andrew, encouraged by Toby, her gentlewoman Maria, her "allowed fool" Feste, and Fabian, also in her service, join to trick Malvolio, her sombre, haughty and puritanical steward, an enemy of them all. "Dost thou think because thou art virtuous there shall be no more cakes and ale?" Toby asks him. Presently, told by a forged letter (ostensibly Olivia's, actually Maria's) that Olivia is infatuated with him, Malvolio takes to himself the phrase: "Some are born great, some achieve greatness, some have greatness thrust upon 'em."

Obeying the false command to appear before his mistress smiling and in absurdly cross-gartered yellow stockings ("a fashion she detests", "a colour she abhors"), Malvolio is carried off (Act III) to a dark cell as a presumed madman. Sebastian, who we have realized by now was saved (believing his sister lost), has reached the town with his rescuer Antonio, a piratical captain who had once fought against Orsino's ships. The plotters have persuaded Andrew, jealous of Olivia's obvious love for Cesario, to challenge the page to a duel; while this is being scrambled through, Antonio arrives, mistakes Cesario for Sebastian, draws his sword to help, and is arrested by the Duke's officers.

Soon afterwards (Act IV), Toby, believing Sebastian to be Cesario, attacks him and is sternly rebuked by Olivia. Also mistaken, she begs the young man to go with her; he does so, pleasantly bewildered, and in a brief later scene she urges marriage ("Plight me the full assurance of your faith") and they follow a priest to the chantry. Finally (Act V), confusions are resolved: the twins recognize each other; Viola, herself again, will be Orsino's Duchess, his "fancy's queen"; Toby weds Maria; Malvolio, released, swears revenge on "the whole pack of you"; and the comedy fades in Feste's twilit song.

# IN PERFORMANCE

*Twelfth Night*, as topical references suggest, was probably written about 1601. The Malvolio sub-plot is Shakespeare's, but the fable of the twins and of Orsino and Olivia could have been derived from an old Italian comedy. Shakespeare's Illyria is simply a high-fantastical invention, a stage for the roaming of identical twins, the presentation of various shades of love, and the sub-plot's May-morning skirmish.

The comedy was acted on Candlemas Day (2 February) 1602, in Middle Temple Hall, where a barrister named John Manningham saw and recorded it. Now one of the most loved and familiar romantic comedies, it had to struggle through several adaptations before being accepted for itself in the mid-18th century. "But a silly play, and not related at all to the name of the day," Samuel Pepys had said (in 1662) to Sir William Davenant's version. He was wrong, for *Twelfth Night,* in the words of Anne Barton, was "a period of holiday abandon... in which serious issues and events mingled perplexingly with revelry and apparent madness."

Revivals of the Shakespearian text have flourished since Charles Macklin and Hannah Pritchard were Malvolio and Viola at Drury Lane in 1741. In the late 19th century — according to the production's Viola (Ellen Terry) — Henry Irving's Malvolio (Lyceum, 1884) was "fine and dignified, but not good for the play" in a production oddly dull. During the Edwardian period, Herbert Beerbohm Tree, firmly realistic, filled the stage of His Majesty's with Olivia's terraced garden; less realistically, he had four minor Malvolios to follow him wherever he went. Granville-Barker broke with tradition in his famous Savoy Theatre revival (1912) in a black-and-silver setting, with Henry Ainley and Lillah McCarthy as Malvolio and Viola.

After 1918 most revivals were divided between Stratford (and from 1960 the Aldwych), the Old Vic and pastorals at the Open Air Theatre, Regent's Park. The play's popularity has resulted in many productions by all the leading companies. It has a Chekhovian quality, not least in the ways in which productions can mingle comedy with melancholy.

In 1922 Granville-Barker wrote an illuminating review of Jacques Copeau's long-lived Paris production (1914–) with designs by Duncan Grant who "was not called on to amuse himself, but to interpret Shakespeare." The 1933 production by Tyrone Guthrie at the Old Vic elicited a beautiful review from Virginia Woolf (reprinted in *The Death of the Moth*, 1942, etc.) Laurence Olivier played Sir Toby also at the Old Vic in 1937, with Alec Guinness a walking wraith as Sir Andrew. Michel St-Denis's Old Vic production, with Peggy Ashcroft as Viola, was the first Shakespeare play to be televized from a theatre. Peggy Ashcroft was Viola again at the Old Vic in 1950, directed by Hugh Hunt. At Stratford in 1955 Olivier, directed by Gielgud, was a parvenu Malvolio whose speech suggested his origins by a lisping, affected veneer that flaked away to reveal the barrow-boy vowels. In 1958 Peter Hall directed Dorothy Tutin's exquisite, boyish Viola, in beautiful settings designed by Lila de Nobili. Max Adrian was an intensely poignant Feste, his eyes streaming with tears at his failure to redeem Malvolio. John Barton's autumnal Stratford production of 1969 has become a classic. Judi Dench, in one of her greatest performances, was a tenderly vulnerable Viola, Donald Sinden a masterly Malvolio, the production subtly nuanced and infinitely responsive to the play's shifting moods. Peter Gill's 1974 RSC version, dominated by a painting of Narcissus gazing at his own reflection in the water, explored the play's psychological and erotic subtexts. The set for Ian Judge's 1994 RSC production prettily evoked a skyscape of chimneys as seen from the garden of New Place but diminished the play with cheap gags. Also at Stratford in 2001 Lindsay Posner's production went still further in exploring the play's sexual ambiguities; on his first appearance, Sebastian was leaving Antonio's bed. An all-adult-male, Elizabethan-style production by the Globe company with Mark Rylance as Olivia who skimmed the stage Japanese-style was seen to best advantage in the stately surroundings of the Middle Temple, where John Manningham had seen it 400 years before. Simon Russell Beale's Malvolio won great plaudits in a production by Sam Mendes at the Donmar Warehouse (later seen in New York) described by Michael Billington as "the best since John Barton's thirty years ago, and filled with the same rich Chekhovian texture."

In the United States *Twelfth Night* was staged first in Boston (1794). Among numerous New York productions were Augustin Daly's (1894), with Ada Rehan, E.H. Sothern and Julia Marlowe's between 1905 and 1919, and one in 1940 with Maurice Evans and Helen Hayes. More recently, the Shakespeare Stage Company revived it at the Samuel Beckett Theater (1988). A Stratford, Connecticut, revival (1960), with Katharine Hepburn insecurely cast as Viola, was set in a 19th-century English seaside town. In 1957, Tyrone Guthrie opened the permanent theatre at Stratford, Ontario, with an exhilarating treatment in Stuart costume.

# IN OTHER TERMS

An operatic version at Covent Garden (1820) included "Songs, Glees, and Choruses, the poetry selected entirely from the Plays, Poems, and Sonnets of Shakespeare." There is an opera, *Viola* (1881) by Smetana. A BBC television film of 1970 had Alec Guinness as Malvolio and Ralph Richardson as Sir Toby. In the BBC series, Sinead Cusack played Olivia, Felicity Kendal Viola. Kenneth Branagh's wintry Renaissance Theatre production, with Richard Briers as Malvolio, was filmed for television and video in 1988. The most successful film version is Trevor Nunn's of 1996, with textual adjustments, filmed on location in Cornwall and with Imogen Stubbs as a would-be macho Viola.

# CHIEF CHARACTERS

**Orsino** The high-romantic Duke of Illyria, who is in love with love, but his raptures should not be theatrically heightened.

**Viola** Dressed as a male page like her brother, she must not be simply a pert masquerader.

**Sebastian** Should look enough like Viola not to make nonsense of Antonio's perilous comparison in Act V: "An apple cleft in two is not more twin/Than these two creatures."

**Antonio** Sea captain and pirate. Granville-Barker called him "an exact picture of an Elizabethan seaman-adventurer…. I am always reminded of him by the story of Richard Grenville chewing a wine-glass in his rage."

**Olivia** This "virtuous maid", at first in love with grief, was once acted as a stately contralto, but is now usually an affected girl. Geraldine McEwan (Stratford, 1958), was a *poseuse* who seemed to have escaped from a columbarium for slightly cracked doves.

**Maria** A gentlewoman and not a kitchen soubrette. She says of herself: "I can write very like my lady… On a forgotten matter we can hardly make distinction of our hands." Supposed to be small, possibly a reference to the original boy player.

**Sir Toby Belch** With the longest part in the play, he is a boisterous reprobate but a gentleman, Olivia's uncle ("Am I not of her blood?" he asks).

**Sir Andrew Aguecheek** Olivia's gullible wooer, "a very fool and a prodigal" whose hair "hangs like flax on a distaff". He has a wistful line — "I was ador'd once" — at the end of the drinking scene, and ought not to be unwisely burlesqued.

**Malvolio** Olivia's self-loving and pompous steward: "Contemplation makes a rare turkey-cock of him." His ultimate treatment, as even Toby realizes ("I would we were all rid of this knavery"), goes beyond a joke.

**Feste** Olivia's Fool, never a twirling, conventional clown, but a mature, privileged and bitter-sweet onlooker, guardian of the play's latent melancholy. He sings the famous songs, "O mistress mine" (II.3), "Come away, death" (II.4), and the "When that I was and a little tiny boy". Created by Robert Armin, the subtle comedian who joined Shakespeare's company in 1599.

# Hamlet, Prince of Denmark
## 1601–2

 **THE CHARACTERS**

Claudius, King of Denmark
Gertrude, Queen of Denmark, Hamlet's
    mother
Hamlet, son to the former King and
    nephew to Claudius
Ghost of Hamlet's father
Polonius, Lord Chamberlain
Laertes, son to Polonius
Ophelia, daughter to Polonius
Horatio, Hamlet's friend
Rosencrantz, Guildenstern, courtiers,
    former schoolfellows of Hamlet
Fortinbras, Prince of Norway
Voltemand, Cornelius,
    ambassadors to Norway

Marcellus, Bernardo, Officers
Francisco, a soldier
Osric, a foppish courtier
Reynaldo, servant to Polonius
A Gentleman
A Priest
Players
Two gravediggers
A Norwegian Captain
English Ambassadors
Lords, Ladies, Officers, Soldiers, Sailors,
    Messengers

**THE SCENE**
Denmark

## SYNOPSIS

Hamlet, Prince of Denmark, has not succeeded his father as King. On the throne is his uncle Claudius, who married Queen Gertrude immediately upon the death of her husband, the first King Hamlet. At midnight the ghost of the dead King (whom Claudius had poisoned) appears to his son on the battlements of the castle and commands revenge. "If thou hast nature in thee, bear it not."

Hamlet, unsure at first, simulates madness (Act II) which overwhelms Ophelia (daughter of the Lord Chamberlain, Polonius) whom he loves. When a company of actors arrives, Hamlet asks for the performance of a play with a plot much like his father's murder, so that he can see how the King responds. Claudius, deeply alarmed, plans (Act III) to send Hamlet at once to England. Before this can be done, Hamlet, going to his mother's closet, fiercely reviles her for yielding to Claudius; then, hearing a noise, he stabs through the curtain, killing Polonius who had concealed himself there.

Two courtiers (Act IV) conduct Hamlet towards the voyage to England, bearing letters that order his death when he arrives. Meanwhile, Laertes, son of Polonius, enraged by news of his father's end finds that his sister Ophelia is helplessly mad, and swears to kill Hamlet (now coming home after a sea-fight in which he was saved by pirates).

Ophelia drowns herself; Hamlet is in time to see her burial (Act V). Later, at a fencing match where Laertes, after plotting with the King, seeks to stab Hamlet with a poisoned rapier, both men are wounded; Queen Gertrude drinks, in error, the poisoned wine Claudius has prepared for Hamlet as a second device. Laertes and Gertrude die; Hamlet, after killing Claudius, collapses in the arms of his friend Horatio and dies. Fortinbras, Prince of Norway, whose army has invaded Denmark, enters to take the throne that Hamlet, with his "dying voice", has bequeathed. Fortinbras orders him to be borne up with military ceremonial: "For he was likely, had he been put on,/To have prov'd most royal."

## IN PERFORMANCE

"This is I, Hamlet the Dane." As we hear the actor's challenge (V.1), we must always ask if he is entitled to it. A Hamlet must be stricken to the heart; no superficial grief. Everything he speaks has been argued in the mind. He is a young man in the darkest mental fight, balancing and indeterminate, swayed — as Matthew Arnold said long ago — by a thousand subtle influences, physiological and pathological. This study of the divided mind in a play of revenge deferred is probably the most famous part in world drama. It is supposed Shakespeare based his tragedy, among other sources, on a vanished play known as the *Ur-Hamlet*.

It is all marvellously theatrical; nothing has been so often acted or more stringently analysed. A standard dictionary of quotations contains 210 references to *Hamlet*, covering well over 800 lines. Full-scale productions in the theatre (this is the longest of all Shakespeare's plays) take about five hours. Though these are more frequent than they used to be, as a rule we get a cut version of about $3\frac{1}{2}$ to 4 hours. Cuts are fairly stereotyped, e.g. Polonius with Reynaldo (II.1), some of IV.7, the beginning (always a sad choice) of the Hamlet-Horatio colloquy (V.2). One of the least expected cuts was the opening on the guard-platform of Elsinore, the challenge and counter-challenge in the midnight cold, the hushed questioning, the sudden "Peace, break thee off; look where it comes again." — "In the same figure, like the king that's dead."

*Hamlet* moves forward in a sequence of astonishments, unfailing, however familiar. The play endures, not simply for its wisdom or acted excitements, but because, though he is by no means Everyman, there is at least a trace of Hamlet in us all.

Every actor sees the man differently, but none should forget — as is often done — that Hamlet should not differ in essence from the Prince Ophelia remembers (III.1): "Th'expectancy and rose of the fair state", "That unmatch'd form and feature of blown youth". He is sometimes over-subtilized; it is a pleasure now and then to find an actor who has the voice, the bearing and the intelligence, and who is not afraid to simplify.

Hamlets, in all their variations, defy pigeonholing. Any record of the 17th century must name Thomas Betterton, whose face, when he saw the Ghost, turned as white as his neckcloth; in the 18th century, David Garrick, with his rhetorical pauses and quick transitions, and John Philip Kemble (Drury Lane, 1783; black velvet court dress, powdered wig), a nobly introspective romantic. From the 19th century we may think of Edmund Kean (not at his meridian); Macready's intellect; Charles Fechter's naturalism; Henry Irving (Lyceum, 1874), princely, tender, hypnotic; Tree (Haymarket, 1892), dying to the sound of an angelic chorus; Johnston Forbes-Robertson (Lyceum, 1897), with "the courtier's, scholar's, soldier's, eye, tongue, sword."

Nearly every speech can be fitted into a mosaic of effects from the acting of the part. From myriad English Hamlets of the 20th century we can choose Ernest Milton (Old Vic, 1919), "lonely, prehensile, mysterious"; Colin Keith-Johnston in modern dress (Kingsway, 1925), "the prose side of the medallion", said Ivor Brown; John Gielgud (Old Vic, 1930; New, 1934; Lyceum, 1939; Haymarket, 1944), lofty in spirit and mind, violin-music searchingly scored; Donald Wolfit (Stratford, 1936; various stages), forcible without physical grace; Laurence Olivier (Old Vic and Elsinore, 1937); and players of such contrasting methods as Paul Scofield (Stratford, 1948; Phoenix, 1955), with his doomed gentleness; Alec Guinness (Old Vic, 1938; New, 1951); Michael Redgrave (New, 1950; Stratford, 1958), who could have been a Double First and Double Blue of Wittenberg; John Neville (Old Vic, 1957), David Warner (Stratford/Aldwych, 1965–6), Peter O'Toole (National at Old Vic, 1963), Alan Howard (Stratford, 1970), Ian McKellen (Cambridge, 1971), Derek Jacobi (Old Vic, 1977), Albert Finney (National at Old Vic, 1975, and the National itself, 1976), and Jonathan Pryce (Royal Court, 1980) a "chilling, demonic ventriloquist's act". Roger Rees was Hamlet for the RSC (with Branagh as Laertes in his first Stratford season (Stratford, 1984–5). Mark Rylance played over 400 performances for the RSC (Stratford/Barbican, 1988–9), directed by Ron Daniels.

Still in pyjamas, he took the role again at the Globe in 2000. In 1987 the National Theatre hosted the Royal Dramatic Theatre of Stockholm in a Swedish adaptation, the stage debut by the film director Ingmar Bergman (Lyttleton, 1987) in which the main focus was the collapse of the nation, with strong parallels drawn with the West in the late 20th century. Ian Charleson took over from Daniel Day Lewis for Richard Eyre at the National (Olivier, 1989). Both remarkable performances were dogged by illness — the understudy, Jeremy Northam, was on stage most often. Michael Bryant was, memorably, "the best Polonius since Polonius". Two excellent visiting productions: Yuri Lyubimov's, first shown in Russia in 1971, (Old Vic/Leicester Haymarket, 1989), and the marvellous Bulandra Theatre Company from Bucharest, hosted by the National Theatre (Lyttleton, 1990). The Russian element showed again with Robert Sturura's unsuccessful venture with Alan Rickman (Riverside Studios, 1992–3). Meanwhile at the RSC Adrian Noble's highly popular Edwardian-dress production had Kenneth Branagh, Jane Lapotaire (Gertrude) and John Carlisle (Polonius) (Barbican/Stratford, 1992–3). Alan Cumming was an entrancing Hamlet in a less memorable production by Stephen Unwin for Century Theatre (Donmar Warehouse and tour, 1993). Simon Russell Beale won great acclaim as an exceptionally sensitive, beautifully spoken Hamlet at the National, directed by John Caird, in 2000. Back at Stratford, Samuel West, directed by Steven Pimlott, gave a technically assured performance which connected easily with the young people of the day. Michael Boyd's first production as Artistic Director of the RSC in 2004 had Toby Stephens as a more aristocratic, if excitable, Prince in a production which, among other textual oddities, included the Horatio/Gertrude scene from the 1603 quarto. Also in 2004 Trevor Nunn directed a youth-centred production at the Old Vic with a Claudius (Tom Mannion) who cleared up the mess after the killing of Polonius, and a Gertrude (Imogen Stubbs) whose taste for the bottle gave new meaning to "Do not drink, Gertrude."

The New York sequence is comparable. We can name here Edwin Booth (from 1857), patrician, gentle, melancholy, probably the nonpareil of American Hamlets; John Barrymore (1922; London, 1925), powerful and original; Walter Hampden (e.g. 1925, 1929); the English actor, Maurice Evans (New York, 1938), who had acted it at the Old Vic three years earlier; Donald Madden (1961); Richard Burton (modern dress, 1964). Christopher Plummer played Hamlet at Stratford, Ontario (1957); and Kenneth Welsh (1969). Two productions from Europe were Ingmar Bergman's Swedish adaptation at the Brooklyn Academy of Music (1988), and Ron Daniels' RSC production with Mark Rylance, at the American Repertory Theatre, Boston (1991).

The Orange Coast Theatre played it as an analogy for the Kennedy myth, with on-stage cameras following the royal family's every move for late-night TV reports — as Jan Herman said "turning Denmark into Camelot"; Robert Sicular was Hamlet (1993).

Among European Hamlets have been Sarah Bernhardt, Jean-Louis Barrault (France), Alexander Moissi (Germany), Giorgio Albertazzi (Italy), and Miklós Gábor (Hungary, early 1960s), a great actor little known outside his country.

## IN OTHER TERMS

Laurence Olivier's (1948), in black and white, was set elaborately, with odd textual shredding and patching. Grigori Kozintsev directed a Russian film (1964) with Innokenti Smoktunovsky as Hamlet and music by Shostakovich. Nicol Williamson was directed as Hamlet by Tony Richardson in a British one (1969). Franco Zeffirelli's 1990 film, with Mel Gibson and Glenn Close, aimed for popular appeal, but was bland. Kenneth Branagh confounded received opinion by using a full text in his grandiose feature film (1996), playing Hamlet himself with a strong supporting cast including Derek Jacobi as a particularly fine Claudius. Very different is Michael Almereyda's film (2000) in which Denmark becomes a corporation located in modern New York and Ethan Hawke plays Hamlet as a film student of limited articulacy.

A romantic opera by Ambroise Thomas (1868) which has alternative endings, one happy the other sad, is still occasionally performed, mainly for its coloratura mad scene for Ophelia. An opera by Humphrey Searle (1968) given at Covent Garden has not sustained its place in the repertoire. Tchaikovsky's fantasy overture (1888), which he drew on for incidental music for a production of 1892, has been used for a ballet by Robert Helpmann. Many other ballets have been based on the play, including one to music by Michael Tippett created by John Neumeier in 1986 for the Royal Danish Ballet.

A 17th-century German version exists, entitled *Hamlet, Der bestrafte Brudermord* (Fratricide Punished), inspired by travelling acting troupes. Tom Stoppard's *Dogg's Hamlet, Cahoot's Macbeth* applies linguistic philosophy to the two plays; *Rosencrantz and Guildenstern Are Dead* follows the conversations of these two minor characters while off-stage during a performance of Hamlet.

## CHIEF CHARACTERS

**Hamlet** "The time is out of joint. O cursed spite,/That ever I was born to set it right" (I.5). This (1,530 lines in the uncut text) is the longest part in Shakespeare. Soliloquies: "O, that this too too solid flesh would melt" (I.2); "O, what a rogue and peasant slave am I!" (II.2); "To be, or not to be" (III.1); "How all occasions do inform against me" (IV.4).

**Claudius** Murderer, seducer, drunkard, "bloat king"; yet on stage he can be a suave and regal diplomatist.

**Gertrude** Hamlet's foolish, sensual mother is allowed one pictorial speech, the description of Ophelia's death, "There is a willow grows aslant the brook" (IV.7).

**Polonius** An elder statesman some critics say was based on Lord Burghley. Garrulous and shrewd, as in the precepts to Laertes (I.3).

**Ophelia** The "rose of May". Best acted simply, with no superfluously embarrassing developments of her madness.

**Horatio** Personification of loyalty, who need not be turned into a veteran tutor. He is a man of Hamlet's own age (about 30).

**Laertes** The grieving son and brother is as impetuous as Hamlet is indecisive.

**Rosencrantz** and **Guildenstern** One of Shakespeare's "pairs", Hamlet's Wittenberg fellow-students; court spies for the King. Nothing to tell them apart, but they have had more luck in Tom Stoppard's play, *Rosencrantz and Guildenstern Are Dead*.

**Osric** The affected "water-fly", sometimes presented in these days as a mildly sinister man-about-court.

**Bernardo** (or Barnardo). Has arguably the most tingling lines in the world's drama, the two words "Who's there?", which begin the play in the Elsinore midnight.

**Marcellus** He has the "bird of dawning" speech (I.1).

**First Player** More than an opportunity for old-school declamation; Shakespeare delighting in a chance to talk shop (II.2).

**Gravediggers** Not an enthralling pair of clowns; but the First Gravedigger at least provides Hamlet with Yorick's skull (V.1).

**Fortinbras** The Norwegian prince who will reign in Denmark after Hamlet's death, and who makes a commanding entry in the last few minutes. Restored, after a long absence, in Forbes-Robertson's production at the Lyceum in 1897.

**Ghost** Worrying in today's theatre (where there have been sundry experiments with echoes, off-stage speaking and vast shadows). Still, an imaginative actor can hold us without seeming, in Shaw's words, to have anything else to "while away eternity".

# Troilus and Cressida
## 1601–2

**THE CHARACTERS**

Priam, King of Troy
Hector, Troilus, Paris, Deiphobus and
   Helenus, his sons
Cassandra, Priam's daughter; a
   prophetess
Margarelon, a bastard son of Priam
Andromache, Hector's wife
Aeneas and Antenor Trojan commanders
Calchas, Cressida's father, a
   Trojan priest taking part with
   the Greeks
Cressida, daughter of Calchas
Alexander, Cressida's servant
Pandarus, Cressida's uncle

Agamemnon, the Greek general
Menelaus, his brother
Helen, wife to Menelaus
Achilles, Ajax, Ulysses, Nestor,
   Diomedes and Patroclus, Greek
   commanders
Thersites, a deformed and scurrilous
   Greek
Trojan and Greek soldiers;
Attendants; Servants

**THE SCENE**
Troy and the Greek camp before it

## SYNOPSIS

Seven years after the Greek army has landed to seek Helen, the Spartan queen carried off by a Trojan prince, Troy is still beleaguered. Young Troilus loves Cressida, niece of Pandarus and daughter of a Trojan priest who has defected to the Greeks. Hector, Priam's son, sends to the Greeks a challenge of single combat but, because the great Achilles, "the sinew and the forehand of our host", is sulking in his tent, Ulysses suggests that if the chance is offered to the "blockish" Ajax, Achilles will return to reason. Again the Greeks offer to abandon the siege if Helen is returned but, though Cassandra prophesies woe if the offer is refused, the Trojans decide to continue the fight (Act II).

The Greeks consent (Act III) to exchange a Trojan prisoner for Cressida, and Diomedes is despatched to bring her from the city. Troilus and Cressida part sadly, having sworn everlasting faith, but in the Greek camp (IV.5) Cressida responds to every salute, to the distaste of Ulysses who calls her a "daughter of the game". Achilles boasts that in the next day's fighting he will meet Hector "fell as death". Troilus learns during a brief truce that Diomedes has wooed Cressida. Conducted by Ulysses he sees her give his love-token to the Greek (Act V). In the next day's battle Troilus fails in his vengeance on Diomedes; Achilles treacherously kills the unarmed Hector. Wearily, the Trojans retire.

# IN PERFORMANCE

This magnificent, long-ignored play — Chapman's translation of Homer's *Iliad* is among the sources — had to wait more than three centuries for its quality in the theatre, as in the text, to be rightly recognized. Though its classification — comedy, history or tragedy — has been in doubt, it is above all a satire. A First Quarto edition (1609) said that it had been acted at the Globe; a second edition, in the same year, said nothing about this and in a preface added that it was "a new play never staled with the stage". Probably — though we can only surmise — it had been performed at one of the Inns of Court before a sophisticated audience. After some perplexity, the First Folio editors (1623) inserted it between the histories and the tragedies.

Here, in effect, Shakespeare is a traitor inside the walls of Troy. The heroes of the *Iliad* are lost in harshest satire and the thorny mazes of debate; the great contention over Argive Helen turns to "cormorant war". And yet, among this, the play can move miraculously into the love scenes of Troilus and Cressida or shape the ice-flowers of Ulysses in those speeches on Degree (I.3) and Time (III.3). Its examination of values, its quick splendours, its dark mocking at love and strife, the ultimate confusion in the dying day — a director in the theatre has somehow to sort out this complexity. When he manages to do so the play (as in certain RSC productions) can be a stage marvel. Shakespeare had always been fascinated by the Troilus story: consider only a long section of *The Rape of Lucrece*, and a number of incidental references, e.g. Pistol calls Doll Tearsheet a "lazar kite of Cressid's kind" (*Henry V*, II.1).

Theatre history until the 20th century is brief. The play was performed during the Restoration at the Smock Alley Theatre in Dublin. Dryden cut and expanded the text to *Troilus and Cressida; or, Truth Found Too Late* (Dorset Gardens, 1679), acted on several occasions until 1734. A gap then until an insignificant production at the Great Queen Street Theatre, London (1907, Lewis Casson as Troilus), and William Poel's eccentrically cut version (King's Hall, Covent Garden, 1912) which brought to the stage a 24-year-old amateur, Edith Evans, as Cressida, with her pennon-fluttering voice and eloquent hands, the perfect "encounterer glib of tongue".

In 1922 the Marlowe Society of Cambridge staged it (Everyman, London): one of several Marlowe revivals, later under George Rylands. Professional work was undistinguished, except for Ion Swinley's Troilus (Old Vic, 1923), and Pamela Brown's lisping Cressida and Donald Wolfit's Ulysses (Stratford, 1936), until Michael Macowan's modern-dress version at the Westminster (1938), with the Ulysses of Robert Speaight. John Byron was Troilus (Open Air, 1946), and Paul Scofield and Laurence Harvey in, respectively, the

Stratford revivals of 1948 and 1954. Tyrone Guthrie satirized the satire in his celebrated Old Vic production (1956) with its Hohenzollern Greeks undermined by faction, its Ruritanian Trojans undermined by frivolity, and the poetry sadly wasted.

More recent important productions include Stratford (1960, by John Barton and Peter Hall) and the Aldwych (1962, Peter Hall alone). The play was presented in a symbolic cockpit (as a critic described it): on this shallow, white-sanded, octagonal platform, before an abstract torrid backcloth, love and chivalry were grated to dusty nothing. John Barton directed other RSC treatments (1968–9, 1976–7). Also at Stratford, Howard Davies directed Juliet Stevenson and Anton Lesser (1985), and the young Sam Mendes directed Amanda Root, Ralph Fiennes and Simon Russell Beale (1989–90) with Simon Russell Beale as an outstandingly bizarre Thersites. In Ian Judges's RSC production of 1996, which amply exploited opportunities for homoerotic display, Philip Voss brought exceptional understanding and a virtuoso vocal technique to Ulysses's great speeches. Trevor Nunn's magnificent production at the National (1999), with black Trojans and white Greeks, made impressive use of the Olivier auditorium.

Most American productions have been amateur ones in universities. Professional versions in New York (1932; Otis Skinner as Thersites, 1955; and 1975, with the same actress playing Cressida, Cassandra and Helen) had little popular response. At Stratford, Connecticut (1957), the play was set during the period of the American Civil War, with the Trojans played as the Confederacy.

In 1949 Luchino Visconti directed the play in the Boboli Gardens at Florence, with half the characters on horseback.

## IN OTHER TERMS

The BBC television film (1981) was imaginatively directed by Jonathan Miller. Sir William Walton's opera *Troilus and Cressida* (1954), after Chaucer's poem rather than Shakespeare's play.

## CHIEF CHARACTERS

**Hector** Chivalrous paladin of the Trojans, but futile in argument (II.2).

**Troilus** 22 years old. The longest part, and far from a simple hero. Against ending the war (II.2); passionately hurt by Cressida. Ulysses says of him (IV.5), "His heart and hand both open and both free;/For what he has he gives, what thinks he shows."

**Paris** The Trojan prince whose seizure of Helen began the war. "Well may we fight for

121

her whom we know well/The world's large spaces cannot parallel" (II.2).

**Cassandra** The prophetess of Troy must not be underplayed. Her entry, "raving", at II.2, should be genuinely exciting.

**Cressida** At the heart of the play. A searching portrait of a woman who, though dismissed by Ulysses as a "daughter of the game", does know her frailty.

**Pandarus** Cressida's uncle and matchmaker. Early exuberance declining to utter hopelessness at the very end of the play (V.10).

**Agamemnon** "Great commander, nerve and bone of Greece" (I.3).

**Helen** Her scene (III.1) offers no reason why the Trojan war should have lasted so long, or why, in the words of Troilus (not Marlowe here), she is "a pearl whose price hath launch'd above a thousand ships" (II.2).

**Menelaus** Helen's cuckolded husband.

**Achilles** Despicably arrogant Greek champion; treacherously murders the unarmed Hector (V.8).

**Ajax** Although the Homeric hero becomes a "beef-witted" block, he has a telling couplet (V.9) when he hears that Achilles has slain Hector: "If it be so, yet bragless let it be;/Great Hector was as good a man as he."

**Ulysses** Prince of Ithaca. He has the wise speeches on Degree (I.3) and Time (III.3).

**Nestor** "Most reverend, for thy stretch'd out life," says Ulysses (I.3).

**Diomedes** The Greek "sweet guardian" of Cressida.

**Thersites** Rancid camp-follower of the Greeks. "Crusty batch of nature" (V.1). William Poel (1912) saw him as a jester and cast for the part a Scots-accented actress, Elspeth Keith. He has sometimes been a scrubby journalist.

**Andromache** Hector's wife. A pallid remembrance of Calphurnia (*Julius Caesar*), V.3.

# All's Well that Ends Well
## 1602–3

**THE CHARACTERS**
King of France
Duke of Florence
Bertram, young Count of Rousillon
Countess of Rousillon, Bertram's mother
Helena, a gentlewoman protected
  by the Countess
Lafeu, an old lord
Parolles, a follower of Bertram
Two French Lords, named
  Dumain, serving with Bertram
Renaldo, steward, Lavache, a clown,

a Page, servants to the Countess of
  Rousillon
A Widow of Florence
Diana, the Widow's daughter
Violenta (non-speaking) and Mariana, the
  Widow's neighbours and friends
Lords, Officers, Soldiers, etc.,
French and Florentine

**THE SCENE**
Rousillon, Paris, Florence, Marseilles

# SYNOPSIS

Helena, an orphan, loves Bertram, son of the dowager Countess of Rousillon, who has brought her up. When the haughty young man goes as a ward to the French King, Helena — whose father had been a celebrated physician — follows him, hoping that she may cure the King of a painful illness. She does so (Act II) with one of her father's remedies; and being offered her choice of husband from the gentlemen at court, chooses Bertram. Snobbishly, he objects — "A poor physician's daughter my wife!" — but forced by the King, agrees to the match. Immediately afterwards he runs away to Florence as a volunteer in the Tuscan wars — the Florentines against the Sienese — with a cowardly braggart, Parolles, as his companion.

Back at Rousillon (Act III) Helena learns that Bertram will take her as his wife when she has got from his finger a prized heirloom-ring and borne him a child. She goes, in pilgrim's dress, to Florence, where Bertram is seeking to seduce a widow's daughter, Diana. Helena persuades Diana to yield to him but to ask for his ring and to make an assignation which she, Helena, will keep.

Meanwhile, the fellow-officers of Parolles (Act IV) trick him into exposing his cowardice. Diana, having got Bertram's ring, duly arranges a midnight meeting with him; hidden by darkness, Helena takes Diana's place and gives Bertram as a keepsake a ring she had received from the King of France. Hearing that Helena is dead, Bertram returns to Rousillon, where his mother and the old lord, Lafeu, also believe the story.

Lafeu (Act V) arranges a match between his daughter and Bertram, who prepares to give to her the ring from Helena. The King recognizes it and orders Bertram's arrest. Diana, newly arrived, accuses Bertram of seducing her; when he denies it, the King orders her to prison as well, but her mother, the widow, produces "bail", Helena herself, who is to have Bertram's child. "All yet seems well", says the King comfortably, "and if it end so meet/ The bitter past, more welcome is the sweet."

# IN PERFORMANCE

*All's Well That Ends Well*, based on a story by Boccaccio in the *Decameron*, has not been a popular play, largely because Helena (though Granville-Barker approved) can come through as an unlikeably persistent opportunist. Actresses and directors can overcome this: we accept her single-mindedness for the sake of some gravely haunting verse. The couplets in II.1 cannot be glibly dismissed; in performance they have a curious spirit of incantation. Though the dark comedy may be "a mingled yarn, good and ill together", it can grow on readers of the text and listeners in the theatre: unadorned productions so far have been scarce.

There was no theatrical success until the mid-18th century (1741, Goodman's Fields; 1742, Drury Lane, with Peg Woffington as Helena). Thereafter various revivals emphasized the romance less than the comedy: Parolles, a favourite part of Henry Woodward, was always prominent. John Philip Kemble restored the balance when he played Bertram (1794) at Drury Lane, with Mrs Jordan as Helena. By 1832 the comedy was being played at Covent Garden as an opera (sub-title, *Love's Labour's Won*), with a sheaf of songs from elsewhere in Shakespeare and an added masque. Twenty years later Phelps did the Folio text at Sadler's Wells.

The play then slept until Frank Benson, immediately after receiving his knighthood, appeared as Parolles at Stratford in the tercentenary year (1916). William Poel directed an eccentric "vocal recital" (Ethical Church, Bayswater, 1920), with a uniformed nurse wheeling on the King in a bath-chair, and Edith Evans and Winifred Oughton as the brothers Dumain. In 1922 Bridges-Adams's Stratford production pushed the play, as he said, an inch or two towards Cinderella. Young Laurence Olivier was a glossy Parolles in Barry Jackson's modern-dress version (Birmingham Repertory, 1927); Iden Payne had a dull Stratford revival (1935); and in 1940 (Vaudeville) Robert Atkins — probably with the title in mind — bravely directed the piece for three weeks of matinées during heavy daylight air raids, with Catherine Lacey as Helena and Ernest Milton as the King.

Since then, the play has had more attention: Old Vic (1953), a production ruined by the clowning of the King into senile hypochondria; Stratford (1955) in Louis XIII costume; Stratford (1959) in an inconsequential fantastication by Tyrone Guthrie (from which he cut Lavache); Stratford again (1967; Aldwych, 1968), directed by John Barton, with Lynn Farleigh's transforming Helena; and Greenwich (1975), a modern-dress performance under Jonathan Miller. Peggy Ashcroft was the Countess of Rousillon for Trevor Nunn at Stratford (1981), while Peter Hall's revival was his first Shakespeare since leaving the RSC (Stratford/Barbican, 1993). Gregory Doran's sensitive Swan Theatre production (2003) brought Judi Dench back to Stratford as the Countess in a performance of consummate artistry.

Tyrone Guthrie staged his version first at Stratford, Ontario (1953), with Alec Guinness as the King, Irene Worth as Helena; and David Jones directed the play there (1971) with Martha Henry. Nancy Wickwire was Helena in the New York Shakespeare Festival (1959); Barbara Barrie in 1966.

# IN OTHER TERMS

Elijah Moshinsky's BBC television version (1981), with designs inspired by Dutch masters, is one of the best of the series.

# CHIEF CHARACTERS

**King of France** Generous and grateful, his autumnally wistful regal dignity must not be dispersed in the kind of fooling that shattered an Old Vic revival (1953).

**Duke of Florence** Insignificant in the text. Tyrone Guthrie used the little scene III.3 as the basis of a ten-minute comic interlude.

**Bertram** One of Shakespeare's weaker (and snobbish) young men. There has been much special pleading for him — a suggestion that he has been corrupted by Parolles — but any actor has some trouble in commending him to us. "War is no strife/To the dark house and the detested wife" (II.3).

**Countess of Rousillon** The finest Shakespearian grande dame, described by Shaw as "the most beautiful old woman's part ever written."

**Helena** Heroine, opportunist, or both. Rouses mixed feelings, though she has some good lines: "Twere all one/That I should love a bright particular star/And think to wed it, he is so above me" (I.1); "My friends were poor, but honest" (I.3); should be barefooted in the pilgrim scene (III.5), but seldom is.

**Lafeu** A sage old lord with a daughter, Maudlin, who is mentioned in the text but unseen in the theatre.

**Parolles** A hollow, parasitic coward, thoroughly exposed in the blindfold scene where he betrays his own side.

**Lavache** An inferior clown; played at Stratford (1955) as a dwarf. Guthrie cut him altogether from Canadian and English revivals.

**Widow** The useful hostess of Florence, whose daughter, Diana, aids Helena's plan.

**Diana** The widow's daughter. Replies unanswerably and mockingly to Bertram's first refusal to yield his ring (IV.2): "Mine honour's such a ring;/My chastity's the jewel of our house.../Which were the greatest obloquy i'th' world/In me to lose."

**A gentleman** Met in Marseilles (V.1). Described, agreeably, in the Folio as "A Gentle Astringer" (falconer).

---

# Measure for Measure
## 1604

### ✹ THE CHARACTERS

Vincentio, Duke of Vienna
Angelo, the Deputy
Escalus, an ancient lord
Claudio, a young gentleman
Isabella, Claudio's sister
Juliet, beloved of Claudio
Mariana, formerly betrothed to Angelo
Lucio, a fantastic
Two other Gentlemen
Varrius, a gentleman, servant to the Duke
Provost
Thomas, Peter, two friars

Francisca, a nun
Mistress Overdone, a bawd
A Justice
Elbow, a simple constable
Froth, a foolish gentleman
Pompey, a clown and servant to Mistress
    Overdone
Abhorson, an executioner
Barnardine, a dissolute prisoner
Lords, Officers, Citizen, Boy, Attendants

### ✹ THE SCENE

Vienna

---

# SYNOPSIS

Vincentio, Duke of Vienna, resolving on the enforcement of the city's ignored laws against immorality, proclaims his departure to Poland; actually he remains, disguised as a friar, to see what his Deputy, the severe Angelo (whose "blood is very snow-broth") will do. One of Angelo's first acts is to imprison Claudio for getting his betrothed, Juliet, with child, an offence that carries the death penalty.

Isabella, Claudio's sister, a potential novice in a religious order, comes (Act II) to plead with Angelo and he invites her to return next day. When she does he tells her that, if she will be his mistress, he will pardon her brother. Horrified, she visits her brother (Act III) who entreats her to agree. She refuses; but the disguised Duke/Friar suggests that she give way, and that Mariana, once Angelo's spurned love, take her place at night.

Mariana (Act IV) accepts the plan; Angelo, faithlessly, has ordered Claudio's death which is prevented by the Duke/Friar and the Provost. The Duke returns as himself (Act V). In a complex scene Angelo, after compulsorily wedding Mariana, is pardoned, Claudio will marry Juliet, and the Duke confesses his own love for Isabella.

# IN PERFORMANCE

"Haste still pays haste, and leisure answers leisure;/Like doth quit like, and Measure still for Measure" (V.1). Here Shakespeare, who got much of his material from an unacted drama in two parts (*Promos and Cassandra* by George Whetstone, set in Hungary), wrote an intricate tragi-comedy about justice and mercy. It is an examination of moral values that has become something of a chameleon-play in our time, principally because the enigmatic Duke of Vienna (Vincentio), who in disguise watches the behaviour of his Deputy, can be interpreted in so many ways. We have seen him as divine power personified, as a sinister hypocrite, as a complacent statesman and as a master-intriguer; the play has appeared as an allegory, an attack on dictatorship and a sociological exercise.

Whichever the choice, and in spite of its shameless use of the "bed-trick" whereby one girl takes the place of another, *Measure for Measure*, written with absorbing strength and eloquence, can usually hold the stage. One absurd revival (Stratford, 1974) turned the Duke into a vulgar sham. Isabella, setting honour above her brother's life, is not an easy heroine; it has been proposed plausibly that in her notorious line, "More than our brother is our chastity" (II.4), she is speaking in terms of her religious order. The comedy rests principally on Lucio, a libertine "fantastic", whose morals are as deplorable as his insolence is amusing, and Pompey, a cheerful ruffian in both Vienna's sultry days and its sultrier nights before "the unfolding star calls up the shepherd".

After the customary free versions, Shakespeare's text was revived at Drury Lane (1738) with James Quin as the Duke and Mrs Susannah Cibber as Isabella. The great Isabella was Sarah Siddons (between 1783 and 1811), using all her passionate emotional integrity; John Philip Kemble often acted the Duke with her. In spite of intermittent revivals — e.g. Adelaide Neilson's Isabella at the Haymarket, 1876 and 1878 — the play was not for Victorians, who suspected its morality. Oscar Asche and his wife, Lily Brayton, were Angelo and Isabella (Adelphi, 1906); William Poel (first in 1893) treated *Measure for Measure* less strangely than some of his productions. Between the wars Baliol Holloway appeared, variously, as Lucio (Stratford, 1922), the Duke and Angelo; and Randle Ayrton was a grittily impressive Duke at Stratford (1931), during the cinema-stage "interregnum" between the two theatres.

Tyrone Guthrie, who had a particular feeling for the piece (interpreted diversely), directed a Vic/Wells revival (1933), with Charles Laughton's Angelo, the unarguable success of his Shakespearian career, and Flora Robson as Isabella. Guthrie also directed at the Old Vic (1937; Emlyn Williams as Angelo, with Marie Ney), at Stratford, Ontario (1954), and at Bristol Old Vic (1966). Peter Brook (Stratford, 1950; John Gielgud as a man in torment, and the youthful Barbara Jefford's Isabella) insisted on a daring pause when Isabella knelt to plead for Angelo's life: a silence that lasted originally for 35 seconds, and now and then as long as two minutes. Judi Dench was Isabella at Stratford (1962). John Barton's RSC production of 1970 famously denied the play a conventional happy ending by causing Isabella (Estelle Kohler) to show uncertainty about whether to accept the Duke's proposals of marriage. As if in reaction, Michael Rudman's National production (Lyttelton, 1981), set on a Caribbean island with a largely black cast (Norman Beaton a powerful Angelo) adjusted the text to steer the play in the direction of romantic comedy. Adrian Noble's 1985 Stratford production had Juliet Stevenson as Isabella to Daniel Massey's Duke. In Nicholas Hytner's RSC production of 1987 Roger Allam's Duke was close to nervous collapse as the action began, his opening speech a recorded address to the city. At The Other Place in 1991 Trevor Nunn set the play firmly in Freud's Vienna. Three years late Declan Donnellan's Cheek by Jowl version, though played on a minimal set (Nick Ormerod), also used realistic detail; Isabella got Claudio to recite the 23rd Psalm in preparation for death. In the same year, Steven Pimlott's RSC version used townspeople of Stratford as Viennese citizens. Isabella (Stella Gonet) responded hysterically to the Duke's proposal with a disconcerting mixture of ace-slapping, kisses, and tears. Michael Boyd directed at Stratford in 1998, and in 2004 at the National, Théâtre de Complicité's outstanding production, with an acutely observed Angelo from Paul Rhys, used film and video in its exploration of the play's sexual and social complexities.

The New York Shakespeare Festival have offered it twice: in 1987, and again in 1993, with Blair Underwood as Claudio, in Central Park. It was also the 1993 choice of the California Shakespeare Company, with Brenda Kenworthy and Aaron Craig.

Peter Brook directed the play in what has been called "the mosque-like ruin" of his Théâtre Bouffes-du-Nord, Paris (1978).

# IN OTHER TERMS

Kate Nelligan, in an otherwise indifferently spoken version (BBC television, 1979), was a moving Isabella who from her habit seemed to have been admitted prematurely to the sisterhood.

# CHIEF CHARACTERS

**Vincentio, the Duke** Chooses to wander, disguised, in Vienna. A long part (fifth longest in the plays; 835 lines). At Bristol Old Vic (1966) Vincentio, as Power Divine, showed the stigmata to the Provost (IV.2): "Here is the hand and seal of the Duke."

**Angelo** The puritan who falls. Acted definitively by Charles Laughton (Vic/Wells, 1933), a shuddering glance at a cankered mind.

**Isabella** A testing part ("a thing enskied and sainted") that can be potently affecting. Her plea for mercy (II.2) outmatches Portia's.

**Mariana** Romantically "of the moated grange", she will be Angelo's wife. She has (IV.1) a tempting line for actresses, the simple "I have sat here all day."

**Juliet** Shakespeare this time uses the name for Claudio's unlucky betrothed.

**Escalus** The "ancient lord" is one of Shakespeare's expressions of experienced wisdom.

**Claudio** Comes out sharply in his fear of death, "Ay, but to die, and go we know not where" (III.1).

**Lucio** The "fantastic" who has, reluctantly, to marry Kate Keepdown.

**Elbow** A faint glimmer of Dogberry (*Much Ado*).

**Pompey** Cannot restrain his natural exuberance, even in gaol where (IV.3) he evokes the procession of prisoners (Rash, Caper, Deepvow, and the rest); and becomes assistant to the executioner, Abhorson ("Can you cut off a man's head?" the Provost asks him, IV.2).

**Barnardine** Most independent of prisoners, he "will not die today for any man's persuasion" (IV.3).

**Francisca** A nun with nine lines. Memorable because Ellen Terry played the part for one performance (with Oscar Asche, Adelphi, 1906) to mark her stage jubilee.

**Mistress Overdone** The Viennese bawd whose name says all.

# Othello, the Moor of Venice
## 1604

 **THE CHARACTERS**

Othello, The Moor, in the service
  of Venice
Desdemona, Brabantio's daughter and
  Othello's wife
Cassio, his honourable Lieutenant
Iago, his ensign, a villain
Emilia, Iago's wife
Bianca, a courtesan, in love with Cassio
Roderigo, a fooled Venetian gentleman
Duke of Venice
Brabantio, a Venetian Senator,

Desdemona's father
Gratiano, Brabantio's brother
Lodovico, Brabantio's kinsman
Montano, Governor of Cyprus before
  Othello
Clown, servant to Othello
Senators, Gentlemen of Cyprus,
  Sailors, Officers, Messenger,
  Musicians, Heralds, Attendants, etc.

 **THE SCENE**

Venice, Cyprus

## SYNOPSIS

Iago, ensign to the Moorish general Othello, in the service of the Venetian republic, is a man inwardly malevolent and envious, outwardly an honest soldier. Resolved, for his own reasons, to revenge himself upon Othello, he begins one midnight in Venice by getting Roderigo — Desdemona's foolish suitor — to rouse her father with the news that Othello has stolen her. Brabantio at once accuses Othello at the Duke's hastily convened council which is considering a threatened Turkish attack on Cyprus; but the Moor's tale of his wooing, and Desdemona's testimony, persuade all the senators except Brabantio himself. Othello is despatched to govern Cyprus with his new lieutenant Cassio (of whom Iago is feverishly jealous), Desdemona following them with Iago and his wife Emilia.

The Turkish fleet has been dispersed in a tempest by the time (Act II) the travellers reach Cyprus. (Roderigo, still pursuing Desdemona, is also there.) On a night of celebration Cassio, who at Iago's prompting has drunk unwisely, is involved in a brawl and disgraced ("Never more be officer of mine," says Othello). At Iago's suggestion (Act III) Cassio implores Desdemona to plead his cause; Othello, already distressed by Iago's hints at infidelity, grows progressively inflamed. Iago makes diabolical play with a handkerchief (Othello's gift) that Desdemona has dropped and that he ensures Cassio will unwittingly find.

When Othello is overwhelmed by the falsehood that Desdemona is untrue, Iago arranges other "proof" (Act IV). Othello swears to kill her; and envoys from Venice, who have come to recall him, leaving Cassio as governor, are horrified to see him strike his wife. Iago (Act V) urges Roderigo to murder Cassio, and when the effort fails, stabs the dupe to death. Othello smothers Desdemona in her bed; Emilia, rousing the citadel, tells the truth about Iago, confirmed when in desperation he kills her. Whereupon Othello stabs himself, Iago is borne off to torture, and Cassio rules in Cyprus.

# IN PERFORMANCE

Iago, Othello's "ancient", or ensign, says, "I do hate him as I do hell pains" (I.1). This is the tragedy of a "free and open nature" (also, surprisingly, Iago's phrase) wrecked by an apparently honest soldier. For all his anxiously sought reasons, his resentment at Cassio's appointment over him, and the utterly implausible suggestion that Othello has seduced Emilia (I.3), Iago is a man in love with evil for its own sake. The First Folio cast list describes him simply as "a villain". He has a ready imagination: directors ought not to cut his first urging of Roderigo to call aloud "with like timorous action and dire yell/As when, by night and negligence, the fire/Is spied in populous cities." We know at once that nothing will change the mind behind the mask. The tragedy of Othello is its inevitability, beginning with Cassio's humiliation and continuing to the deaths of Desdemona and the Moor. On the way the fooled Roderigo must die, and, at length, Iago's own wife; but we can say (with Albany at the end of *King Lear*), "That's but a trifle."

Othello, the victim, shattered as much by his loss of faith in an ideal as by sheer jealousy, is a wonderfully planned part, a man caught — as it has been said — at the meeting-point of two cultural and spiritual traditions. The actor needs temperament and voice: one quality alone will not serve. There are scenes when Othello is possessed by a barbaric ancestry; but for the famous speeches — "Most potent, grave, and reverend signiors" (I.3), "O, now for ever/Farewell the tranquil mind" (III.3), "It is the cause", "Behold, I have a weapon", and "Soft you; a word or two before you go" (all V.2) — we should have a fitting splendour; towards the end, the arched fury of the breaking wave.

In the text the time scheme of *Othello* is impossible but in performance no one questions it. The tragedy, suggested by an Italian tale in the *Hecatommithi* of Cinthio, has been played steadily since 1604 when we suppose the "grievèd Moor" was Burbage. Margaret Hughes, presumed to have been Desdemona in Thomas Killigrew's company (Vere Street, Clare Market, 1660), could have been the first professional actress on the English stage: "Here comes the lady; let her witness it."

Revisers have left the play alone. Down the centuries there have always been leading players for Othello and Iago, sometimes alternating incautiously. Betterton ("When he wept his tears broke from him perforce") was Othello during the Restoration and afterwards; James Quin, white-attired, imposing, slow, and not very tender, played at intervals between 1722 and 1751. David Garrick (more assured as Iago) was too violent, but his rival, silver-tongued Spranger Barry, became the day's most feeling Othello, profoundly distressed. John Philip Kemble needed emotional authority. Edmund Kean (from 1814) gave one of his lightning-flash portraits, kindling in the third act and with a final speech (said Hazlitt) like "the sound of years of departed happiness." Macready (whose Iago could be darkly smouldering) seemed overstudied.

Samuel Phelps was better as Othello, Charles Fechter as Iago. Henry Irving, lachrymose and restless, threw Othello away, but not his sardonic, irregular Iago, during his alternation with the American Edwin Booth. Forbes-Robertson (Lyric, 1902), chivalrous always, never a man for the "steep-down gulfs of liquid fire", was too gentle in a multilated text. Though critics praised Matheson Lang (New, 1920) for Shakespearian excellence at matinées, his public preferred him at night in *Carnival*, a facile modern treatment of the Othello theme. Wilfrid Walter (Stratford, 1930) looked, and sometimes sounded, superb, with George Hayes as his demi-devil Iago; Paul Robeson's Othello (Savoy, 1930) ebbed into monotony; and Tyrone Guthrie failed in a Freudian attempt (Old Vic, 1938) to show that Iago (Laurence Olivier) was attracted to Othello (Ralph Richardson) homosexually.

The next quarter-century brought a few debated performances. Frederick Valk, a thunderously passionate Czech (Old Vic company at New, 1942) mauled the verse but worked closely with his Iago (Bernard Miles), a coarse, chilling fox. Godfrey Tearle, who had been Othello as early as 1921 (Royal Court), was nobly commanding (Stratford, 1948) but failed to blaze. Orson Welles (St James's, 1951) was unresourceful; and John Gielgud (Stratford, 1961) had to dissipate his glorious speech in a tiresomely scenic Zeffirelli production. Three years later (National at Old Vic) Laurence Olivier proved the Othello of his age, with wind-tossed harmonies, bursts of barbaric music, and volcanic temperament. Paul Scofield's performance for the National company in the Olivier Theatre (1980) was valuable. In an entirely straight production by Peter Hall, Scofield was gravely dignified in mind and breeding, and had at the last a sudden agonized fury at "Whip me, ye devils!" when Othello saw too clearly and too late. Donald Sinden (Stratford/Aldwych, 1979–80) was similarly eloquent, affecting and truthful, and overcame perilous eccentricities in direction. Since then few directors have dared to cast a white actor as Othello – a socially well-meaning policy which may have deprived audiences of great performances. Terry Hands directed Ben Kingsley

(Othello) and David Suchet (Iago) for the RSC (1986) in another production that proposed an erotic attraction between Othello and his ensign. At The Other Place (1991) Trevor Nunn directed a novelistically detailed production with the black opera singer Willard White as a physically dominating Othello and Ian McKellen hypnotically evil as Iago. In Stratford's main house Michael Attenborough directed Ray Fearon, with Richard McCabe as a psychotic in a powerfully straightforward production which gave full weight to the love between Othello and Desdemona (Zoe Waites). At the Swan (2004) Gregory Doran directed a strong modern-dress production with Sello Maake ka Ncube (Othello) and Antony Sher (Iago); on tour, Declan Donnellan's Cheek by Jowl company had the young black actor Nonso Anozie as an impassioned Moor in a more adventurous production.

Ben Kingsley and David Suchet were Othello and Iago for the RSC (1986). The RSC production, with Willard White as Othello, Ian McKellen as Iago, and Imogen Stubbs as Desdemona, directed by Trevor Nunn, was televized (The Other Place/Young Vic, 1991–2).

American stage history, from New York (1751), is governed by two men: Edwin Forrest's massive-bull Othello (1826 to 1871); and, between 1860 and 1891, America's greatest player, the intellectual Edwin Booth. He acted both parts, more surely his Machiavellian Iago, plausible, precisely enunciated, and with frightening inner fires. Paul Robeson had a long New York run, 1943–4; by 1959, when he came across to Stratford-upon-Avon, his voice had become an oddly distant bass rumble.

Italy bred two celebrated Othellos, the sensual, tempestuous Tommaso Salvini, a marvellous tragic actor (New York, 1873; London, 1875), and the savage Sicilian, Giovanni Grasso (London, 1910). Salvini was criticized for his treatment of Othello's death and the fierce hacking at his throat. Edmund Kean in the same scene had been applauded. Leigh Hunt said of him ("piercing himself to the heart with a poignard"): "Can you not mark the frozen shudder as the steel enters his frame?... Death by a heart wound is instantaneous. Thus does he portray it; he literally dies standing."

## IN OTHER TERMS

1955, directed by Orson Welles (Welles as Othello); 1955, directed by Sergei Yutkevitch (largely shot in the Crimea); 1965, National Theatre production (Olivier as Othello, Frank Finlay as Iago), directed by Stuart Burge. *Otello* (Rossini, 1816); *Otello* (Verdi, 1887). Verdi was 74 when he composed his magnificent opera to the libretto Arrigo Boito based upon Shakespeare. *Catch My Soul*, a rock musical adapted from the play, was on the London stage in 1971. On its re-release in 1992, Orson

Welles's film, damned on its first showing in 1952, was hailed as a pioneering masterpiece. In Serge Yutkevitch's Russian film (also 1952) Iago leads Othello into temptation through a tangle of fishing nets; Othello's hair turns suddenly white after the murder of Desdemona. John Dexter's National Theatre production, with Olivier as Othello, as redirected on film by Stuart Burge (1965), sadly fails to achieve the changes in perspective needed to translate a great stage production into filmic terms. Janet Suzman's politically loaded Market Theatre Capetown production, with John Kani as Othello, was filmed in 1988. Anthony Hopkins plays Othello in the BBC television film (1981). Oliver Parker's 1995 film, strong on narrative and with Kenneth Branagh as a commanding Iago, leaves no room for doubt that Othello's marriage was consummated.

Rossini's 1816 opera, which requires three star tenors, is notable especially for a beautiful setting of the Willow song. It has been overshadowed by Verdi's supreme masterpiece *Otello*, with a brilliant libretto by Arrigo Boito which omits the first act; a fine film with Placido Domingo was directed by Franco Zeffirelli (1986).

Patrick Stewart evaded the ban on white actors in a photo-negative production in Washington (1997).

# CHIEF CHARACTERS

**Othello** One of the most taxing parts in the canon, he must be more than simply passionate or (the usual simplification) soldierly. He should be a majestic speaker, and we must always be aware of the racial depths. Cassio speaks his epitaph: "For he was great of heart".

**Desdemona** Has been played too often as a wilting lily. But her marriage was courageous; and we should not be allowed to forget her response to Brabantio (I.3), "My noble father,/I do perceive here a divided duty."

**Iago** The longest part (1,070 lines). "Honest Iago" speaks for himself in I.1: "For necessity of present life,/I must show out a flag and sign of love,/Which is indeed but sign." He is an affirmation of evil for its own sake; behind him is the midnight, and he brings chaos with him. "The pity of it, Iago!" says Othello (IV.1), but Iago has never known pity.

**Emilia** Iago's wife, Desdemona's attendant and confidante. Anxious to please her husband, she gives him the fatal handkerchief (III.3). "Have we not affections,/Desires for sport and frailty, as men have?" (IV.3).

**Cassio** The Moor's "honourable lieutenant", impulsive and weak. Iago: "He hath a daily beauty in his life/That makes me ugly" (V.1).

**Roderigo** Iago's foolish dupe, whom the Folio calls "a gull'd Venetian gentleman". Still vainly pursuing, he is killed (V.1) with "O damn'd Iago! O inhuman dog!" as his last words. He should be played with discretion —not, as frequently, turned into an Andrew Aguecheek.

**Montano** Former Governor of Cyprus, injured by Cassio in a brawl (II.3).

**Brabantio** Desdemona's father. Othello, in Iago's net, may remember Brabantio's last couplet — as we can be sure Iago does — "Look to her, Moor, if thou hast eyes to see;/ She has deceived her father, and may thee" (I.3). We hear in V.2 of his grieving death.

**Lodovico** The Venetian envoy, Brabantio's kinsman, who is present (IV.1) when Othello strikes Desdemona. "My lord, this would not be believ'd in Venice,/Though I should swear I saw't."

**Gratiano** Brabantio's brother and Desdemona's uncle appears (V.1) just in time to know of Roderigo's death; in the next scene he says of Brabantio that Desdemona's marriage was "mortal to him, and pure grief/Shore his old thread atwain." In the play's final speech Lodovico says: "Gratiano, keep the house,/And seize upon the fortunes of the Moor,/For they succeed on you."

**Bianca** Cassio's Cypriot courtesan, impudent and brave.

# King Lear
## 1605

 **THE CHARACTERS**

Lear, King of Britain
Goneril, Lear's daughter and wife to Duke of Albany
Regan, Lear's daughter and wife to Duke of Cornwall
Cordelia, Lear's daughter, who becomes Queen of France
King of France
Duke of Burgundy
Duke of Cornwall
Duke of Albany
Earl of Kent
Earl of Gloucester
Edgar, Gloucester's son

Edmund, bastard son to Gloucester
Curan, a courtier
Old Man, tenant to Gloucester
Doctor
Lear's Fool
Oswald, Goneril's steward
A Captain, employed by Edmund
Gentleman attendant on Cordelia
A Herald
Knights attending on Lear, Officers, Messengers, Soldiers, Attendants, Servants to Cornwall

**THE SCENE**
Britain

# SYNOPSIS

Lear, King of Britain, aged and choleric, has resolved to divide his realm between his three daughters, supposedly in accordance with the depth of their professed love. Though Goneril (married to the gentle Albany) and Regan (cruel Cornwall's wife) extravagantly declare their love for him, the youngest, Cordelia, disdaining this, says simply: "I cannot heave/My heart into my mouth." Wrathfully, Lear disinherits her, banishing Kent who has spoken on her behalf, but the King of France takes her, dowerless, as his Queen. Lear gives her share to her sisters, proposing to live alternately with them, with his retinue of 100 knights.

Edmund, Gloucester's bastard son, foments discord between his legitimate brother Edgar and their father. Kent, disguised, returns to serve his master Lear. Goneril receives Lear with contempt; invoking a curse upon her (I.4), he leaves for Regan. At the same time (Act II) Regan and Cornwall reach Gloucester's castle, whence Edgar has fled. Regan proves to be even harsher than Goneril; believing madness will supervene, Lear goes out with his Fool into the night storm on the heath, where the loyal Kent finds him. Gloucester, braving the anger of the two sisters and Cornwall, gets shelter for them in a hovel (Edgar is there, disguised as a half-witted "Poor Tom") and urges Kent to take the endangered King to Dover ("There is a litter ready; lay him in 't"). Returning to his castle, Gloucester is reviled and savagely blinded by Cornwall, who is then slain by a servant.

Edgar, still as "Poor Tom" and unknown to his blinded father, sets off with him towards Dover. There is a strange meeting (Act IV) between the mad King and the blind man. Soon afterwards Cordelia, who has come from France, is reunited with the enfeebled Lear. Captured (Act V) in a battle which the French forces have lost, they are sent to prison where by Edmund's instructions they are to be murdered. But Edmund — who has been deceiving both the infatuated Goneril and Regan — is killed by Edgar (as a nameless knight) in single combat. Goneril has poisoned Regan; she now stabs herself. Cordelia has been hanged in prison; Lear bears her in, and within minutes he himself has died. "The wonder is he hath endur'd so long." Edgar, at Albany's wish, will look to the state; but Kent will follow Lear: "My master calls me; I must not say no."

# IN PERFORMANCE

*King Lear*, dawn-in-Britain tragedy of retribution, is an anguished, storm-ridden journey of the mind and spirit. With many of the most searching passages in Shakespeare, it has still to be for some listeners an acquired taste in the theatre, though no one now will talk, as Charles Lamb did, of "An old man tottering about the stage with a walking-stick, turned out of doors by his daughters on a rainy night... The Lear of Shakespeare cannot be acted." The great play has been a normal part of the repertory for most of the 20th century, though no one has succeeded without reservation as the wilful patriarch driven to madness.

Among the sources for his tragedy of "unaccommodated man" (III.4), Shakespeare worked most directly from an old chronicle drama, *King Leir*. The first version to be printed, in 1608, differs considerably from the revision in the Folio. Since the publication of the Oxford edition in 1986 editors have tended to base their text firmly on one or the other; directors usually continue to pick and mix. Shakespeare's play fared unhappily from 1681 when it fell into the hands of Nahum Tate, who produced a ridiculous mutilation, with Edgar and Cordelia as lovers, the Fool eliminated, and a happy ending ("Old Kent throws in his hearty wishes too"). For 150 years Tate's was practically the only version that audiences would accept, though one by David Garrick, with Tate's plot retained but much of the original verse restored, was familiar at Drury Lane for 30-odd years from 1756.

In the course of two revivals by Robert Elliston, with Edmund Kean as Lear (1823 and 1826), more of the original returned; but it was left to William Charles Macready (Covent Garden, 1838) to bring back an abridged Shakespearian text, with the Fool assigned to an actress, Priscilla Horton. Once the changes had been made, *King Lear* — cut according to managerial taste — remained Shakespeare's. Samuel Phelps gave the Fool to a male actor at Sadler's Wells, 1845. In England before 1928, and in spite of several renowned players, only Macready's Lear (1838) and Ellen Terry's Cordelia (with Henry Irving, 1892) were really eminent.

Ernest Milton, his Lear cut to the brains, was powerfully individual (Old Vic, 1928; Jean Forbes-Robertson as Cordelia); John Gielgud, larch rather than oak, had a first clear look at the part (Old Vic, 1931 and 1940); Randle Ayrton (Stratford, 1931, and on Komisarjevsky's variously levelled staircase-set, 1936) abounded in pathos, especially at "We two alone will sing like birds i'th' cage" (V.3); William Devlin, in his early twenties (Westminster, 1934; Old Vic, 1936) was an Olympian figure who needed only a more flexible voice.

Donald Wolfit (Scala, 1944) had played Lear earlier without marked response but the critic James Agate now became as much of a cheer-leader for Wolfit as Hazlitt had been for Kean's Othello. Unarguably affecting, especially in the hovel scene, III.6 ("The little dogs and all... see they bark at me"), the performance did suffer from a creeping monotony of intonation; some preferred Wolfit as the unexampled Kent he had acted at Stratford (1936). Olivier's Lear (Old Vic at New, 1946) was closely considered; Gielgud (Stratford, 1950) returned with undimmed impact, especially in the colloquy with Gloucester (IV.6) and the Recognition (IV.7); Michael Redgrave (Stratford, 1953) had a massive quietness.

A sequence of later performances included Gielgud's final portrait (Palace, 1955), ruined by the caprices of Japanese décor. Charles Laughton (Stratford, 1959) added little. Paul Scofield, in a pitilessly Brechtian production by Peter Brook (Stratford/Aldwych, 1962), resembled for a moment an ancient sea captain commanding the bridge of his vessel, defying the cosmic fates as he drove, unmanned, towards death. Donald Sinden played Lear in Trevor Nunn's ruritanian-style RSC production (1976). In 1982 Adrian Noble's production, also for the RSC, Michael Gambon's Lear took his revenge on the scene-stealing brilliance of Antony Sher's Fool by stabbing him to death in a barrel. Two very different productions opened within weeks of each other in 1990. In Deborah Warner's austere version at the National, Brian Cox careered on in a wheelchair on his first entrance, clearly having a whale of a time at his 80th birthday party; later he wheeled on the dead Cordelia in the same chair. At the RSC Nicholas Hytner directed a vocally self-conscious John Wood in an elaborate production based closely on the Folio text, though importing the trial scene from the Quarto. Adrian Noble returned to the play at Stratford in 1993 with Robert Stephens impassioned and tender as Lear, Simon Russell Beale bringing great depth to the difficult role of Edgar, and David Bradley as a profoundly suffering Gloucester. At the National (Cottesloe) in 1997 Richard Eyre directed Ian Holm, fiery yet tender, as a metric Lear, every centimetre a king, in a thoughtful production played in "timeless" costumes and graced by Paul Rhy's well-conceived Edgar. Also in 1997 a production by Helen Kaut-Howson seen first in Leicester presented the play as the dream, or hallucination, of a dying patient in a geriatric hospital, with Kathryn Hunter as Lear. The Japanese director Yukio Ninagawa directed Nigel Hawthorne as Lear, with a Japanese Fool, in an RSC production (1999) that opened in Tokyo before moving to London and Stratford.

Anthony Hopkins was Lear at the National, directed by David Hare and with Bill Nighy (Edgar) and Douglas Hodge (Edmund) (Olivier, 1986).

In America, where the Shakespeare text did not return until Macready visited New York (1844), the most famous 19th-century Lears were Edwin Forrest (only 20 when he essayed it first in 1826), Edwin Booth (1875), and John E. McCullough (1877). In the 20th century: Robert Mantell (1905), Louis Calhern (1940), and at Stratford,

Connecticut (1963, 1965), the exceptional Morris Carnovsky. Kenneth Branagh's Renaissance Theatre Company took repertory stagings of *Dream* and *King Lear* to the Mark Taper Forum in 1990.

## IN OTHER TERMS

Grigori Kozintsev's marvellous film (1970) used a translation by Boris Pasternak; viewers of the video can hear Pasternak in Russian while reading Shakespeare on the English sub-titles. At around the same time Peter Brook directed Paul Scofield in a shortened but devastating version deriving from his stage production but more ostensibly naturalistic in setting. Both these versions were shot on location. In the somewhat studio-bound Granada television film (1983) Michael Elliott directed Laurence Olivier, who, though visibly weakened by illness and age, gives a brilliantly original and affecting performance as Lear. Akira Kurosawa's great film *Ran* (chaos, civil war) adapts the play no less radically than Shakespeare adapted *King Leir*, transferring the action to feudal Japan and metamorphosing Lear's daughters into sons. Jean-Luc Godard's film (1987) is bizarrely post-modern.

John Gielgud made a sound recording (1993) with an all-star cast based on the Renaissance Theatre Company to celebrate his ninetieth birthday. Aribert Reimann's opera (1978) was written for Dietrich Fischer-Dieskau.

*King Lear* has inspired other plays, notably Edward Bond's bleak *Lear* (1971) and Elaine Feinstein's *Lear's Daughters* (1987). Prose fiction indebted to the play includes Turgenev's novella *A King Lear of the Steppes* (1870) and Jane Smiley's novel *A Thousand Acres* (1991). There are fine paintings by, among others, William Blake, Heinrich Fuseli, Sir Joshua Reynolds, John Runciman, and Benjamin West.

## CHIEF CHARACTERS

**Lear** King of Britain (752 lines in the full text). A mighty part, though it can often fare better in the imagination than in performance.

**Earl of Kent** The most loyal of Lear's followers, who will not long outlive his master: "I have a journey, sir, shortly to go" (V.3).

**Earl of Gloucester** The blinding scene is as painful as anything in the canon: Lilian Baylis would have it played immediately after the interval, so that the more sensitive in the audience could avoid it.

**Edgar** The actor needs to give a protean performance ("Poor Tom"; peasant; Edmund's challenger in that blazingly theatrical passage, V.3).

**Edmund** Gloucester's bastard son, the play's Iago, "A most toad-spotted traitor" (V.3). "Yet Edmund was belov'd," he says with almost his last breath.

**Fool** Lear's personified conscience. Lost to the theatre for 150 years, then restored, in Macready's 1838 revival, by an actress.

**Cordelia** The loving daughter who will not "heave [her] heart into [her] mouth", thereby prompting her banishment and the beginning of Lear's decline.

**Goneril** Possibly, though it is a hard choice, marginally the less repellent of the elder daughters; the subject of Lear's curse (I.4).

**Regan** "Go thrust him out at gates," she says of blinded Gloucester (III.7), "and let him smell his way to Dover." Her body and that of Goneril should be on the stage at the last; it is a piece of tragic symmetry, sometimes forgotten, that the play begins with an old man and his three daughters, and ends with them, now all dead.

**King of France** Cordelia's romantic rescuer in the first act does not reappear. In IV.3 we hear that he has returned suddenly to France, leaving behind him one of Shakespeare's faintest personages, the Marshal of France ("Monsieur La Far") of whom we hear no more.

**Duke of Cornwall** Regan's abominable husband, who blinds Gloucester ("Turn out that eyeless villain", III.7) and is, rightly, slain.

**Duke of Albany** Goneril's gentle husband proves his mettle in the final scenes.

**Oswald** Goneril's steward, whose death (IV.6) is fitting. The young Gordon Craig acted the part with Irving.

# Macbeth
## 1606

 **THE CHARACTERS**
Duncan, King of Scotland
Malcolm and Donalbain, his sons
Macbeth and Banquo, Generals of the
   King's army
Lady Macbeth
Gentlewoman attending on Lady Macbeth
Fleance, son to Banquo
Macduff, Lennox, Ross, Menteith, Angus,
   Caithness, Noblemen of Scotland
Lady Macduff
Siward, Earl of Northumberland, General
   of the English forces
Young Siward, his son
Seyton, an officer attending on Macbeth

The Weird Sisters
Boy, son to Macduff
A Sergeant
A Porter
An Old Man
An English Doctor
A Scots Doctor
Hecate
Ghost of Banquo, Apparitions, Lords,
   Gentlemen, Officers, Soldiers,
   Murderers, Attendants, Messengers

**THE SCENE**
Scotland and England

## SYNOPSIS

Upon a "blasted heath" near Forres, three Witches, Weird Sisters, meeting the King of Scotland's generals, Macbeth and Banquo, hail Macbeth in a triple prophecy, ending with the promise of kingship. Banquo is told that he shall "get kings, though thou be none". After King Duncan has made him Thane of Cawdor (as the Witches promised), Macbeth knows that he and his unflinching wife are ambitious for the greater honour. She drives him onward; and that night he murders the sleeping King, their guest at the castle of Dunsinane. At dawn (Act II) Macduff and Lennox discover the murder, assumed to be by the King's sons, Donalbain and Malcolm, who fly for safety. Macbeth goes to Forres to be crowned. Remembering the Witches' prophecies, he has Banquo killed (Act III), but Banquo's son Fleance escapes; that night Banquo's ghost appears to Macbeth at a state banquet.

Macbeth goes (Act IV) to the Witches' "pit of Acheron", where he hears that he must beware of Macduff, that he is to fear no man born of woman, and that he will remain unvanquished until Birnam Wood has come to Dunsinane. Macduff, meanwhile, has joined Malcolm in England, where he hears that in Fife the tyrant has had his family murdered. Revenge will follow. At Dunsinane (Act V) Lady Macbeth, burdened by guilt, reveals much during her sleepwalking ("Infected minds," says the doctor, "to their deep pillows will discharge their secrets"). Malcolm's invading army advances under the shelter of branches from Birnam Wood; Macbeth, who has just learned of his wife's suicide ("She should have died hereafter"), hears that Birnam Wood is indeed coming towards Dunsinane. Trusting desperately to a charmed life that "must not yield to one of woman born", he faces in battle Macduff, who cries to him: "Let the angel whom thou still hast serv'd/Tell thee Macduff was from his mother's womb/Untimely ripp'd". Macbeth is slain and Malcolm hailed as King of Scotland.

# IN PERFORMANCE

This is one of the shortest and certainly the most concentrated of the plays — Macbeth himself speaks nearly a third of the lines. It should be acted without an interval, as it frequently now is, though as recently as the 1930s there may have been as many as 20 scene breaks and three long intervals during a performance. That is fatal, for the tragedy of vaulting ambition and overpowering conscience needs to move inexorably and swiftly from the salute on the heath to the last desperate defiance: "Lay on, Macduff;/And damn'd be he that first cries 'Hold enough!' "

The only surviving text, printed in the Folio of 1623, appears to be an adaptation by Thomas Middleton made some time after the first performance. The scenes involving Hecate, generally agreed to be written by Middleton, are almost always omitted in performance. So is the "king's evil" passage (4.3), possibly written in flattery of James I.

*Macbeth* is an astonishing portrait of two creatures, one beset by imagination, the other not but both possessed by the powers of evil. Macbeth is at first urged forward by his wife but, once on the throne, their deed behind them and conscience environing them, he becomes the stronger of the two: "I am in blood/Stepp'd in so far that, should I wade no more,/Returning were as tedious as go o'er." It is there, in mid-tragedy, that Lady Macbeth says "You lack the season of all natures, sleep." We do not meet her again until in the distress of her sleepwalking (V.1), she speaks what she should not.

This is a play of darkness: we think of it in "thick night". "Stars, hide your fires;/Let not light see my black and deep desires." This is the world Shakespeare had written of in *The Rape of Lucrece:* "O comfort-killing night, image of hell!/Dim register and notary of shame!"

Based freely on Holinshed's *Chronicles*, the play has grown to a legend in the theatre, where disasters are said to attend it. Undeniably its record is strange; Sybil Thorndike and Lewis Casson (Princes, 1926; she as Lady Macbeth, he Banquo) sought to exorcize the spirits of evil by reading together the 90th Psalm, "Thou shalt not be afraid for any terror by night".

This aside, it is curious that so few of the many past performances are laurelled: *Macbeth* has been a challenge seldom taken to the full. Sir William Davenant's weird Restoration "improvement", with its *divertissements* of dancing and singing Witches, kept the stage until 1744. David Garrick (though he retained the musical Witches) got back more of the play and appeared himself in the red coat of a British officer, with powdered wig. He, and later John Philip Kemble, were particularly redoubtable Macbeths, Kemble the slower (he could be said to have usurped the time of night). Edmund Kean appeared as a chieftain turned moral coward and crumbling ruin. History remembers Hannah Pritchard's Lady Macbeth (1748–68); Sarah Siddons' performances (1785–1817) of a woman intensely resolved ("Give *me* the daggers"), dignified, and at length piteous in remorse, established the part at a height that few later actresses have reached.

Macready (from 1820 until retirement in 1851) was the Macbeth of the 19th century, a great general devil-ridden by his imagination. Other notables: Samuel Phelps (Sadler's Wells) cut the remnants of the Davenant text; Henry Irving (notably 1888, 1895), whose Lady Macbeth, Ellen Terry, proved to be more kindling than he was; Beerbohm Tree (1911); the resonant American, James K. Hackett, in blood-red hair and beard (Aldwych, 1920); and Eric Maturin, glumly, in modern dress ("This *blasted* heath!") at the Court, 1928. Gielgud (Old Vic, 1930) used a voice like the springing into light of a chain of hilltop beacons, fire answering fire; Komisarjevsky's production, with George Hayes (Stratford, 1933) was textually capricious and set in scrolled aluminium screens; Charles Laughton (Sadler's Wells, 1934) saw Macbeth as a pathological subject; and Olivier (Old Vic, 1937) showed what might come.

Gielgud returned (Piccadilly, 1942) in a grandly spoken performance of a sombre, lonely usurper, after which there was no other Macbeth for history until Olivier's second study (Stratford, 1955) grew to its ultimate agonizing despair in beleaguered Dunsinane. The most discussed revival of its period, Trevor Nunn's in the sparest of settings (Stratford, 1976; Donmar Warehouse, London, 1977–8), rested on one uncanny performance, Judi Dench's Lady Macbeth, unwavering in purpose and so hypnotic in her opening speech that one Shakespearian scholar claimed to have seen the "spirits that tend on mortal thoughts". Adrian Noble directed the play three times for the RSC, most successfully in 1986 with Jonathan Pryce possessed by fear in the dagger scene and intensely involved with Sinead Cusack's lissom Lady. For once the Witches were truly fearful. The play is notoriously difficult to bring off, even with actors as distinguished as Derek Jacobi (RSC, Noble again, 1993) and Alan Howard (National, directed by Richard Eyre, 1993). Peter O'Toole's Old Vic performance (1976) is one of the great all-time flops. The best production since Nunn's at The Other Place was Gregory Doran's in the Swan, with Antony Sher and Harriet Walter, suggesting that its claustrophobic evocation of fear may be best summoned up in smaller spaces. In the Stratford main house in 2004 Greg Hicks was an intense Macbeth with Siân Thomas as a Fuseli-inspired Lady.

In North America (first performances, 1759) some of the most historic players were Edwin Forrest (from 1828), Charlotte Cushman, profoundly expressive (1840s), and Edwin Booth. Orson Welles (1936) staged the play — known as "the Voodoo *Macbeth*" — in Harlem, set atmospherically in 19th-century Haiti with a black cast. Christopher Plummer and Glenda Jackson were strong Macbeths at the Mark Hellinger Theater in New York (1988).

## IN OTHER TERMS

One of the finest literary essays inspired by Shakespeare is Thomas de Quincey's "On the Knocking at the Gate in *Macbeth*" (1823). Verdi's opera *Macbetto* is not on the same uniform level of inspiration as his *Otello* and *Falstaff*, but has a hypnotic sleep-walking scene. Orson Welles directed himself as Macbeth in a technically flawed film (1948). Akira Kurosawa's film set in medieval Japan known as *Throne of Blood* (1957) is a powerful, free adaptation. Roman Polanski's adventurous film has Jon Finch and Francesca Annis as the Macbeths.

A half-hour excerpt from the Old Vic production starring Laurence Olivier and Judith Anderson was shown on television, but Olivier never succeeded in raising the finance for the full-length film that he hoped to make. Nicol Williamson and Jane Lapotaire star in the BBC television film (1983).

Works of visual art inspired by the play include fine paintings by Zoffany and Fuseli of Garrick and Mrs Pritchard. Fuseli also memorably painted Sarah Siddons as Lady Macbeth. John Singer Sargent has two striking paintings of Ellen Terry in the role.

## CHIEF CHARACTERS

**Duncan, King of Scotland** His age (he is usually played as an ancient) must be left to actor and director. But in the theatre the *Macbeth* cast is growing younger with the years.

**Malcolm** Has a long and false self-accusation in the English scene that here clogs the action (IV.3).

**Macbeth** Haunted and possessed, he dwindles from "Bellona's bridegroom lapp'd in proof" (I.2) to the gaunt, famished wolf of Dunsinane. Early in the play — and one is reminded of Iago's appearance in *Othello* after "Chaos is come again" — Macbeth reaches the palace at Forres (I.4) and hears Duncan's memory of the executed Thane of Cawdor: "He was a gentleman on whom I built/An absolute trust." Surprisingly few actors have been able memorably to plot the graph of Macbeth's rise and fall or to sustain the brooding verse.

**Lady Macbeth** Although the ambition-obsessed wife has two superb key scenes (I.5 and V.1), the part is sometimes overestimated. Few actresses have transformed it.

**Banquo** Worthy general and (III.4) menacing ghost.

**Macduff** The avenger. In IV.3, after the tale of his wife and children's murder, he uses the phrase "one fell swoop", which (though it has become a cliché) should not be thrown away.

**Lady Macduff** In the scene of her murder (IV.2) she has to have a plausible Young Macduff ("Poor prattler, how thou talk'st!").

**Ross** The bringer of news, good (I.3) and ill (IV.3).

**Lennox** Enters Inverness with Macduff (II.2) after a night that has been unruly but in which the Macbeths have heard only the owls scream and the crickets cry.

**Siward, Earl of Northumberland** Lives for the epitaph to his son, "God's soldier be he!" (V.8).

**Seyton** Loyal to the end, he is to Macbeth as Catesby to Richard III.

**A porter** (II.3) He admits Macduff and Lennox to Inverness Castle after the "unruly" night. He need not be a figure of low comedy. His references to an "equivocator" may be to the trial of Henry Garnet, the Jesuit hanged for high treason in May 1606.

**The Weird Sisters** (or Witches) "You should be women,/And yet your beards forbid me to interpret/That you are so." For a long time played by men. Directors should remember John Masefield's phrase, "Satan's kingdom does not laugh."

# Antony and Cleopatra
## 1606–7

 **THE CHARACTERS**

Mark Antony, Octavius Caesar and M. Aemilius Lepidus, triumvirs

Cleopatra, Queen of Egypt

Sextus Pompeius

Octavia, Caesar's sister and wife to Antony

Domitius Enobarbus, Ventidius, Eros, Scarus, Dercetas, Demetrius, Philo, friends to Antony

Maecenas, Agrippa, Dolabella, Proculeius, Thyreus, Gallus, friends to Caesar

Menas, Menecrates, Varrius, friends to Pompey

Taurus, Lieutenant-General to Caesar

Canidius, Lieutenant-General to Antony

Silius, an officer in the army of Ventidius

Euphronius, an ambassador from Antony to Caesar

Alexas, Mardian, Seleucus, Diomedes, attendants on Cleopatra

A soothsayer

A clown

Charmian, Iras, ladies attending on Cleopatra

Officers, Soldiers, Messengers, and Attendants

 **THE SCENE**

The Roman Empire

# SYNOPSIS

Mark Antony is one of the triumvirs, the three joint rulers of the Roman world. Cleopatra, in her Alexandrian palace, is Queen of Egypt. They are infatuated with each other; but Antony leaves Alexandria for Rome when he hears that Fulvia, his wife, has died, and that Sextus Pompeius (Pompey), son of Pompey the Great, has risen against Octavius Caesar.

In Rome (Act II) Antony patches up a quarrel by agreeing to marry Caesar's sister, Octavia; the triumvirs attend a friendly feast in Pompey's galley. Still, Antony will not relinquish Cleopatra; Caesar will not keep the peace with Pompey. Ultimately (Act III) Caesar opposes Antony at Actium and in the sea-battle Cleopatra's squadron flies. Antony is defeated. He wins a first day of land fighting (Act IV) but on a second day the Egyptian fleet surrenders.

After hearing a false report of Cleopatra's death, and falling on his sword, Antony is borne, mortally wounded, to Cleopatra in her "monument" (or mausoleum). There he dies. Rather than be taken to Rome as a captive, she has herself arrayed (Act V) in the royal robes and crown of Egypt and dies from the bite of an asp brought to her by a peasant. So she is found with her waiting-women dead beside her; and Caesar orders, "She shall be buried by her Antony;/No grave upon the earth shall clip in it/A pair so famous."

# IN PERFORMANCE

The scene is described embracingly as "the Roman Empire", and the play is imperial. None has more verbal glory, even though its central narrative can be expressed in a line or two from the opening speech. There the inconsiderable Philo (who fades into the dark) says of Antony: "You shall see in him/The triple pillar of the world transformed/Into a strumpet's fool." True, but the ordering of the tragedy is magnificent, and Antony at the last (IV.15) is mourned as no man has been in the world's drama: "The crown o'th'earth doth melt.../There is nothing left remarkable/Beneath the visiting moon." The speaker is the Egyptian queen of whom Enobarbus had said in the most quoted speech of all (II.2): "Age cannot wither her, nor custom stale/Her infinite variety."

Soon after Antony's death, Cleopatra herself has gone, with Charmian, to speak her epitaph (V.2): "Now boast thee, death, in thy possession lies/A lass unparallel'd." Whatever Antony and Cleopatra were, they are transfigured in a play of 42 scenes — several very short — that surges across "the wide arch of the rang'd empire". Here is the flexibility of Shakespeare's theatre. In a swift progress Ventidius and the Roman forces should be appearing at one side of the stage upon a plain in Syria, while Enobarbus and Menas on the other are moving towards a cabin in Pompey's galley. Today the tragedy has its problems. The lovers are hard to cast. Moreover a director obsessed by spectacle is doomed. The splendour is in the language and the speed.

Shakespeare's main source was North's translation of Plutarch's *Lives*. For 200 years little happened to the play in London; Dryden's adaptation, *All For Love* (Drury Lane, 1678), held the stage for a century. Garrick used a much altered version of Shakespeare (himself as Antony, Mrs Yates as Cleopatra) that ran for only six nights (1759). John Philip Kemble (1813) mingled Dryden and Shakespeare in transient chaos. When Tree, changing the order of the early scenes, revived it at His Majesty's (1906), it appeared almost furtively — in spite of Constance Collier's imperious Cleopatra — among a mass of scenic effects including a procession through the streets of Alexandria with Cleopatra as the goddess Isis.

Robert Atkins (Old Vic, 1922) typically let the play speak for itself on a bare stage, as judicious directors have done since. Dorothy Green, with Bridges-Adams at Stratford (1927) and with Gielgud (Old Vic, 1930), was the Cleopatra of her time — "Royal Egypt", and not an operatic contralto. The worst production between the wars was Komisarjevsky's (New, 1936), in retrospect a catalogue of disaster, with a charming but unintelligible Russian comedienne as Cleopatra and a variety of insensitive changes. (Even so, the performances of Margaret Rawlings as Charmian and George Hayes as

Soothsayer and Clown were gratefully acknowledged.)

Edith Evans twice played Cleopatra with only mild success (1925, Old Vic, to Baliol Holloway; 1946, Piccadilly, to Godfrey Tearle). Vivien Leigh (St James's, 1951, with Laurence Olivier) was intelligent, low-keyed and small-scale. The most realistic post-war performances were those of Michael Redgrave and the beautifully sensitive Peggy Ashcroft (Stratford and Princes', 1953), Barbara Jefford (Old Vic, 1978), and Glenda Jackson and Alan Howard (Stratford/Aldwych, 1978–9), directed with extreme clarity by Peter Brook with an uncut text and set austerely in a glazed pavilion. Trevor Nunn's RSC production of 1972 (available on video) had Janet Suzman as a volatile, forceful Cleopatra. Michael Gambon and Helen Mirren gave splendid performances in Adrian Noble's production at The Other Place (1982), which showed that for all its world-encompassing language, the play can work well in a chamber production. Peter Hall returned to the grand scale in his National Theatre production of 1987, with Anthony Hopkins as Antony and Judi Dench as Cleopatra who encompassed every facet of this immensely demanding role, from self-mockery through passionate anger to tragic grandeur. John Caird's version (RSC, 1992), in which Suzman's Antony, Richard Johnson, returned to the role again with Clare Higgins's Cleopatra, was grand-operatic in style to the extent of providing a pre-interval tableau of the lovers with their offspring. Away from the subsidized companies, the multi-racial group Talawa gave the play at the Bloomsbury Theatre in 1991, and Barry Rutter's Northern Broadsides returned to simplicity of setting in a strong production on tour in 1995. In 1999 Mark Rylance was (intentionally) a more than usually comic Cleopatra in an all-male "original practices" production at the Globe. Sinead Cusack outplayed her Antony in Michael Attenborough's RSC production (2002).

Rose Eytinge's revival (Broadway Theatre, 1877) was the richest of the 19th century in New York. Later, there were performances as misguided as Tallulah Bankhead's (1937) — "She barged down the Nile and sank," said John Mason Brown — and as properly balanced as Katharine Cornell's (1947), with the experienced Antony of Godfrey Tearle. Maggie Smith and Keith Baxter led the Stratford, Ontario, cast in 1976.

## IN OTHER TERMS

Charlton Heston's respectful and well-cast film (1972), in which he plays Antony, has Hildegard Neil as a seductive Cleopatra. Jane Lapotaire (Charmian for Heston) plays Cleopatra in the BBC television film with Colin Blakely as Antony. Vanessa Redgrave played Cleopatra on stage and on American television (1985–6).

# CHIEF CHARACTERS

**Mark Antony** Though his vigour remains, he is a great soldier in his autumn; "Beguil'd... to the very heart of loss" (IV.12).

**Cleopatra, Queen of Egypt** "whose every passion fully strives/To make itself... fair and admir'd" (I.1). Few actresses have fully realized the long adagio of her end ("My desolation does begin to make/A better life").

**Octavius Caesar** Standing marmoreally for Rome, he is usually played ice-cold.

**Octavia** Caesar's sister, Antony's wife: "the piece of virtue, which is set/Between us as the cement of our love" (III.2).

**Lepidus** As we see in *Julius Caesar*, the weakest of the triumvirate, or "three world-sharers". He gets rapidly drunk in Pompey's galley (II.7). Soon Caesar deposes and imprisons him (III.5, 6).

**Pompey (Sextus Pompeius)** "Rich in his father's honour, creeps apace/Into the hearts of such as have not thrived/Upon the present state" (I.3). Pompey the Great's younger son, he concludes a treaty with the triumvirs at Misenum, but in III.4 and 5 we hear of Caesar's resumed war against him and of his death.

**Enobarbus** The blunt soldier who from being Antony's dearest friend, deserts his cause and dies of a broken heart. He speaks the renowned description (transmuted from the prose of North's *Plutarch*) of Cleopatra upon the river Cydnus: "The barge she sat in, like a burnish'd throne,/Burned on the water" (II.2).

**Eros** Antony's attendant who commits suicide rather than obey Antony's command to kill him. "Thus do I escape the sorrow/Of Antony's death" (IV.14).

**Charmian** Waiting-woman to Cleopatra, she has the great farewell, "Now boast thee, death" (V.2).

**Iras** Cleopatra's second waiting-woman, she hardly speaks (19 lines to Charmian's 84), but when she does it can be memorable: "Finish, good lady; the bright day is done,/And we are for the dark" (V.2). She dies, as Enobarbus does in an earlier scene, of a broken heart.

**Thyreus** Caesar's messenger to Cleopatra is whipped at the order of Antony, who has seen him kissing the Queen's hand (III.13).

**Euphronius** Antony's schoolmaster, sent as ambassador to Caesar (III.12). A passing figure, he dwells for ever in the four lines beginning "Such as I am, I come from Antony."

**A Soothsayer** In a few revivals there has been an unwisely economical habit of coupling him with Euphronius. They could hardly be less alike.

**A Clown** If the country fellow who brings the asps to Cleopatra (V.2) is played too broadly, he will endanger the transcendent scene that follows. The repetition of "worm" is perilous, even though Cleopatra herself does give the cue, "Hast thou the pretty worm of Nilus there?" The man should be quiet and strange.

---

# Timon of Athens
## 1607–8

 **THE CHARACTERS**
Timon, an Athenian nobleman
Lucius, Lucullus and Sempronius,
   flattering lords
Ventidius, one of Timon's false friends
Alcibiades, an Athenian commander
Phrynia, Timandra, mistresses to
   Alcibiades
Apemantus, a churlish philosopher
Flavius, Timon's steward
Flaminius, Lucilius, Servilius,
   Timon's servants
Caphis, Philotus, Titus, Hortensius,
   servants to Timon's creditors

Poet, Painter, Jeweller, Merchant, Mercer
An old Athenian
Three strangers
A page
A fool
Cupid, Amazons, in the Masque
Lords, Senators, Officers, Soldiers,
   Servants, Thieves and Attendants

 **THE SCENE**
Athens and the neighbouring woods

---

# SYNOPSIS

Timon, a noble Athenian and the most bountiful of men, is the prey of parasites, false friends, whom the professional misanthrope Apemantus despises. Only Flavius, his steward, realizes that — though "to Lacedaemon did [his] land extend" — Timon's money has almost gone.

When (Act II) his creditors ask for payment, he gets nothing but excuses from those he has helped so generously. Belatedly embittered (Act III) he invites all his "friends" to a mock banquet at which he spurns them by throwing lukewarm water in their faces. Cursing Athens (Act IV), he leaves the city for a cave in the woods by the seashore where he dwells as a misanthrope. While digging for roots he discovers gold; some of it he gives to an Athenian commander, Alcibiades, who having been unjustly banished, is now returning to avenge himself on the city. Much of the treasure goes to Flavius who has loyally sought out his master. ("Hate all," says Timon to him, "curse all; show charity to none", IV.3).

Finally (Act V) Timon drives off other former parasites, as well as the Athenian senators. Later, one of the soldiers of Alcibiades finds a tomb by the shore, "upon the very hem o'the'sea", and brings Timon's epitaph ("Here lie I, Timon; who, alive, all living men did hate") to the conquering general. Alcibiades prepares to enter Athens, promising to "use the olive with my sword".

# IN PERFORMANCE

In his apparently ceaseless magnanimity, Timon is the victim of every sycophant. "I am wealthy to my friends," he says, but when he is brought too late to realize that his money has gone ("Tis deepest winter in Lord Timon's purse"), he turns a scorching hatred upon the world that deceived him. The play has a strangely unfinished, unrevised quality. Increasingly, scholars have come to see it as a work written in collaboration with Thomas Middleton. Timon's language in his later misanthropy is sovereign, music borne to us uncannily through the storm, both on the page and — given an actor to speak it — on the stage. This is rare, for the play, hard to animate theatrically, has never been a favourite.

The sources were a brief digression in Plutarch, Painter's *The Palace of Pleasure*, and a dialogue by Lucian, *Timon; or, The Misanthrope*. For 200 years adaptors and revisers were at work. Thomas Shadwell, in his long-approved *The History of Timon of Athens, the Man Hater* (1678) added a "love interest" and two women, Evandra and Melissa. Richard Cumberland, in a more ephemeral version (1771), gave Timon a daughter, Evanthe, whom just before his death he gives to Alcibiades. Shakespeare's text, with a few of Cumberland's additions but no women at all, came to Drury Lane (1816), fortified by the inspiration of Edmund Kean. Samuel Phelps, acting Timon himself, brought back the full Shakespearian tragedy in 1851.

Thereafter, minor revivals aside, little happened until Robert Atkins directed (and played) at the Old Vic in 1922. Wilfrid Walter, pictorially and resoundingly, was Timon for Bridges-Adams at Stratford (1928); Nugent Monck (Westminster, 1935) directed a cut version with Ernest Milton at his most mannered, and incidental music by 21-year-old Benjamin Britten. At Birmingham Repertory (1947), Barry Jackson presented his own modern-dress arrangement of a play that, so he said provocatively, "has a good deal in common with contemporary Birmingham". Tyrone Guthrie (André Morell as Timon) added much exaggerated low comedy (Old Vic, 1952); Ralph Richardson seemed baffled (Old Vic, 1956). There have been exceptional revivals. In Stratford (1965), brilliantly directed by John Schlesinger, Paul Scofield acted and spoke superbly, especially in the curse on Athens — thunder buffeting from crag to crag and ending in the full diapason. Peter Brook urged the play forward with a tingling impulse in the tattered majesty of his Théâtre des Bouffes du Nord in a French adaptation by

J-C Carrière. In 1991 at the Old Vic Trevor Nunn attempted to iron out the play's irregularities with much rewriting that infused the play with contemporary relevance. David Suchet played Timon. Gregory Doran's Stratford version (1999), with Michael Pennington forceful and eloquent as Timon, was more faithful to the original, though the masque became a homoerotic fantasy.

Michael Langham directed the tragedy in modern dress at Stratford, Ontario (1963) and brought it over to the Chichester Festival Theatre in the following year.

## IN OTHER TERMS

The BBC television film directed by Jonathan Miller (1981) has Jonathan Pryce as an acerbic Timon. Stephen Oliver's opera based on the play was presented at the ENO shortly after his death in 1992.

## CHIEF CHARACTERS

**Timon** The betrayed patron turned misanthrope; victim of his own indiscriminate generosity ("Methinks I could deal kingdoms to my friends/And ne'er be weary", I.2). The only fully realized character, he commands the play until he makes "his everlasting mansion/Upon the beachèd verge of the salt flood" (V.1).

**Apemantus** A professional cynic who, in the woods (IV.3), is out-cursed by Timon.

**Lucius** One of the false friends. In Michael Langham's production (Stratford, Ontario, 1963) he denied the request of Timon's messenger for a loan (III.2) while he was receiving a massage and pedicure in a steam-bath. Probably the director was inspired by the messenger's early phrase, "I have sweat to see his honour."

**Alcibiades** The general, outlawed by Athens, who returns to take the city. A part curiously undeveloped.

**Phrynia** and **Timandra** The only women, mistresses of Alcibiades. The note of their single scene (IV.3) is: "Give us some gold, good Timon. Hast thou more?"

**Flavius** The honest, loyally undemanding steward. "All save thee", says Timon (IV.3), "I fell with curses."

**Poet** In "a thing slipp'd idly from me" (I.1) he offers an allegory of the play to come.

# Coriolanus
## 1607–8

 **THE CHARACTERS**

Caius Marcius, afterwards Caius Marcius
   Coriolanus
Titus Lartius and Cominius, Generals
   against the Volscians
Menenius Agrippa, friend to Coriolanus
Sicinius Velutus and Junius Brutus,
   Tribunes of the People
Volumnia, mother to Coriolanus
Virgilia, wife to Coriolanus
Young Marcius, son to Coriolanus
Valeria, friend to Virgilia
Gentlewoman attending on Virgilia
A Roman herald
Nicanor, a Roman

Tullus Aufidius, General of the Volscians
Lieutenant to Aufidius
Conspirators with Aufidius
Adrian, a Volscian
A citizen of Antium
Two Volscian guards
Roman and Volscian Senators,
   Patricians, Aediles, Lictors, Soldiers,
   Citizens, Messengers, Servants to
   Aufidius, and other Attendants

**THE SCENE**

Rome and the neighbourhood, Corioli
   and the neighbourhood, Antium.
   Period: 490 BC

## SYNOPSIS

Caius Marcius, arrogant patrician, loathes the common people, the hungry plebeians of Rome, who return his hate. He shows so much personal bravery in the defeat of the Volscians, led by Tullus Aufidius, that he is given the name of Coriolanus (from the town of Corioli, the Volscian stronghold) and, in Rome, is chosen as candidate for the consulship (Act II). Detesting the obligatory display of humility in public, he carries it out with contempt, though the Tribunes of the People are in venomous opposition.

   Accusing him (Act III) of being a traitor to the Roman people, they urge the plebeians to demand his death. At length he goes into exile ("There is a world elsewhere") and seeks his enemy Aufidius who, at Antium (Act IV), is planning a fresh attack. News of this deeply disturbs the Roman citizens; Coriolanus, advancing as a general of the Volscians, remains obdurate until (Act V) he yields to the pleading of his mother, wife and son, and prepares to make a treaty of peace. Aufidius, who has been bitterly jealous, charges him before the Volscian Senate with betraying the cause, and he is stabbed to death. "Struck with sorrow", Aufidius orders the body to be taken up: "He shall have a noble memory."

# IN PERFORMANCE

The play concerns the clash of a proud, obstinate autocrat, his mother's son, with the Roman plebeians ("mutable, rank-scented") led by malevolent tribunes. It is also a narrative of destructive envy. It does not grow with ease, but once its complex battle scenes outside Corioli are over, it does roll forward in a slow, cold and splendid tide.

*Coriolanus* is founded on North's *Plutarch*. Though there were two early variations (1681 and 1719), its 18th-century record was overshadowed by a mosaic-play formed from Shakespeare and (a new work) Thomson's *Coriolanus*, first with alterations by the actor, Thomas Sheridan (1754), and later by John Philip Kemble (Drury Lane, 1789). Kemble and Sarah Siddons, then at their meridian, appeared very often as Coriolanus and Volumnia. Julian Charles Young described Mrs Siddons at the entry of Coriolanus in triumph: "She towered above all around, and rolled, almost reeled across the stage; her very soul, as it were, dilating and rioting in its exultation." Edmund Kean was a disappointment; Macready (notably Covent Garden, 1838) had the mind and the manner; Phelps (from 1848) established the play in the Sadler's Wells repertory; and Frank Benson and Genevieve Ward appeared together many times (from Comedy Theatre, 1901) as Coriolanus (acted by Benson previously) and Volumnia. Henry Irving and Ellen Terry (Lyceum, 1901) were thoroughly miscast; Coriolanus, Irving said, was "not worth a damn."

Among many later actors were the flamboyant Anew McMaster, in gale force (Stratford, 1933); and Laurence Olivier (Old Vic, 1938), with his ominous growl on the word "*mildly*" (III.2), when entreated to "answer mildly" on going to the Forum to face the tribunes. Olivier's second Coriolanus (Stratford 1959, directed by Peter Hall) was devastating in arrogance and irony and sensational in death as, held by the feet, he dangled upside down from a promontory, to be stabbed in the belly by Anthony Nicholls's eloquent Aufidius. Edith Evans was his formidable mother. The National Theatre (Old Vic, 1971) presented a not particularly stimulating production by Manfred Wekwerth and Joachim Tenschert, described glumly as "a reassessment" of the tragedy "viewed through Brechtian glasses, re-ground by experience."

Ian McKellen and Greg Hicks were directed by Peter Hall at the National Theatre, with a portion of the audience on the Olivier stage, playing the crowd (Olivier, 1984). In 1986, the Kick Theatre Company were at the Almeida directed by Deborah Warner, with Douglas Hodge. At Stratford, directed by Terry Hands (1990), Malcolm Storry's Aufidius and Barbara Jefford's outstanding Volumnia proved more authoritative than Charles Dance's over-mild Coriolanus. Michael Pennington was a fine Coriolanus in Michael Bogdanov's modern-dress, Brechtian production for the English Shakespeare

Company (1991). Tim Supple's Chichester Festival theatre production (1992), with Kenneth Branagh as Coriolanus, was memorable mainly for Judi Dench's fine Volumnia. David Thacker's Swan Theatre production (1994) evoked the French Revolution, with Toby Stephens as an exceptionally young, powerfully arrogant Coriolanus. Homoeroticism was suggested in Barry Lynch's response to Coriolanus's embrace; Philip Voss was a wonderfully subtle Menenius. In 1993, the Nottingham Playhouse hosted Robert Lepage's production from Montreal, entitled *Coriolan.*

The play arrived in the United States (Philadelphia, 1767) where the most renowned Coriolanus would be Edwin Forrest (New York, from 1831), a largely external performance; John Edward McCullough (New York, 1878) used a sustained attack. 20th-century actors include Erford Gage (1938), Robert Ryan (1954) and Robert Burr (1965). Steven Berkoff's cut version, low-budget and with minimal staging, was "jagged, percussive" at the Public Theatre, New York (1988), with Christopher Walken as Coriolanus.

In the spring of 1934, when various French anti-republican groups were seeking revolution, the Comédie Française was persuaded to stage a version freely translated and adapted to the politics of the hour. It led to fierce demonstrations, in the theatre and out, but no revolution.

Deborah Warner directed an open-space production with a cast of 200, led by Bruno Ganz, for the Peter Stein Company (Salzburg, 1993).

## IN OTHER TERMS

Günter Grass's sardonic *The Plebeians Rehearse the Uprising* (1966), about Berthold Brecht rehearsing his adaptation, *Coriolan*, was done at the Aldwych (1970). John Osborne "reworked" Shakespeare in *A Place Called Rome* (published 1973). In the BBC television version directed by Elijah Moshinsky (1984), Alan Howard and Mike Gwilym (like John Neville and Ian McKellen at Nottingham in a Guthrie production of 1963) evoked a homoerotic subtext in the relationship between Coriolanus and Aufidius.

## CHIEF CHARACTERS

**Caius Marcius Coriolanus** The disdainful egoist who speaks for what John Masefield described as "the clash of the aristocratic temper with the world"; who is driven from his city by mob law; who later "does sit in gold, his eye/Red as 'twould burn Rome" (V.1); and who yields in the end, as he has always done, to his mother's plea.

**Cominius** Roman general against the Volscians who, after the attack on Corioli, bestows on Marcius the name of Coriolanus. Speaking before the Senate (II.2), he narrates the life of Coriolanus and how at 16, after the fight against Tarquin, he was "brow-bound with the oak".

**Menenius Agrippa** The old patrician, brave and garrulous, devoted friend of Coriolanus, who tells the story of the Belly and its Members — a parable of Senate and People — to the mutinous crowd in I.1, and whom Coriolanus ("This man was my beloved in Rome") refuses to hear as the Volscian army advances.

**Volumnia** The archetypal Roman matriarch (named by Swinburne "Volumnia Victrix") who sways her son from his purpose when Rome seems lost. The First Citizen says of Coriolanus in the play's opening scene that his exploits had been to please his mother.

**Virgilia** Wife to Coriolanus. "My gracious silence" (II.1).

**Sicinius Velutus** and **Junius Brutus** Tribunes of the People. "The tongues o'th' common mouth," exclaims Coriolanus (III.1); "I do despise them,/For they do prank them in authority,/Against all noble sufferance." The tribunes, usually acted as lamentable demagogues, return his bitterness.

**Tullus Aufidius** The Volscian leader who after swearing revenge on Coriolanus (I.10), welcomes him as an exile to Antium (IV.5), is possessed with envy, and calls at last for his death (V.6).

**Valeria** The Roman lady who flashes into an early domestic interlude (I.3). In the Supplication scene with Volumnia and Virgilia (V.3) Coriolanus salutes her eloquently: "The moon of Rome, chaste as the icicle/That's curdied by the frost from purest snow,/And hangs on Dian's temple."

# Pericles, Prince of Tyre
## 1607–8

 **THE CHARACTERS**

Gower, as Chorus
Antiochus, King of Antioch
The daughter of Antiochus
Pericles, Prince of Tyre
Simonides, King of Pentapolis
Thaisa, daughter to Simonides
Marina, daughter to Pericles and Thaisa
Helicanus, Escanes, Lords of Tyre
Cleon, Governor of Tarsus
Dionyza, wife to Cleon
Lysimachus, Governor of Mytilene
Cerimon, a lord of Ephesus
Thaliard, a lord of Antioch

Lychorida, Marina's nurse
Philemon, servant to Cerimon
Leonine, servant to Dionyza
A pander
Boult, his servant
A bawd
Diana, the goddess of chastity
Marshal, Lords, Ladies, Knights,
   Gentlemen, Sailors, Pirates, Fishermen
   and Messengers

**THE SCENE**

Dispersedly, in various Mediterranean
   countries

# SYNOPSIS

John Gower, the mediaeval poet, acts as Chorus throughout. His *Confessio Amantis* (1385–93), in which he retells the story of Apollonius of Tyre, was one of Shakespeare's main sources.

Pericles solves the riddle propounded by Antiochus, King of Antioch, to his daughter's suitors. The answer, which no one has found (death is the penalty of failure), is that father and daughter have had an incestuous relationship. When Pericles shows that he knows the meaning and Antiochus is suspiciously hospitable, the young Prince realizes that he must escape; back in Tyre he leaves Helicanus to govern in his absence and sets off for Tarsus where he relieves the famine-stricken city.

Still pursued by a minion of Antiochus, he puts again to sea (Act II), only to be wrecked on the shores of Pentapolis; there the King is celebrating with a tournament the birthday of his daughter Thaisa. Pericles wins, and he and Thaisa are betrothed. They expect ultimately to go to Tyre (where Pericles will now be safe), but in a great sea-storm (Act III) Thaisa, after giving birth to a daughter, Marina, is thought to be dead and is thrown overboard in a waterproof chest, with a letter. When it comes to land in Ephesus the noble Cerimon ("'Tis known I ever have studied physic") revives Thaisa who, believing herself to be the only survivor, becomes a priestess of Diana's temple. Pericles, meantime, returns to Tyre, entrusting the infant Marina to the care of Cleon, Governor of Tarsus, and his wife Dionyza.

Some 14 years pass. Pericles is in Tyre; Marina has grown up in Tarsus. Dionyza, jealous of a girl who overshadows her own daughter, is about to have her murdered when pirates kidnap Marina (Act IV) and take her to a brothel in Mytilene. When Dionyza and Cleon tell Pericles his daughter is dead, he vows (says Gower) "Never to wash his face or cut his hairs." In Mytilene Marina, whose purity bewilders her employers and startles the Governor, Lysimachus, manages to leave the brothel and work in an "honest house". Pericles, in utter dejection, chances to visit the city; Lysimachus (Act V) sends for Marina to comfort the stranger, and there, in his anchored ship, Pericles realizes that this is his daughter. In a dream Diana urges him to go to her temple at Ephesus, where presently he relates his tale to the priestess. She is Thaisa; and all griefs are over. Marina and Lysimachus (to whom she is now betrothed) will rule in Tyre, and Pericles and Thaisa spend the rest of their lives in Pentapolis.

# IN PERFORMANCE

"From ashes ancient Gower is come", a phoenix-figure on whose version of an old plot Shakespeare, almost certainly writing in collaboration with George Wilkins, based a picaresque romance. It delighted Jacobeans with its wandering narrative, its music, and its masquing, and was the envy of other dramatists, soured as Ben Jonson was (he called *Pericles* "a mouldy tale") by another man's success. Gower, courier in his rough couplets, leads us on the oldest of pleasures, the telling of a story. *Pericles* is little more than a fantastic and beguiling stage exploit, beginning with a blunt record of events and then, as Shakespeare takes over, adding the bounty of sometimes major verse to "glad" the ear. Directors have talked about neo-Platonic allegories; *Pericles* is not material for such an exercise as that.

In his share Shakespeare is both remembering some of his old ideas and looking forward to later work. His rambling narrative, from which the sound of the sea is never far distant, can hold us from the riddle, the appearance of the unnamed daughter of Antiochus, through shipwreck and wooing, storm and loss, to the final reunion of Pericles and Thaisa in Diana's temple. The Levantine tour drifts us from Antioch to Tyre, Tarsus, Pentapolis, to the gale-swept Mediterranean, to Mytilene and Ephesus. The prince gains a king's daughter. He calls, in grand Shakespearian phrase, upon "the god of this great vast" to "rebuke these surges/Which wash both heaven and hell" (III.1). A princess rises, alive, from a wave-tossed chest. Her daughter's innocence shines through the murk of a brothel. The "goddess argentine" summons Pericles to "do upon mine altar sacrifice", and there before him is a wife miraculously restored.

Applauded (and mocked) in its own day, *Pericles* did not appear in the First Folio, possibly because the received text was known to be corrupt. It is a great moment when Shakespeare's unmistakable voice enters with the third act.

Oddly, *Pericles* was the first Shakespeare play staged at the Restoration, with Thomas Betterton, then 25, as Pericles. In 1738 the play suffered from a feeble adaptation by George Lillo, called *Marina*. Indeed, until a pictorial revival by Samuel Phelps (Sadler's Wells, 1854), it had no real luck. Silence after this until old John Coleman's legendary and preposterous adventure (Stratford, 1900), a *Pericles* eccentrically (in Coleman's own words) expunged, eradicated, eliminated, and omitted, and a good deal of rubbish added. Robert Atkins put back Shakespeare and directed with loving simplicity at the Open Air Theatre, Regent's Park, 1939, where Robert Eddison's romantic, lyrical Prince grew as the play did. Nugent Monck disposed of it all in 90 minutes at Stratford (1947) with the first act cut and Paul Scofield as Pericles, a part he acted once more, in a full production by John Harrison, at the Rudolf Steiner Hall, London (1950). Richard Pasco gave his gentle truth to Pericles at the Birmingham Repertory (1954); a strained Stratford revival (1958) turned Gower to a calypso-singer; and in 1969, also at Stratford, Ian Richardson — who looked at the last as if he had risen from a mosaic in the cathedral of Torcello — played Pericles with shining imagination. Derek Jacobi (Her Majesty's, 1973) was at the centre of a production planted in a male brothel throughout; and a small-scale treatment (Other Place, Stratford, 1979; Donmar Warehouse, London, 1980) had Peter McEnery as the Prince. Cheek by Jowl presented *Pericles* in its second season, for which it won an Olivier Award for Best Newcomer (1985). David Thacker's 1989 Swan Theatre production made intelligent use of the Oxford editors' reconstructed text and had Rudolph Walker as a beguiling Gower. Adrian Noble's highly picturesque production (2000), with Ray Fearon as Pericles, played in the round at London's Roundhouse before moving to Stratford. It had many members of its audience wondering why they had not seen the play before. Stratford, Ontario, 1973–4: Nicholas Pennell as Pericles.

## IN OTHER TERMS

*The Painfull Adventures of Pericles, Prince of Tyre* (1608) is generally supposed to have been based on the play, with one or two additions from the story in Laurence Twine's *The Patterne of Paynfull Adventures* (1576).

# CHIEF CHARACTERS

**Pericles, Prince of Tyre** The wanderer who lives through many hazards, and whose recognition scene with Marina (V.1) is affectingly reminiscent of Lear and Cordelia.

**Antiochus** Evil author of the riddle Pericles solves (I.1).

**Simonides** Thaisa's benevolently playful father.

**Cleon** The Governor of Tarsus whose first scene (I.4) is sincerity in distress. Later he is punished for his wife's crime. Gower's last chorus (V.2) explains how the wrathful citizens burn Cleon and Dionyza in their palace.

**Dionyza** Cleon's wife. Though she becomes a paltry villainess, we may think of her as she is seen first, in the "misery of Tarsus" (I.4) that Pericles relieves.

**Thaisa** (pronounced Ty-eesa). Daughter of Simonides of Pentapolis. Cast into the sea after childbirth, apparently dead, revived by a noble physician, and later Diana's priestess.

**Marina** Daughter of Pericles. One of the enchanting lost girls of Shakespeare's final period. The speed with which she gets from shore to ship at Mytilene, V.1, is reason enough for her to say she has "been gazed on like a comet". Marina should not be doubled with Thaisa, as some directors attempt, for (as with Sebastian and Viola in Twelfth Night)we lose the effect of the key moment of reunion.

**Lysimachus** The Governor of Mytilene rapidly overcome by Marina. But there should be credit to an unnamed lord (V.1) who first suggests that Marina would "win some words" of the silent Pericles.

**Cerimon** A lord of Ephesus with medical knowledge. It would be agreeable to think that Shakespeare intended Thaisa's restorer to be a compliment to his Stratford son-in-law, Dr John Hall.

**A pander, Boult, a bawd** The deplorable and baffled staff of the Mytilene brothel in Act IV.

**Gower, the Chorus** He has been played variously by a handsome actress, as an avuncular ancient, as a black calypso-singer, and as a kind of Welsh bard.

# Cymbeline
## 1609

### ❀ THE CHARACTERS

Cymbeline, King of Britain

The Queen, Cymbeline's second wife

Imogen, Cymbeline's daughter by his
former Queen

Cloten, son to the Queen by a former
husband

Posthumus Leonatus, a gentleman,
Imogen's husband

Helen, a lady attending on Imogen

Belarius, a banished lord, disguised under
the name of Morgan

Guiderius and Arviragus, Cymbeline's
sons, disguised under the names of
Polydore and Cadwal and supposed
sons to Belarius

Philario, Italian friend to
Posthumus

Iachimo, friend to Philario

A French gentleman, friend to Philario

Caius Lucius, General of the Roman
forces

A Roman captain

Two British captains

Pisanio, servant to Posthumus

Cornelius, a physician

Two Lords of Cymbeline's court

Two gentlemen of the court

Two gaolers

Apparitions: Jupiter and the Leonati

Lords, Ladies, Roman Senators,
Tribunes, a Soothsayer, a Dutch
Gentleman, a Spanish Gentleman,
Musicians, Officers, Captains, Soldiers,
Messengers, Attendants

### ❀ THE SCENE

Britain and Italy

## SYNOPSIS

Cymbeline, king of Britain, has an evil second wife who wishes to see her own oafish
son, Cloten, wedded to Cymbeline's daughter, Imogen. But Imogen, against her
father's will, has married Posthumus Leonatus, who is banished; before parting he
gives a bracelet to Imogen. Iachimo, in Rome, boasts to the angry Posthumus that
Imogen is corruptible; later, in Britain, he arranges to be secreted in a trunk in her
bed-chamber, and when she is asleep (Act II) he emerges and steals her bracelet.
Posthumus, persuaded, vows to be revenged on Imogen. Writing to her to meet him
at Milford Haven, he orders his servant, Pisanio, to kill her on the journey.

Rome demands from Britain tribute that the King (Act III) refuses. Pisanio, faithful
to the bewildered Imogen, tells her to disguise herself as a boy and seek the invading
Roman general. Losing herself in Wales, she is sheltered under the name of Fidele by a
long-banished lord, Belarius, who calls himself Morgan, and two youths who are actually
sons of the King (and Imogen's brothers), stolen in infancy and brought up in a mountain
cave. In sickness, Imogen/Fidele takes a sleeping drug that gives the appearance of death.

Cloten, in the clothes of Posthumus, has followed her with evil intent, but one of the youths meets and kills him (Act IV). Returning, the brothers and Belarius find "Fidele" apparently dead; when she wakes, alone, she mistakes Cloten's headless body for her husband's. Profoundly grieved, she joins the Roman general, whose forces are ready to attack Cymbeline.

The courage of Belarius and the princes win the battle for Britain ("This was a strange chance:/A narrow lane, an old man, and two boys", V.3). All come at length before the King, and swiftly, one revelation growing from another, the plot is resolved. There is happiness for all except the dead Queen; Cymbeline magnanimously submits to Rome, and even Iachimo is pardoned, who has fought with the Romans. Imogen and Posthumus are reunited.

# IN PERFORMANCE

"A father cruel and a step-dame false;/A foolish suitor to a wedded lady/That hath her husband banish'd." That is Imogen speaking in I.6. Already the plot of *Cymbeline* is coiling itself: an intricacy that mingles *The Decameron* with Holinshed and the fairy-tale of Snow White, and Renaissance Italy with the classical Rome of Caesar Augustus — a pattern which the rashly dogmatic critic Samuel Johnson described as "unresisting imbecility". The play, flowering again and again into the loveliest of Shakespeare's late verse, has suffered from the convolutions of a narrative that actually, as Sir Arthur Quiller-Couch made clear in a famous essay, is a miracle of technique. Not all of its people rise easily from the text. Neither the much-troubled Cymbeline nor his evil Queen is a personage; Posthumus is usually functional; Cloten is a blown-up Thurio (*Two Gentlemen of Verona*). Still, in the theatre, two parts — Imogen, the princess who is the nonpareil of Shakespeare's women, and Machiavellian Iachimo, the "slight thing of Italy" — are intensely rewarding.

Though the Folio sets it among the tragedies, *Cymbeline* is a romance; it would have suited audiences at the candle-lit Blackfriars Theatre which Shakespeare's company, the King's Men, used from 1608. Simon Forman commenting on a performance at the Globe in 1611 noted the heroine's name as "Innogen", a form restored by the Oxford editors in 1986 and used in some more recent performances. The inevitable supplanting play during the Restoration, *The Injured Princess; or, The Fatal Wager*, was written by Thomas D'Urfey and revived as late as 1738. Covent Garden used Shakespeare's text (1746); and David Garrick's acting (from 1761 at Drury Lane, in a version slightly altered) could transform Posthumus. John Philip Kemble played Posthumus in 1785, and again in 1787, with his elder sister Sarah Siddons as a celebrated Imogen. Helen Faucit was the crown of 19th-century Imogens (between 1837 and 1865) until Ellen Terry's creation (Lyceum, 1896), with Irving indifferently as Iachimo, "a statue of romantic melancholy", said Shaw. Sybil Thorndike, who had been an Old Vic Imogen (1918) came back to her at the New in 1923, a year when Barry Jackson, at the Birmingham Repertory, began the fashion for modern-dress Shakespeare. Other distinguished Imogens since then, all at Stratford: Peggy Ashcroft (1957), Vanessa Redgrave (1962), Susan Fleetwood (1974), and Judi Dench (1979). The best Iachimos have also been at Stratford: Eric Porter (1962), Ian Richardson (1974), Joanne Pearce, and Anton Lesser (2003).

Bill Alexander directed Harriet Walter in a sensitive RSC production at The Other Place (1987) with David Bradley as the evermore-bemused King. Peter Hall's National Theatre production (Cottesloe, later Olivier, 1988), with Geraldine James as (this time) Innogen, was masterly in its handling of the multiple denouements of the final scene. Dominic Cooke directed an intelligent and affecting revival at the Swan in 2003, with Emma Fielding as Imogen. Theatre for a New Audience's western-style production (2002) was the first American production to be put on by the RSC in Stratford, at The Other Place.

## IN OTHER TERMS

Bernard Shaw, who considered the last act to be "a tedious string of unsurprising dénouements sugared with insincere sentimentality after a ludicrous stage battle", rewrote the last act himself (1936) as *Cymbeline Refinished*, a superfluous and flippant exercise that was performed at the Embassy Theatre (1937) at the end of an otherwise Shakespearian text.

## CHIEF CHARACTERS

**Cymbeline**, vacillating King of Britain. One of the lesser title roles. No one in the First Folio is more progressively puzzled than he is during Act V.

**Queen** Cymbeline's wife. The nameless Queen has one speech out of character when she defies Rome (III.1). Elsewhere she is the evil stepmother of a fairy-tale. She expires (V.5) "with horror, madly dying, like her life".

**Imogen** Cymbeline's daughter. The soul of beauty, honour and faith.

**Cloten** The Queen's dire son has one happy moment, his defiance of Caius Lucius (III.1). Otherwise, he is rejected by Imogen, listens to music that he detests, and is decapitated in conflict with Guiderius (IV.2). The key to the pronunciation of his name is the line in IV.2, "I have sent Cloten's clotpoll down the stream."

**Posthumus** Imogen's husband has a long part, but it is generally unrewarding.

**Belarius** (alias Morgan). The grand old man of wild Wales has something of the firm-set oaken quality of Kent (*King Lear*).

**Guiderius** and **Arviragus** (Polydore and Cadwal). The two "princely boys" who speak the dirge, "Fear no more the heat o'th'sun/Nor the furious winter's rages" (IV.2). They speak it because Guiderius (Polydore) cannot sing ("I'll weep, and word it with thee") — a line that brings us close to one of Shakespeare's boy players.

**Iachimo** "Slight thing of Italy" (also "bold Iachimo, Sienna's brother"), a natural conspirer who needs a hypnotic utterance to express such language as "the crickets sing" (II.2).

**Pisanio** Another example of personified loyalty.

**Soothsayer** His name is Philarmonus; and he has his moment (V.5) when he interprets the "tablet" left on the breast of Posthumus after the vision of Jupiter.

**A Gaoler** A few minutes of determined black comedy; but with the celebrated phrase, "O, the charity of a penny cord! It sums up thousands in a trice" (V.4).

---

# The Winter's Tale
## 1611

**❀ THE CHARACTERS**

**In Sicilia:**
Leontes, King of Sicilia
Hermione, Queen to Leontes
Mamillius, his son, the young Prince of
   Sicilia
Perdita, daughter of Leontes and Hermione
Camillo, Antigonus, Cleomenes, Dion,
   lords of Sicilia
Paulina, wife to Antigonus
Emilia, a lady attending on the
   Queen

**In Bohemia:**
Polixenes, King of Bohemia

Florizel, his son, Prince of Bohemia
Archidamus, a lord of Bohemia
Old shepherd, reputed father of Perdita
Clown, his son
Mopsa and Dorcas, shepherdesses
Autolycus, a rogue
A mariner
A gaoler
Time, as Chorus
Other Lords, Gentlemen, Ladies, Officers,
   Servants, Shepherds, Shepherdesses

**❀ THE SCENE**
Sicilia and Bohemia

# SYNOPSIS

Leontes, King of Sicilia, grows so wildly and unreasonably jealous of Polixenes, King of Bohemia, for nine months a visitor at his court, that he believes his wife Hermione has been unfaithful and that her unborn child is not his own. Through Camillo, a Sicilian lord, he seeks to poison his guest, but Camillo warns Polixenes and they depart at once for Bohemia.

Leontes (Act II) orders his wife to be imprisoned and their elder child Mamillius removed from her. In prison she gives birth to a daughter; when Paulina brings the babe to Leontes, hoping to soothe him, he commands her husband Antigonus to abandon the "bastard by Polixenes" in some desert place.

At the trial of Hermione (Act III) a message from the Delphic oracle declares the Queen's innocence; Leontes, refusing to credit it, hears immediately of the death of young Mamillius. Hermione faints and is carried out; presently Paulina tells Leontes that his Queen is dead and he vows life-long mourning. Antigonus, meantime, has left the babe on the Bohemian shore, with the name he gives her (Perdita) and gold in a bundle. Then he vanishes for ever ("Exit, pursued by a bear"). A shepherd and his son find the child.

Sixteen years pass. In Bohemia (Act IV) Florizel, the King's son, is in love with Perdita, brought up as a shepherdess. At a sheep-shearing feast a disguised Polixenes (with Camillo) reveals himself, threatening to disinherit his son and to put Perdita to death if they do not leave each other. Camillo advises them to go to Leontes in Sicilia, but he also tells Polixenes, hoping there may be a reconciliation.

All (including Shepherd and Clown, with their proofs of Perdita's discovery) leave, variously, for Sicilia, where (Act V) Leontes and Polixenes are reconciled; so is Polixenes to Florizel and Perdita. They go to Paulina's chapel to see a remarkable "statue" of Hermione; kissing it, Leontes finds that, after the gulf of years, his wife — long cared for by Paulina — is still alive.

# IN PERFORMANCE

Some titles and names are fated in print, but possibly none more than *The Winter's Tale* which again and again is given the indefinite article — no doubt a recollection of Mamillius when he says "a sad tale's best for winter". The play, which has been called a cycle of life, death and resurrection, is among the later romances of Shakespeare's autumn, and it has to be treated as *Cymbeline* is, with no grumbling about the unlikelihood of the narrative. Largely, Shakespeare based it, with his own enrichment, upon Robert Greene's romance of *Pandosto* (1588), which in 1607 had been reprinted as *Dorastus and Fawnia*. (Yet the changes are radical, and Paulina, Antigonus and Autolycus are Shakespeare's own: so, too, is the bear.)

Briefly, it is a Janus-play of winter and spring, a Sicilia of the passions contrasted with those scenes from a Bohemian world that are direct from rural Warwickshire.

The early verse dialogue is packed and knotted; still, what is difficult in the text can come over in the theatre if it is swiftly spoken. It is the third of Shakespeare's main treatments of jealousy, a sin that obsessed him. In *The Merry Wives of Windsor* Ford is farcical; in *Othello* jealousy is the cause of high tragedy; Leontes, in *The Winter's Tale*, seized by a destroying fever, is spared after a passage of 16 years from the first terrifying attack that takes him to the rim of madness. The plot is in three movements: the King's fury; the flowered idyll of the Bohemian pastoral, lit by the speeches of Perdita and the songs of Autolycus; and finally the grave beauty of peace and reconciliation.

*The Winter's Tale* does not appear to have been staged for over a century before 1741, when there were productions at Goodman's Fields and (with Hannah Pritchard as Paulina) at Covent Garden. Garrick's abridgment, *Florizel and Perdita* (Drury Lane, 1756), was founded on the fourth and fifth acts, all else condensed into a 150-line prologue by Garrick, himself as Leontes: this served until the beginning of the 19th century, when Kemble (Leontes) brought back most of the original to Drury Lane (1802) and Sarah Siddons was Hermione. The century's truest Leontes was Macready, who from 1823 often played a part temperamentally suited to him. Charles Kean's accustomed archaeological pageantry (Princess's, 1856; Bohemia changed to Bithynia) is recalled because Ellen Terry, at nine years old, had her first speaking part, Mamillius.

Mary Anderson captivatingly doubled Hermione and Perdita (Lyceum, 1887); Ellen Terry, at her professional jubilee, was Hermione for Tree (His Majesty's, 1906); and in 1912 (Savoy) Granville-Barker, cutting only six lines, directed his apron-stage revival, with Henry Ainley and Lillah McCarthy. Rehearsing his company almost to weariness, he urged them until his sensitive ear was satisfied, to speak rapidly but to remember the musical structure of the verse: all must be quick, continuous, intimate, vital. That would remain the definitive production until Peter Brook's at the Phoenix (1951) uncompromising in its restraint except for the blizzard through which Time emerged as Chorus. Gielgud's voice in the remorse of "Stars, stars, and all eyes else dead coals!" (V.1) rings from half a century's acted Shakespeare. Judi Dench's doubling of Hermione and Perdita (Stratford, 1969) was the most distinguished personal feat in any revival of the play since the war. Peter Hall's distinguished production at the National as part of his "Late Shakespeare" series (1988, Cottesloe, then Olivier) stressed the provisionality of the happy ending: Leontes (Tim Pigott-Smith) and Hermione (Sally Dexter) had still a long way to go. Théâtre de Complicité's brilliant and innovative production (Lyric, Hammersmith, etc., 1992) had Simon McBurney as an exciting (and excitable) Leontes, Marcello Magni as an Autolycus who was apt to improvise in both Italian and English, and Kathryn Hunter in a virtuoso quadrupling as Mamillius, Paulina, Time, and the Old Shepherd. Terry Hands's bear-dominated version (RSC, 1986) had Jeremy Irons as a Leontes who ended the play, stricken, in a wheelchair. Paulina (like Emilia in *Othello*) rarely fails to touch the audience's hearts; Gemma Jones made the most of her in Adrian Noble's 1992 pretty — lots of balloons — if unsearching RSC production in which Richard McCabe played Autolycus in the best traditions of the English music hall. Probably the most powerful Leontes since Gielgud was the pathologically jealous Antony Sher in Gregory Doran's fine RSC production (1999), with Alexandra Galbreath as Hermione; Mamillius was doubled with Perdita.

Henry Daniell (Leontes), Eva Le Gallienne (Hermione), and Florence Reed (Paulina) had a popular triumph in a Theatre Guild revival in New York (1945–6). Christopher Plummer was Leontes at Stratford, Ontario (1958).

## IN OTHER TERMS

The BBC television film directed by Jane Howell, was strongly cast, with Jeremy Kemp (Leontes), Anna Calder-Marshall (Hermione), Robert Stephens (Polixenes), and Margaret Tyzack (Paulina).

## CHIEF CHARACTERS

**Leontes, King of Sicilia** Morbidly irrational, he brings disaster upon himself. But it is his memory of Hermione (V.1) and his reunion (V.3) that stay with us when the play is done.
**Mamillius** The young prince who tells his own winter's tale ("There was a man… dwelt by a churchyard", II.1). Ellen Terry's tripped over her go-cart at her début (Princess's, 1856).
**Camillo** Important in the movement of the plot (I.4, IV.4).
**Antigonus** Paulina's husband, who brings the infant Perdita to the Bohemian coast ("Blossom, speed thee well"), and who is killed by a bear as the Clown describes in III.3.
**Polixenes, King of Bohemia** Wronged guest and stern parent.
**Florizel** An impetuous prince for a fairy-tale. "When you do dance," he says to Perdita (IV.4), "I wish you/A wave o'th'sea, that you might ever do/Nothing but that."
**Shepherd** and **Clown** They are from the inner sheepfolds of Warwickshire Arden and

should be so performed. Paul Scofield's Clown (Stratford, 1948) was the subject of a painting by Laura Knight.

**Autolycus** The "snapper-up of unconsidered trifles" (IV.3) is a vagrant rich in ballads, songs and snatches; a rogue, sharp of mind and eye, who in his time has served the prince. Some comedians, given an inch, will turn the part into "a gallimaufry of gambols".

**Time** As Chorus, carries us forward 16 years.

**Third Gentleman** Paulina's steward in an hour of fleeting splendour (V.2); he reports events that Shakespeare failed to show in action.

**Hermione** The Emperor of Russia's daughter. A heroine of patient nobility. After her eloquence at the trial and her collapse on hearing of the prince's death, she speaks no word until her "statue" takes life at the end of the play: "You gods, look down."

**Perdita** Shakespeare's Bohemian girl. Princess in a shepherd's cottage, she strews the verse with flowers ("Daffodils that come before the swallow dares", IV.4).

**Paulina** Wife of Antigonus. Candid and courageous, the heart of common sense. "I pray you, do not push me. I'll be gone" (II.3).

---

# The Tempest
## 1611

 **THE CHARACTERS**
Alonso, King of Naples
Sebastian, his brother
Prospero, rightful Duke of Milan
Miranda, Prospero's daughter
Antonio, his brother, usurping Duke of
   Milan
Ferdinand, son of the King of Naples
Gonzalo, an honest old counsellor
Adrian, Francisco, lords
Caliban, a savage and deformed slave
Ariel, an airy spirit

Iris, Ceres, Juno, Nymphs, Reapers, spirits
Trinculo, a jester
Stephano, a drunken butler
Master of a ship
Boatswain
Mariners
Other Spirits attending on Prospero

 **THE SCENE**
A ship at sea; afterwards an uninhabited
   island

---

## SYNOPSIS

Twelve years before the play begins, Antonio, helped by the King of Naples, Alonso, usurped his brother Prospero's dukedom of Milan and put Prospero and his child Miranda to sea in a rotten boat. They reached a far-off island where Prospero resorted to the books on magic that a loyal lord, Gonzalo, had sent with him. He freed Ariel, an "airy spirit" whom the dead witch, Sycorax, had imprisoned in a cloven pine, and he attempted to educate the witch's son, the deformed Caliban. When Caliban sought to rape Miranda, Prospero made him into a slave.

Prospero tells the story to his daughter just after the raising of a magical storm that has cast upon the island Alonso and Antonio with Alonso's son Ferdinand, his brother Sebastian, and attendant lords. Ariel leads Ferdinand to Prospero's cell; there the youth falls in love with Miranda, and Prospero sets him to the hardest of menial tasks. The King (Act II) believes that Ferdinand is drowned; Antonio and Sebastian plan to murder Alonso, but thanks to the invisible Ariel, the deed is prevented. Stephano and Trinculo, Alonso's butler and jester, are involved drunkenly with Caliban.

Aided by Ariel (Act III) Prospero uses his magic art to baffle the royal party. Agreeing to the betrothal of Miranda and Ferdinand, he summons a masque for them (Act IV). Later (Act V) he decides to abandon his revenge, to forgive his enemies, and break his magic staff. Then he reveals himself, demands back his dukedom, shows Ferdinand at chess with Miranda, sets Ariel free, and speaks a wistful epilogue before sailing home.

Shakespeare has obeyed the "unities" here: the action of *The Tempest* is on a single day and in the same place.

# IN PERFORMANCE

"The isle is full of noises,/Sounds, and sweet airs, that give delight and hurt not." That, unexpectedly, is Caliban (III.2) during an adventure of the spirit that was Shakespeare's last unaided play. The isle, like Alonso's daughter and offstage Queen, Claribel of Tunis, is ten leagues beyond man's life, a meeting-ground of elemental forces. It was once fashionable to suggest that Prospero could be Shakespeare, and that the breaking of his staff and the burial of his magic book symbolized a farewell to the theatre. But there are opinions for all tastes: one, rather dreary, is that the piece is a study in colonialism (an idea treated without luck in a London revival). It is simpler to regard *The Tempest* as a haunted poem inspired vaguely by many sources — folk-tales, romantic comedies, and some of the pamphlets about the wreck in Bermuda ("the still-vexed Bermoothes" of the text) of a ship from an English fleet that had sailed for Virginia in 1609.

The play is Prospero's. Though its other people — except for Ariel and Caliban, who stand for the spirit and the flesh — are relatively conventional, it can be strong magic both in the text and the better stage performances. True, not many revivals have been more than intermittently right, and some writers hold that theatrically the poem is inaccessible.

During the Restoration, Davenant and Dryden (1677) devised an unfortunate perversion, *The Tempest; or, the Enchanted Island*, that contained, among its characters, "Hippolito, one that never saw Woman, right Heir of the Dukedom of Mantua; Miranda and Dorinda, daughters to Prospero, that never saw Man; Caliban and Sycorax, his sister, two Monsters of the Isle; Milcha, a female spirit". It was all extremely silly, but much loved for nearly a century, a period during which there were adaptations of the adaptation, one (with Purcell's music) by Thomas Shadwell. For a long period from 1757 Garrick regularly returned Shakespeare's text to Drury Lane, yet the Davenant-Dryden muddle, readjusted, continued to keep its hold, under Kemble, for some time after 1789.

Macready, as we would expect, reverted to Shakespeare (Covent Garden, 1838), playing Prospero himself, with Priscilla Horton as Ariel. Afterwards, Phelps and Charles Kean treated the poem in their familiar ways: the first, solid and straightforward; the second burying the verse in spectacular effects and "scenic appliances" (the masque was like an uninhibited harvest festival). Tree (His Majesty's, 1904) was as scenically unrestrained as Kean, playing Caliban himself in a production, with actor-managerial transpositions, that A.B. Walkley of *The Times* called *The Girl from Prospero's Island*. Between the wars (1919–39) *The Tempest* survived most reasonably in a Robert Atkins production (Old Vic, 1924), with Ion Swinley as Prospero; under Bridges-Adams (Stratford, 1934, with its great galleon in distress); and again under Atkins (Open Air, 1936 and 1937), Swinley once more in Prospero's "beating mind". Elsa Lanchester's silver Ariel, all spirit, was the one relief of Tyrone Guthrie's sparse Vic/Wells revival (1934).

Gielgud acted Prospero three times (Old Vic, 1940; Stratford and Drury Lane, 1957; Old Vic, for National company, 1974); on the third occasion he was an El Greco figure. Michael Redgrave (Stratford, 1951) resembled one of Blake's prophets, and in the Ariel of Alan Badel it was as if a Donatello figure, given quivering life, moved through the island air. Later interpretations of Prospero tended to depart from the traditional image of a benign, all-forgiving sage. John Barton's RSC production (1970) had Ian Richardson as a stern but youthful Prospero. Derek Jacobi, dignified and beautifully spoken at Stratford in 1983, returned to the role in a Sheffield production directed by Michael Grandage also seen at the Old Vic in 2003. In 1988 at the RSC Nicholas Hytner directed John Wood as a mellifluously paternal Prospero; at the National in the same year Michael Bryant, in Peter Hall's production, offered a bitterer interpretation. Sam Mendes' highly metatheatrical RSC production of 1993 had Simon Russell Beale as an Ariel who (in some performances) spat at Alec McCowen's Prospero in his farewell. Adrian Noble's RSC production of 1998, with David Calder as Prospero, offered a lofty, philosophical, even religious interpretation. Malcolm Storry was authoritative in Michael Boyd's RSC production, seen first at the Roundhouse before transferring to Stratford, of 2002.

New York: 1916, 1945 (directed by Margaret Webster, with Arnold Moss as Prospero), 1974 (Prospero, Sam Waterston). Stratford, Ontario: 1962. Julie Taymor's production for the Theatre for a New Audience, New York, was memorable.

## IN OTHER TERMS

Derek Jarman's film (1980) entertainingly deploys a gay sensibility, reaching a climax with Elisabeth Welch's singing of "Stormy Weather". In Peter Greenaway's far more cerebral *Prospero's Books* (1991), visually stunning, John Gielgud, well into his eighties, appears naked in the opening sequence and speaks not only Prospero's lines but most of the rest of the play too. In Giorgio Strehler's long-running Italian production (1978–), inspired by Jan Kott, Prospero's magic was equated with the magic of theatre.

*The Tempest* has been a great stimulus to other artists. Fine early settings of "Full Fathom Five" and "Where the bee sucks" by the lutenist Robert Johnson (c.1582–1633) may have been written for the first performances. Later composers who have set the songs include Thomas Arne and Michael Tippett. Operatic versions include *Der Sturm* (1956) by the Swiss composer Frank Martin and Thomas Adès's profoundly original *The Tempest* (Covent Garden, 2003), handicapped by a feeble paraphrase of Shakespeare's text as a libretto; the role of Ariel requires a coloratura soprano with the range of a bat. Hector Berlioz's orchestral fantasy was incorporated in *Lélio, or The Return to Life* (1832). Arthur Sullivan's incidental music (1862) for the play was his first great success. Literary offshoots include W.H. Auden's sequence of poems *The Sea and the Mirror* (1942–44) and Marina Warner's novel *Indigo* (1992).

## CHIEF CHARACTERS

**Alonso, King of Naples** Except for one outburst of grief for Ferdinand, this is a grey, subdued part.

**Sebastian** His brother; a serviceable minor villain.

**Prospero** Controls the play as he controls the island. A man of powerful eloquence, he is tedious in the theatre only when his actor is: the opening exposition, as much for the audience as for Miranda, can be troublesome. But the great speeches are unfailing when well uttered. Prospero is a potent magician, not a tired schoolmaster.

**Miranda** A girl, about 15, is a rare portrait of innocence. "O brave new world/That has such people in 't" (V.1).

**Antonio** Prospero's usurper and Sebastian's fellow-cynic.

**Ferdinand** "I might call him/A thing divine," says Miranda (I.2), "for nothing natural/I ever saw so noble."

**Gonzalo** The good old lord who imagines an earthly paradise (II.1) is among Shakespeare's wise veterans. "O rejoice/Beyond a common joy, and set it down/With gold on lasting pillars" (V.1).

**Caliban** "Hag-born — not honour'd with a human shape". Yet this son of Sycorax has a sudden touching awareness at "the isle is full of noises" (III.2).

**Ariel** "On the bat's back I do fly/After summer merrily" (V.1). The "airy spirit" has been imagined in many ways. Some Prosperos do not look at their Ariel but use the reading, "I *think* thee [instead of "thank"], Ariel; come" (IV.1).

**Iris, Ceres, Juno** Their betrothal masque (IV.1) is tranquil and underrated; directors are given to incomprehensible experiments with it.

**Trinculo** Part of the obligatory fooling.

**Stephano** The drunken butler.

**Francisco** Describes Ferdinand in the water after the wreck, "Sir, he may live" (II.1); otherwise insignificant.

# Henry VIII
## 1612–13

**❁ THE CHARACTERS**
King Henry VIII
Queen Katharine, King Henry's wife, afterwards divorced
Anne Bullen, her Maid of Honour, later Queen
Cardinal Wolsey
Cardinal Campeius
Capucius, Ambassador from Emperor Charles V
Cranmer, Archbishop of Canterbury
Duke of Norfolk
Duke of Buckingham
Duke of Suffolk
Earl of Surrey
Lord Chamberlain
Lord Chancellor
Gardiner, Bishop of Winchester
Bishop of Lincoln
Lord Abergavenny
Lord Sands
Sir Henry Guildford
Sir Thomas Lovell
Sir Anthony Denny
Sir Nicholas Vaux
Cromwell, in Wolsey's service

Griffith, gentleman-usher to Queen Katharine
Patience, Queen Katharine's woman
An old lady, friend to Anne Bullen
Three gentlemen
Dr Butts, physician to the King
Garter King-at-Arms
Surveyor to the Duke of Buckingham
Brandon, and a Sergeant-at-arms
Doorkeeper of the Council Chamber
Porter, and his Man
Page to Gardiner
A Crier
Lord Mayor, Aldermen, Lords and Ladies in the Dumb Shows; Woman attending upon the Queen; Secretaries to Wolsey; Scribes, Officers, Guards, and other Attendants; Spirits

**❁ THE SCENE**
London, Westminster, Kimbolton. Henry VIII ruled from 1509 to 1547. In 1509 he married, as the first of six wives, his elder brother's widow, Katharine of Aragon

## SYNOPSIS

Henry VIII dances with Anne Bullen at Cardinal Wolsey's London mansion, York Place. The Duke of Buckingham (Act II) is condemned to execution on a charge of high treason raised by Wolsey. At the inquiry into Henry's marriage, Queen Katharine (also worked against by Wolsey) leaves the court at Blackfriars to "appeal unto the Pope". Wolsey's efforts to stop the King from marrying Anne are discovered, and more evidence of intrigue that will lead to his dismissal.

Secretly, the King marries Anne who (Act IV) is crowned Queen. Katharine (who has heard of the death of her enemy, Wolsey) dies at Kimbolton. Gardiner, malicious Bishop of Winchester, tries to bring down Cranmer, the new Archbishop of Canterbury (Act V), but the King intervenes. Cranmer, as godfather of Anne's child, Princess Elizabeth, prophesies at her christening that she will be "A pattern to all princes…"

# IN PERFORMANCE

A collaboration between Shakespeare and John Fletcher, *Henry VIII* is a loose chronicle rather than a play tautly contrived. It was originally acted as *All is True*; the title *Henry VIII* derives from the 1623 Folio.

Primarily a play of farewells — to the world, to life, to greatness — it has an October sense, a pervading melancholy that is set off by its ceremonial which, if instructions are obeyed, has more pomp than anything else in Shakespeare (no wonder that Charles Kean rose to it). Often used as a pageant for a celebration, it has also been a play of disaster. Fire, caused by the discharge of "chambers" (stage cannon), at Henry's entry to Wolsey's masque, destroyed the first Globe Theatre on Bankside, Southwark, during a performance on 29 June, 1613.

Shakespeare and/or Fletcher drew on the chronicles of Edward Halle and Raphael Holinshed. At the Restoration and after, Thomas Betterton enjoyed playing the King and did so until 1709, the year before he died. The 18th century had such actresses as Hannah Pritchard and the imperative Sarah Siddons ("Lord Cardinal, to you I speak") as Katharine. Mrs Siddons, appearing with her brother John Philip Kemble (Wolsey), was in fullest grandeur many times between 1788 and 1816. By the 19th century Wolsey had become the principal male part, acted by Macready, Charles Kean (who had a moving barge and a historical panorama of London in a Princess's scenic orgy), and Henry Irving, whose Lyceum production (January 1892, with Ellen Terry as Katharine) was even more extravagant than Kean's. Tree's revival (His Majesty's, 1910–12), dialogue cut for the pageant's sake, ended with Anne's coronation; Tree himself was a hard, brooding Wolsey (and in New York, 1916). Sybil Thorndike was a magnificent Katharine (Empire, 1925; few people noticed a youth, Laurence Olivier, as First Serving Man).

In Tyrone Guthrie's production (Sadler's Wells, 1933) Henry became for a while the main character because Charles Laughton, in a popular film, had recently acted him as a gross sensualist. On the stage Laughton's husky sibilance could not recreate his former vitality, and the night belonged to Flora Robson as Katharine. Guthrie's production at Stratford (1949), in spite of an overplus of "business", did quicken the sprawling pageant; Michael Benthall (Old Vic, 1953 and 1958) balanced the processional play and personal drama. Trevor Nunn's (Stratford/Aldwych, 1969–70) was mildly Brechtian, with Donald Sinden's Holbein Henry in strong, relishing charge. Richard Griffiths was Henry for the RSC (Stratford, 1983–4). Gregory Doran's golden RSC production (1997) which achieved great spectacle even in the relatively small space of the Swan auditorium, foregrounded the original title, *All is True*, and had Jane Lapotaire as an immensely dignified Queen.

New York: 1946, directed by Margaret Webster, with Eva Le Gallienne (Katharine) and Walter Hampden (Wolsey).

## IN OTHER TERMS

The BBC television production (1970), filmed largely on location at Leeds Castle, Kent, in rooms once occupied by Henry, has Claire Bloom as Queen Katharine and Timothy West as Wolsey.

## CHIEF CHARACTERS

**Henry VIII** Shakespeare manages to be as tactful as possible; and several actors have filled out the part.

**Queen Katharine** A woman of unremitting courage and regality, both at the trial and in her fading. "Though unqueened, yet like/A queen, and daughter to a king, inter me." The angelic vision she sees in IV.2 can worry directors.

**Anne Bullen** "I would not be a queen" (II.3). "No, we'll no Bullens," says Wolsey (III.2). But she will be crowned in pomp (IV.1).

**Cardinal Wolsey** The "scarlet sin". Beginning sourly, exorbitant in arrogance, he falls (III.2) "like a bright exhalation in the evening." His farewell elegy, with its drooping cadences, may be Fletcherian.

**Cranmer** Archbishop of Canterbury. At the centre of Act V, where Henry saves him from the malice of Gardiner, and he speaks the christening eulogy on the child who one day will be Queen Elizabeth I (V.1).

**Duke of Buckingham** First vigorous, then submissive. His farewell, "All good people" (II.1), before "this long divorce of steel", has long been a showpiece.

**Cromwell** In Wolsey's service; afterwards the King's. A loyally sympathetic listener in III.2.

**Griffith** Katharine's gentleman-usher at Kimbolton. "Such an honest chronicler as Griffith" (IV.2).

**An old lady** Her brief scene with Anne (II.3) is a small, shrewd and racy masterpiece.

# The Two Noble Kinsmen
## 1613–14

 **THE CHARACTERS**

Theseus, Duke of Athens
Hippolyta, Queen of the Amazons and
   then wife of Theseus
Emilia, her sister
Pirithous, Theseus' friend
Palamon and Arcite, cousins from Thebes;
   the two noble kinsmen
Artesius, an Athenian soldier
Valerius, a Theban
A herald
A boy
A gentleman
Six knights assisting Palamon and
   Arcite
Gaoler
The gaoler's daughter
Wooer of gaoler's daughter

Two friends of gaoler
Gaoler's brother
A doctor
Three queens, widows of Kings killed in
   the siege of Thebes
Six countrymen, one dressed as a baboon
Nell and four other country wenches
A schoolmaster
A taborer
Hymen, god of marriage
A woman, Emilia's servant
Nymphs, Attendants, Countrymen,
   Garland-bearer, Hunters, Maids,
   Executioner, Guard of soldiers

 **THE SCENE**
Athens, Thebes, country near Athens

# SYNOPSIS

Three mourning queens urge Theseus, Duke of Athens — at the celebration of marriage to Hippolyta — to attack Creon, King of Thebes, who slew their husbands; Theseus agrees. Palamon and Arcite, Creon's nephews, two noble kinsmen, fight for Thebes, but Theseus captures and imprisons them. From the window of their prison (Act II) they see Emilia, sister of Hippolyta, and both fall in love with her. Arcite, released but banished from Athens, goes disguised into Emilia's service. The gaoler's daughter, passionately infatuated with Palamon, enables him to escape and later goes mad for his loss (Act III). The two kinsmen meet and fight with each other; sparing them on the intercession of Emilia (who cannot say whom she loves) and Hippolyta, Theseus orders them to return in a month and fight again; the winner will have Emilia, the loser will be executed. To restore the sanity of the gaoler's daughter (Act IV), a wooer is advised to impersonate Palamon.

The month passes. Arcite (Act V) prays to Mars and Palamon to Venus for success, and Emilia prays at Diana's altar. Arcite wins the combat but later, falling from his horse, is mortally wounded. With his last breath he gives Emilia, and with her all the world's joy, to Palamon (who is saved from execution). The gaoler's daughter has recovered and is about to marry.

## IN PERFORMANCE

There is now general agreement that this romance, deriving from Chaucer's *Knight's Tale*, was a Shakespeare-Fletcher partnership. Shakespeare — though the play did not get into the Folio of 1623 — is usually allowed the whole of Act I, the first scene of Act III, and the whole of Act V, except the second scene. The subplot of the gaoler's daughter is assigned to Fletcher, but how much each dramatist edited the other none can speculate. Jacobean theatre taste is mirrored in the incidental pageantry.

The piece is seldom performed; the few revivals have strengthened belief in its theatrical power, if not in the consistent quality of its verse.

Davenant adapted the play as *The Rivals* (1664), removing the gaoler's daughter. No more was heard until 1928, when Andrew Leigh put on the true text at the Old Vic, with Ernest Milton and Eric Portman as Palamon and Arcite, and Jean Forbes-Robertson as the gaoler's daughter. Richard Digby Day adapted the text for an imaginatively simple Open Air Theatre revival in Regent's Park (1974). Barry Kyle directed the play to open the Swan Theatre in Stratford (1976). Gerard Murphy and Hugh Quarshie played the kinsmen, and Imogen Stubbs stole the show as the Gaoler's Daughter.

## CHIEF CHARACTERS

**Theseus** Duke of Athens, "all-noble Theseus" (I.3).

**Hippolyta** "Most dreaded Amazonian.../That equally canst poise sternness with pity...(I.1).

**Emilia** Cannot make up her mind between Palamon and Arcite. She does not catch our imagination, though Arcite's May-morning speech (III.1) is an enchantment. "What a mere child is fancy", she says in IV.2, "that having two fair gauds of equal sweetness,/Cannot distinguish, but must cry for both!"

**Palamon** "Melancholy becomes him nobly" (V.3).

**Arcite** (pronounced "Ar-sight") "Mercy and manly courage are bedfellows in his visage" (V.3). In V.1 he has the glorious invocations to Mars.

**The Gaoler's Daughter** In her love for Palamon, a nymphomaniac.

**The Three Queens** Their first-act appeal to Theseus is profoundly dignified and touching. Later, the Third Queen speaks the couplet (I.5) transmuted from Chaucer: "This world's a city full of straying streets,/And death's the market-place, where each one meets."

# THE POEMS AND SONNETS

In 1592, as we have seen, Shakespeare was obliged to abandon the stage for poetry. The immediate fruits of this change of tack were two narrative poems, *Venus and Adonis* and *The Rape of Lucrece*, and possibly also the earliest Sonnets. The Sonnets have not been to everyone's taste — Lord Byron dismissed them as "the most puling, petrifying, stupidly platonic compositions", and the 18th century, which favoured clarity over complexity in poetry, found them too obscure. But more recently they have won high praise.

The narrative poems, by contrast, remain relatively unpopular. Their genre, especially that of *Venus and Adonis* is difficult for the modern reader to come to terms with. If one expects power and sincerity of feeling, one is likely to be disappointed, except perhaps in Tarquin's guilty wrestling with his conscience in *The Rape*.

*Venus and Adonis* deals with mythical figures. Venus is the goddess of love; Adonis a beautiful youth out hunting with whom she falls in love. He declines her advances, returns to the chase, and is killed by a wild boar. He is transformed into a flower. The story occurs in Ovid's *Metamorphoses*, where it occupies about 75 lines. Shakespeare's version takes nearly 1200. One way to approach it is to think of it as an exercise in verbal and imaginative ingenuity. More than most, such a poem is implicitly about the power of the imagination, and its success is less a matter of being true to an experience or emotion, as it is of the poet coaxing as much as possible out of his subject with techniques of elaboration and amplification. The reader is being invited all the time to notice what the poet is doing.

Besides making it longer, Shakespeare also changes the story so that Adonis becomes the unwilling object of Venus's attentions. The usual roles are reversed: the woman woos, and Adonis the hunter becomes the hunted. Adonis meets his end through another such reversal, when the boar he is hunting turns and kills him. The poem thrives on such ironic parallels and inversions. Venus, mourning Adonis's death, goes so far as to say that she would have killed Adonis, like the boar, given the chance:

Had I been tooth'd like him, I must confess,

With kissing I should have kill'd him first.

 (ll.1117–8)

This forms part of a pattern of imagery; Venus is elsewhere associated with birds of prey — eagle, vulture, falcon. Adonis figures as the tame victim: a dabchick or a deer. In one way this is natural imagery, but it is used in a way that contributes to the poem's air of conscious artifice, in which the sexual comedy is played out, as for example, when

Venus offers herself to Adonis as a park for him to play in:

Within this limit is relief enough,
Sweet bottom grass and high delightful plain,
Round rising hillocks, brakes obscure and rough,
To shelter thee from tempest and from rain:
Then be my deer, since I am such a park,
No dog shall rouse thee, though a thousand bark.
(ll.235–40)

Such witty eroticism contributed greatly to the poem's popularity in its day.

*Venus and Adonis* is an unusual kind of high comedy; *The Rape of Lucrece* is a tragedy. *Venus*'s subject is mythical; that of *Lucrece* would have been considered historical. The main characters are the virtuous Lucrece, and Tarquin, king of Rome, who lusts after her. The poem presents her rape, her grief and suicide. But the story is told less by the dramatist's natural means of action and interaction, than by means of symbols and setpiece monologue. Tarquin en route to Lucrece engages in a protracted debate "'Tween frozen conscience and hot burning will" (l.247), which is often seen as anticipating Macbeth's debate with himself before he kills Duncan. Lucrece, after the rape, identifies and reflects upon three things that have aided the crime: Time, Night and Opportunity. Such abstraction enlarges the scope of the poem, but, the reader may feel, at the cost of almost detaching it from the character of Lucrece.

The only other piece worth mentioning before turning to the Sonnets is an enigmatic poem, 'The Phoenix and Turtle'. It is a mysteriously emblematic piece about the perfect union of the two symbolic birds of the title, which is presented in mystic, Platonic terms:

So they loved, as love in twain
Had the essence but in one:
Two distincts, division none;
Number there in love was slain.
(l l.25–8)

It is a union which in a mysterious way is both lost and completed by their death.

# THE SONNETS

In 1609 Thomas Thorpe published Shakespeare's Sonnets in an edition which was probably not authorized. However, as early as 1598, Francis Meres had sung Shakespeare's praises, specifically mentioning several works, including "his sugared Sonnets among his private friends". In the following year a pirate volume of poems called *The Passionate Pilgrim* appeared under Shakespeare's name, including three extracts from *Love's Labour's Lost*, versions of Sonnets 138 and 144, and other work that was clearly not his. There are two conclusions to be drawn from this. Firstly, that Shakespeare's Sonnets were probably intended for manuscript circulation, which was common at the time. Secondly, since *The Passionate Pilgrim* included only a couple of stray sonnets, that they probably did not exist as a whole sequence — at any rate not at first.

Thorpe published a collection of 155 poems. The last of them, 'A Lover's Complaint', is not a sonnet, but a poem of 44 stanzas, whose subject is exactly as its title indicates. Whether it should be seen in relation to the preceding sonnets is, like so much else about this collection, a matter for debate.

The other 154 poems are sonnets. A sonnet is usually a rhyming 14-line poem, although in Shakespeare's collection Sonnet 99 has 15, and Sonnet 126 12 lines. Together they are said to make up a sequence.

In the 1590s sonnet sequences enjoyed a short-lived vogue. Sir Philip Sidney had set the trend with his posthumously published *Astrophil and Stella* (1591). Where he led, others followed. Such sequences normally consisted of pleas addressed to some hard-hearted, but idealized, woman: Samuel Daniel poured out his sonnets to Delia, Thomas Lodge to Phillis, Henry Constable to Diana, and so on. By the time Shakespeare's Sonnets appeared in 1609 the fashion had waned, though it is possible that Thorpe was trying to cash in on an Elizabethan revival.

The Shakespearean sonnet rhymes thus: ABABCDCDEFEFGG. This effectively divides the sonnet up into sections, according to where the rhymes change: three quatrains and a closing couplet. The poet can exploit these to articulate his meaning. A common pattern in the Shakespearean sonnet involves a shift in gear, so to speak, between the first eight lines and the last six, and a 'turn' before the closing couplet, which often has an air of solving a problem posed in the rest of the poem, or of summing it up. For example:

When I do count the clock that tells the time,
And see the brave day sunk in hideous night;
When I behold the violet past prime,
And sable curls all gilded o'er with white;
When lofty trees I see barren of leaves,
Which erst from heat did canopy the herd,
And summer's green, all girded up in sheaves,
Borne on the bier with white and bristly beard;

Then of thy beauty do I question make,
That thou among the wastes of time must go,
Since sweets and beauties do themselves forsake,
And die as fast as they see others grow.
And nothing 'gainst Time's scythe can make defence
Save breed to brave him when he takes thee hence.     (Sonnet 12)

In the first two quatrains the poet notes things which remind him of decay and the passage of time. Then his attention shifts to the person he is addressing ("Then of thy beauty…"). Finally, having posed the problem of mortality and decay, the closing couplet offers the solution: have children.

Shakespeare varies his use of internal structure, but it does tend to create a sense of movement within each poem, while the brief 14-line form encourages density and economy of expression. An individual sonnet is therefore tightly organized. Its appeal, as a contemporary poet put it, lay in its compactness, since it was "most delightful to see much excellently ordered in a small room" (Samuel Daniel, *A Defence of Rhyme*). But while individual sonnets are tightly structured, the "sequence", especially as Shakespeare uses it, seems at first glance to be at odds with such economy. Where the individual sonnet is strictly limited, the sequence seems capable of indefinite expansion, piling on sonnet after sonnet, and, as Shakespeare was ironically aware, often appearing to say the same thing over and over, or as he put it, "I must each day say o'er the very same" (Sonnet 108).

Shakespeare's sequence is not conventional. The author of these lines was not playing the usual game:

My mistress' eyes are nothing like the sun;
Coral is far more red than her lips' red;
If snow be white, why then her breasts are dun;
If hairs be wires, black wires grow on her head.     (Sonnet 130)

The normal, idealized mistress was white-skinned, blonde, red-lipped and, like Juliet, blessed with eyes that rivalled the sun. Instead of an ideal, but cold, mistress, Shakespeare's sonnets are concerned with at least three other people: a young, well-born man, a dark-haired (and disquietingly sexual) woman, and a rival poet. In the sequence as Thorpe published it Sonnets 1–126 appear to be addressed to the young man. Number 126, consisting of just twelve lines in rhyming couplets, serves as a conclusion to this group. Sonnets 127–152 are concerned with the woman. The last two consist of general reflections on love.

All this, of course, assumes that Thorpe's order is the author's. And it is not clear that it is. The sequence, and sonnet sequences generally, are sometimes spoken of as if they tell a story. But sonnet sequences, with the exception of *Astrophil and Stella*, are not good vehicles for narrative; there may be shifts in mood which prompt one to look for a story, and in most sequences the reader can imagine one because the basic situation is clear. But the poet concentrates on the exploration of a situation more than on the development of a story.

However, with Shakespeare the situation is not so simple. To the extent that there is any kind of story to be discerned behind the Sonnets, Shakespeare outlines it in Sonnets 40–42, and here in 144:

Two loves I have, of comfort and despair,
Which like two spirits do suggest me still;
The better angel is a man right fair,
The worser spirit a woman coloured ill.
To win me soon to hell, my female evil
Tempteth my better angel from my side,
And would corrupt my saint to be a devil,
Wooing his purity with her foul pride.
And whether that my angel be turned fiend
Suspect I may, yet not directly tell;
But being both from me, both to each friend,
I guess one angel in another's hell.
Yet this shall I ne'er know, but live in doubt
Till my bad angel fire my good one out.          (Sonnet 144)

The poet has two loves, both in the sense of persons whom he loves and also types of love: an intense friendship with the man (taking Sonnet 20 as disproving homosexual interest in him, though its tone may cast doubt on what it asserts), and a sexual relationship with a woman of whom he speaks in the harshest terms, sometimes out of disgust at sexuality per se (see Sonnet 129). Then, as Sonnet 144 above indicates, the man and woman seem to get together and betray him. It is an intense, bitter, and bawdy poem; the idea of the man being in the woman's hell, for example, is charged with vicious, sexual significance.

However, there are many sonnets which, taken by themselves, have no necessary relation to this story. And while there are discernible connections between particular sonnets, even within clusters of them, both in theme and grammar, these do not help to develop a story. For example, Sonnet 28 is so tightly linked to 27 that its first line would not make proper sense out of context. Sonnet 27 presents the poet, weary after a journey, seeking rest in bed, but finding his mind so preoccupied with the young man that he cannot sleep. It ends:

Lo, thus by day my limbs, by night my mind,
For thee, and for myself, no quiet find.

Sonnet 28 follows directly:

How can I then return in happy plight
That I am debarred the benefit of rest,
When day's oppression is not eased by night,
But day by night and night by day oppressed.

Connections such as these require that certain sonnets not be separated. Other connections of theme or image associate certain sonnets with each other without binding them. For example, Sonnets 46 and 47 both use the idea of playing off eyes against heart. But they do not *need* to be juxtaposed. Equally, there are sonnets which relate to similar subjects, and are separated. For example, Sonnets 34, 44, 109, 50 and 51 all use the idea of travel or distance.

Is the sequence then jumbled up? There have been many attempts to rearrange the Sonnets into a more logical sequence. Yet none of them make much better sense. Part of the problem lies in the false expectations raised by the word "sequence". One inevitably reads the Sonnets one after another; hence one's experience of them is of a sequence, whether in the same order as they're printed or not. But as they live in one's imagination one can make cross-connections between them which break free of such linearity. "Constellation" or "pattern" might be preferable to "sequence".

No matter what order one puts them in, the experience of the Sonnets remains tantalizing and fragmentary. They hold out the promise of revelation, but pluck it away again. Wordsworth remarked of the Sonnets that "with this key Shakespeare unlocked his heart", and many have sought to read them as a kind of autobiography. The unusual situation, the evident intensity of the feeling communicated, and those Sonnets that pun on Shakespeare's name, "Will" (Sonnets 135 and 136), encourage the doomed attempt. Gallons of ink have been spilt in trying to identify the young man and the dark lady. Thorpe's dedication to "Mr. W.H." as the "onlie begetter" of the poems has been taken as a clue. Candidates have been rooted out from the records; ingenuity has suggested others. For example, it has been argued that "W.H." could refer to "Will Himself'. But "onlie begetter" needn't mean more than that "W.H." passed on the manuscript to Thorpe, and so preserved the Sonnets, rather than inspired them.

No one is much the wiser for this sleuthing. Critics sometimes insist rather huffily that one should read the poems purely as poems and ignore this question. Fair enough. But part of the fascination of such sequences lies in the way they tempt the reader to identify real-life dramas behind the poetic masks. In Sidney's sequence, for example, it is known that Astrophil and Stella are poetic projections of Sidney himself and his cousin, Penelope Devereux. Renaissance culture was fascinated by the possibility of fusing art and life. Most famously, Queen Elizabeth I was reinvented in mythic and allegorical terms, as Gloriana, Spenser's *Faerie Queene*.

There are good reasons why the experience of the Sonnets should be fragmentary. Time is a central problem in them. Time is the medium in which we live, but it also inflicts decay and death. Time is also the medium of narrative, as events follow one another. The Sonnets are fascinated by "Time's tyranny" (115), by "Devouring Time" (19). They repeatedly invoked the self-renewing cycle of the seasons, but with the ironic awareness that for the individual time is not self-renewing and cyclical, but linear and terminal: a one-way passage to the grave.

In Sonnet 98 the poet complains that "From you I have been absent in the spring", and comments on the "spirit of youth" that reinvigorates the natural world. But in the man's absence the poet feels no such renewal:

Yet seemed it winter still, and, you away,

As with your shadow I with these did play,

To seek a clear meaning in Shakespeare's use of the medium of time, as one does in trying to connect all the elements of the Sonnets into a lucid story, is to seek for exactly the wrong kind of thing. This is one of the central problems posed by the Sonnets, as here in Sonnet 60:

Like as the waves make towards the pebbled shore,

So do our minutes hasten to their end;

where again the repetitve cyclicity of the waves stands against the linearity of individuals who hasten, like the minutes, "to their end".

There is another reason why we long to know more of the young man and the dark lady (assuming that there is only one of each). While the Sonnets are addressed to them, and they are part of this compelling, fragmentary drama, we learn very little of them. The young man is elusive. Of course this is often the point: he has turned away from the poet, and betrayed him, or is at any rate absent from him. We cannot get a clear picture of him just as the poet cannot make satisfactory contact with him. And the poet faces the further dilemma that the more his imagination dwells on the young man, he risks dissolving him so that the image becomes merely imaginary; in Sonnet 53 he starts by wondering whether the young man is real at all:

What is your substance, whereof are you made,

That millions of strange shadows on you tend?

In the case of the Dark Lady, though we learn that she's dark-haired, 'obscure' seems equally appropriate. The poet is ruefully aware that what she means to him and what she actually is are two different things (see Sonnet 150). Where his imagination risks losing the young man, in the case of the lady it distorts his vision, so he wonders "O me, what eyes hath love put in my head..." (Sonnet 148). He cannot see either of them clearly, because he has to look at both through the mist of his own feelings, which in the case of the lady take the form of ferocious sexual (self-)disgust (see Sonnet 129). Shakespeare has set the Sonnets up so that we share this frustration.

Other sonnet sequences tend to be addressed to women so idealized that they virtually cease to be flesh and blood, with the poet's changeable nature set against her perfect immutability. Giles Fletcher wrote a sequence to *Licia*, and explained that Licia was not necessarily a woman at all:

If thou muse what my Licia is, take her to be some Diana, at the least chaste, or some Minerva, no Venus, fairer farre: it may be shee is Learning's image, or some heavenlie woonder... perhaps under that name I have shadowed Discipline... it may bee some Colledge; it may bee my conceit, and portends nothing...

But Shakespeare denies himself such appeals to unchanging, ideal values and abstractions. His addressees are flawed and inconsistent, and the sequence gains depth and complexity precisely because it remains anchored in the human world. His imagination may be able to reach out beyond mortal existence, but Shakespeare is aware that in so doing he risks being false to its subject. 'Shall I compare thee to a summer's day?' sets out to praise the young man, in which it succeeds. But it is also about Shakespeare's efforts to find an appropriate image for the man, and in this he fails: he rejects the comparison with a summer's day, insisting at the end of the poem

So long as men can breathe or eyes can see,

So long lives this, and this gives life to thee.

But what sort of life? The reader has no real idea what the young man looks like or who he is. Shakespeare promises elsewhere to immortalize the young man's name, but then omits to tell us what that name is. Seen in this light, the poem returns upon itself.

As the poet sometimes exclaimed with almost hubristic delight, his art could remove itself from time (see Sonnet 55). But this can be a liability; in Sonnet 76 this separation threatens to remove his art from life, and he has to exercise his ingenuity to re-establish the connection:

> Why is my verse so barren of new pride,
> So far from variation or quick change?
> Why with the time do I not glance aside
> To new-found methods and to compounds strange?
> Why write I still all one, ever the same,
> And keep invention in a noted weed,
> That every word doth almost tell my name,
> Showing their birth and where they did proceed?
> O, know, sweet love, I always write of you,
> And you and love are still my argument;
> So all my best is dressing old words new,
> Spending again what is already spent:
> For as the sun is daily new and old,
> So is my love still telling what is told.

There is some ironic reflection here on the nature of the sonnet sequence itself: out of fashion, repeating the same 14-line pattern over and over, seeming on one level, like the sun, to be going round and round in circles. The connection is re-established by the final couplet, but there is an undertow: Shakespeare may claim to be "ever the same", but there is the disturbing possibility of his art itself running down and decaying as (in the early sonnets) he had said the man would do. One can project almost any meaning one wants onto the final couplet. For example, "Spending again what is already spent" can be taken to invoke the image of spending money. Through the magic of his art the poet can metaphorically spend the same money over and over again. But "spent" could also be taken to mean "worn-out", in which case the image is then one of pervasive decay — the subject to which he returns in the next sonnet (though the fact that Shakespeare can contrive such ambiguities implies that his art is anything but worn out).

If Shakespeare felt the need to apologize, albeit ironically, for the inadequacies of his art, what severer penance should be laid upon me for the cursoriness of these comments, so risibly unequal to their subject? There are many other issues one could usefully explore — the sustained negotiation between the permanence of art and the transience of life, the inter-relatedness of presence and absence, the significance of images, especially those drawn from daily life, and so on. But space, like life, is short. It is apt then that the three groups of sonnets get shorter and shorter, as if to communicate the sense of space getting tighter: 126, then 26, then 2. But if I feel my critical art has failed Shakespeare, in my failure, at least, I am in one way true. For if a brooding melancholy seems to hang over the sequence, that's no accident: it betrays an awareness of playing a losing hand. The poet may enjoy longevity in his art; the young man may father an heir and secure the future of his line. But in the long run the poet, the young man and the dark lady are all dead, their perishable flesh having failed to sustain the imaginative life of the poet's conceits. The imagination may be capable of a glorious, self-multiplying, self-reinventing mutability, but there is always the threat that it will be undercut by the grimmer mutability of ageing and death, which will reveal human life, in Hamlet's phrase, as a "quintessence of dust".

# THE APOCRYPHA

Though various plays (known as the Apocrypha), not included in the First Folio, have been attributed to Shakespeare, only *Edward III*, *Pericles* and *The Two Noble Kinsmen* can be considered as his work in any substantial part. It is believed now that he wrote one of the additions — Hand D, in the surviving incomplete manuscript — to a play, *Sir Thomas More*, written by various authors for the Admiral's Men around 1593 or 1601. Sir Edmund Tilney, Master of the Revels, required the revisions. That presumed to be by Shakespeare consists of 147 lines in which More, Sheriff of London, is pacifying the rioting anti-alien apprentices on May Day, 1517. The play — which eventually failed to pass the censor — has occasionally been staged. A critic noticed a phrase (not in the "Hand D" addition): "This tide of rage that with the eddy strives" (I.3: see *The Rape of Lucrece*).

Other plays in the Apocrypha — the dates are those of the earliest editions — have included *Arden of Feversham* (1592), revived occasionally in the 20th century, *Locrine\** (1595), *Mucedorus* (1598), *Sir John Oldcastle\** (1600), *Thomas, Lord Cromwell\** (1602), *The London Prodigal\** (1605), *The Puritan\** (1607), *Yorkshire Tragedy\** (1608), *The Merry Devil of Edmonton* (1608), *Fair Em* (undated; second edition 1631), and *The Birth of Merlin* (quarto edition, 1662). Those marked with an asterisk were added in 1664 to the second issue of the Third Folio. The silliest, betrayed by its title, is *A Pleasant Comedy of Fair Em, the Miller's Daughter of Manchester, with the love of William the Conqueror*.

The plays contain some agreeable stage directions, e.g., in *Locrine*, "Enter Humber alone, his hair hanging over his shoulders, his arms all bloody, and a dart in one hand"; in *The Birth of Merlin*, "Thunder and lightning; two Dragons appear, a White and a Red, they fight a while, and pause"; and, in *The Merry Devil of Edmonton*, "The chime goes, in which time Fabell is oft seen to stare about him, and hold up his hands."

There is also a lost play, *Cardenio*, which the King's Men acted in 1613 and was entered in the Stationers' Register 40 years later as "The History of Cardenio by Mr Fletcher and

Shakespeare". The dramatist, Lewis Theobald (1688–1744) claimed in 1727 that a play which he had written, *The Double Falsehood*, was founded on Shakespeare's. It is based on the story, by Cervantes, of Cardenio and Lucinda in *Don Quixote* (of which an English version had appeared in 1612). Theobald said that he had revised and adapted the piece from an old manuscript.

# SHAKESPEARE IN THE THEATRE
## THE THEATRE IN SHAKESPEARE'S DAY

Before there were theatres there were actors, who trudged the country playing in market places, inn-yards and halls — wherever they could drum up business.

Then an Elizabethan joiner, James Burbage (c.1530–97), saw an opportunity: staying put, in a permanent purpose-built theatre might prove more profitable. Having secured a patent for a permanent London company, in 1576 he built an outdoor theatre which he called, straightforwardly enough, the Theatre. It was here that the Lord Chamberlain's Men, Shakespeare's company, would eventually perform, with Burbage's son, Richard, as their leading man.

As soon as the players were fixed in one spot they needed many more scripts to lure regular playgoers back again and again. The idea caught on. Other outdoor theatres sprang up; The Curtain, the Swan, the Fortune, the Hope, the Rose. At the same time, children's companies became popular and began playing in indoor theatres.

The Theatre occupied a confused position in Elizabethan society. It was a culture deeply wedded to tradition, and it was expected that people be locked into established groups, such as noble households or trade guilds. The first groups of players honoured this requirement by securing a patron. Technically, groups such as Lord Pembroke's Men or the Lord Chamberlain's Men were part of these noblemen's households: they were liveried servants. Without this protection, players would have been at risk of being classified as "Rogues, Vagabonds and sturdy Beggars" under legislation of 1572, designed to reassert traditional social structure.

However, in practice the players were their own masters. The fast-developing professional companies might be servants of a lord, but they were supported by the paying public. In theory, players' companies were permitted to give public performances in London only so that they would be ready to play at Court when required, and Court performances were a valuable source of prestige and extra income. But in practice their regular performances developed new kinds of relationships between the players and the public. By the end of the century theatre-going had developed into a craze.

Although protected by the great and watched by Queen Elizabeth, the players and their London theatres were far from secure. Their novelty and the enthusiasm they aroused alarmed traditionalists and puritans. As early as 1578 a preacher thundered against "the sumptuous theatre houses, a continual monument of London's prodigality and folly", and expressed satisfaction at the theatres being temporarily closed by the plague, as "the cause of plagues is sin, if you look to it well; and the cause of sin are plays; therefore the cause of plagues are plays". Such critics had some powerful support. The City of London, which then, as now, had some jurisdiction within the city walls, tended to be opposed to the theatre. This was partly on the moral grounds that plays moved "wholly to imitation and not to the avoiding of those faults and vices which they represent"— indeed, the drama was relatively free of the ponderous and explicit moralizing of much earlier literature. The City fathers were also concerned for public order, and believed that theatres lured apprentices from their work, attracted horse-stealers, whoremongers and other scum, and were a means of spreading the plague.

So James Burbage built the Theatre to the north of the city. All outdoor theatres were situated outside the city — either to the north, or, like the Globe and the Rose, on the south bank of the Thames, in what was then part of Surrey. The indoor theatre at Blackfriars was inside the city, but, because it had been a monastery, by a legal anomaly it was outside city authority.

By 1594 the Lord Chamberlain's men, including Shakespeare, were resident at James Burbage's Theatre. As the lease was due to expire in 1597, Burbage decided to move to an indoor theatre in Blackfriars. He purchased the site, fashioned the theatre, and then fell foul of what today we would call the residents' association, who did not care for the idea of an adult company drawing lowlife into the neighbourhood. Suddenly the company faced losing their London base, and Burbage had sunk his capital into an unusable theatre. In the midst of this crisis James Burbage died.

The company struggled on for a while in other theatres. Then Burbage's sons, Cuthbert and Richard, pulled off a coup. Their landlord at the Theatre had declined to renew their lease partly because he did not care for plays, and partly because he had his eye on the valuable timber of which the Theatre was built. On the night of 28 December 1598 the Burbage brothers gathered a group of workmen, dismantled the Theatre, and did a flit with it over to the south bank, where they built it anew. This was the first Globe Theatre — the theatre for which most of Shakespeare's plays were intended.

The Globe was open to the sky — probably, according to the research of John Orrell, a polygon 30.5 m (100 ft) across. The polygon held covered galleries which looked into a yard maybe 21.3 m (70 ft) in diameter. Into this yard projected the stage, maybe 1.4 m (5 ft) high, and of something like 305 sq m (1000 sq ft). Admission was cheap: just a penny to stand in the yard and another penny for the comfort of the galleries. The wealthy could, if they wished, lay out sixpence for a place in the Lords' Rooms, which looked down onto the stage from the rear. Spectators in the cheapest places, milling round the stage down in the yard, were the most immediately involved. The capacity of such a theatre was said to be as much as 3000, though the performers probably played to smaller houses most of the time.

Such theatres needed and appealed to a popular audience. The audiences of the outdoor theatres were socially more diverse than those of the indoor, hall-type theatres, where sixpence was the lowest admission charge and one could pay more. In the indoor theatres, the well-off were the most conspicuous, sometimes, according to Thomas Dekker, even sitting on the stage, the better to show themselves off.

Being short of capital in 1599 the Burbage brothers made a unique deal with the leading sharers of the actors' company. Five of them, Shakespeare among them, were to put up part of the capital needed for the Globe. In other companies the theatre-owning impresario and the players' company were formally distinct. This new deal secured for the Lord Chamberlain's Men stability and self-determination unknown to the other acting companies. While other acting companies routinely went to the wall, the Lord Chamberlain's Men (from 1603 the King's Men) remained intact through to the closure of the London theatre business in 1642.

Although the impresario wanted to abandon the outdoor theatres, the acting company had other ideas. In 1609 they were able to move into Blackfriars, where they spent the winter months, from October to May. But every summer they were back at the Globe, from May to September. When the Globe mysteriously burnt down in 1613 the company could have withdrawn to Blackfriars, but instead they rebuilt their Globe. In those ten years from 1599 to 1609 the Globe had evidently proved its worth.

## THE GLOBE

The Globe Theatre favoured two things above all others: actors and the spoken word.

There were no sets. It fell to the actors to establish a sense of place as the play required it. In *As You Like It*, Rosalind arrives disguised as a boy and announces: "Well, this is the forest of Arden" (II iv.12), and with those words she makes it so. The forest has already been established in our minds, so Rosalind has only to speak to reactivate it. In an earlier scene the Duke and his followers had come on "like foresters". Here, as elsewhere in Shakespeare, the costume gave us our key to their world; their words elaborate upon it. The Duke reflects upon the advantages of living in "these woods" rather than in "the envious court", and upon the lessons that life in the forest teaches one. But where he claims to find "tongues in trees, books in the running brooks/Sermons in stones, and good in every thing" (II.i.16–7), we the audience find the trees in their tongues. The place is summoned into life by what people say about it and by what they do.

Setting did not have to be specified, or could be partly defined — we might glean that we are in Rome or in Illyria, but not more than that. In this respect the actors had something of the power of the storyteller. He (and they were all male) was not bound into the fictional world in the way actors in films or naturalistic drama are. Their job was to tell a tale in the most vivid and exciting way possible.

The actors' power requires the active co-operation of the audience. The opening chorus of *Henry V* reviews the scale of the play's subject, and then seems to apologize for the show's shortcomings:

> But pardon, gentles all,
> The flat unraisèd spirits that hath dared
> On this unworthy scaffold to bring forth
> So great an object. Can this cockpit hold
> The vasty fields of France? or may we cram
> Within this wooden O the very casques
> That did affright the air at Agincourt?
> O, pardon!

Prologue, *Henry V*, 8–15

But for all his apologies, the answer to his rhetorical questions is a resounding "Yes!", if — and only if — the audience will play along and "Piece out our imperfections with your thoughts./For 'tis your thoughts that now much deck our kings…" There is some ironic humility here. These players were the leading company of their day, and must have been giving the audience what it wanted. But the need for the audience's co-operation was real.

Such an audience is conscious, not just of the represented world, but also of the reality of the performance as performance. Much of Shakespeare's stagecraft exploits, even requires, this double consciousness. For example, all the female roles were played by boy-actors apprenticed to the company. However good they were, there must have been some continuing awareness that they were not what they seemed, and Shakespeare

191

exploits this when his heroines, like Viola and Rosalind, disguise themselves as boys. Ironies quicken when one watches a boy pretending to be a woman pretending to be a boy. Reality and fiction twist round each other in paradoxical knots. In *Twelfth Night* Orsino entrusts Viola, who is in disguise as a boy, Cesario, with the wooing of Olivia. He then notices that Cesario looks remarkably like a woman:

> Diana's lip
> Is not more smooth and rubious; thy small pipe
> Is as the maiden's organ, shrill and sound —
> And all is semblative a woman's part. I.iv.31–3

The ironies in this passage are complex. As with the creation of a sense of place, Orsino newly creates Cesario's hidden (and at this stage totally imaginary) female self.

Other conventions or features of performance played upon this same kind of double consciousness. There was no controlling the sunlight, so night scenes were played by as much light as any others. The audience would be asked to imagine the darkness by the appearance of torches or candles or of someone in night clothes.

Actors could turn and address the audience directly. The chorus in *Henry V* or *Pericles* obviously does this, but so too does Iago in *Othello*. He works Othello's downfall out of his spite, and turns as he does so to ask the audience "And what's he, then, that says I play the villain?" Iago's character is deeply bound up with the nature of performance — he disguises his feelings like an actor, and stage manages much of the play's action.

Another element in the rapport between stage and audience was to do with the personalities of certain performers. The leading comic actor was an invaluable asset to the company. In the early part of Shakespeare's career it was the boisterous Will Kempe who played Peter in *Romeo and Juliet* and Dogberry in *Much Ado About Nothing*. He was succeeded by Robert Armin (c.1568–1615) who probably played Feste in *Twelfth Night* and the Fool in *King Lear*. Armin seems to have been a more melancholy, reflective comic than Kempe, but both were huge stars, with public personalities which the plays in which they appeared had to use or fall foul of. Though Armin seems to have been more willing to submit to the discipline of the written role, both were expert improvisers — Kempe in particular could engage in banter with the audience, and used the jigs at the end of the play to do so. It must have been like having a stand-up comic appear at the end of a straight play today.

Acting is an evanescent art, of and for the moment. It is therefore frustratingly hard to know with any certainty what it was like then. We know that actors were worked hard; rehearsal in the morning, performance in the afternoon and probably planning and line-learning in the evening. They would have needed to learn lines fast and keep many parts alive in their memories. But they also seem to have rehearsed thoroughly.

There has been some debate about how artificial and obviously rhetorical the acting was. This is an almost unresolvable question. But Shakespeare used different types of language, from the most high-flown to the most colloquial, and it would be strange if his company couldn't communicate these shifts of tone in their delivery. Richard Flecknoe, writing admittedly in 1664, some 45 years after Burbage's death, recorded that he:

...was a delightful Proteus, so wholly transforming himself into his Part, and putting off himself with his Clothes, as he never (not so much as in the Tyring-house) assumed himself again until the Play was done.

But Flecknoe then draws a comparison: Burbage was to ordinary actors as an excellent singer is to a "Ballad-singer who only mouths it", in that he "knows all his Graces, and can artfully vary and modulate his Voice, even to know how much breath he is to give to every syllable". Such a description suggests a high degree of vocal skill, capable of ranging over many styles. Whether such acting would strike us as real or artificial, it seemed real to its spectators.

The interpretation of Shakespeare's plays was originally in his own hands. He wrote the script to suit actors he knew well and worked with. He could explain what he had in mind. On occasion he rewrote in the light of practical experience in performance, as he seems to have done with *King Lear*. Later actors worked in different types of theatre, and without Shakespeare for guidance, developed their own ways of doing things.

## SHAKESPEARE IN THE LATER THEATRE

The theatre's enemies got the upper hand in 1642, and the theatres were closed. When they reopened in 1660 they were different from those Shakespeare had known. In the last few years of his career Shakespeare had had the indoor theatre at Blackfriars available to him — *The Tempest*, for example, reflects its different resources. But his company still played at the Globe. However, the open-air theatres did not survive into the late 17th century. From 1660 Shakespeare's works had to be adapted to suit a different kind of theatre, and a different taste.

Later 17th-century comment on Shakespeare often gives the impression of liking his work without exactly knowing why. Critics and commentators were working with neo-classical literary theory, which Shakespeare cheerfully flouted. And though Restoration writers could flout neo-classical rules in order to exploit the glitzy attractions of their own theatres, they seem never to have grasped that Shakespeare might have known what he was doing when he flouted them. It was also an age which craved reassurance in the wake of the Civil War, a craving which found expression in its adherence to the doctrine of Poetic Justice, meaning, as Miss Prism puts it in *The Importance of Being Ernest*, that the good end happily and the bad unhappily. Shakespeare demonstrably flouts this too. Sometimes they could simply let him be an exception. At other times they reworked him to fit their tastes. Nahum Tate, for example, seized on *King Lear* as a wonderful quarry of raw material which Shakespeare had left in a deplorable mess. He called it "a Heap of Jewels, unstrung and unpolisht... yet... dazzling in their Disorder". His process of stringing and polishing involved cutting the Fool (inappropriate, he thought, to have such a low character in a serious play), making Edgar and Cordelia lovers, and giving the play a happy ending.

The Restoration actor still enjoyed something of his Elizabethan predecessor's intimacy with the audience. He played on a stage that reached out in front of the proscenium arch, behind which stood perspective scenery, painted on flats, and capable of being an attraction in its own right.

Most important at that time, he was now also a she — Margaret Hughes having initiated the profession of actress by playing Desdemona in December 1660.

It was hugely expensive to create new sets of scenery, and the players often just used what was in stock. But when a new tragedy was to be produced they might plan the design in a way that points forward to the modern concept of a production. However, there doesn't seem to have been quite the modern idea of having to *interpret* Shakespeare. Interpretation of Shakespeare's work was implicit in the act of adapting it. The idea of playing the dialogue in new ways hadn't yet caught on. Thomas Betterton (c.1635– 1710), the leading actor of the age, is known to have tried to recover Shakespeares's original instructions for his parts in *Hamlet* and *Henry VIII*.

Traditions continued to dominate the acting of Shakespeare, and for most actors the limitations on time and the deepening cultural conservatism of the 18th century encouraged adherence to established business. However, in seeking to make a name for themselves, some ambitious actors occasionally offered their own interpretation of a role especially by focusing on moments that they could plan and control in isolation from the rest of the cast. Charles Macklin (c.1700–97) scored a huge hit as Shylock when he first played it in February 1741. The part was usually played as low comedy, but Macklin imagined Shylock as a terrifying villain. His conception was most powerfully realized in isolated moments of tremendous force which seemed to encapsulate the whole character. One such moment was his whetting of Shylock's knife, prior to cutting his pound of Antonio's flesh, which he did with such effect that on one occasion a young man in the pit fainted.

David Garrick (1717–79) was the greatest actor of the day. His London debut as Richard III (in the adaptation by Colley Cibber that held the 18th-century stage) had a similar redefining force as Macklin's Shylock. It established Richard as one of the hurdles a candidate for theatrical greatness would have to attempt. Garrick in fact gained a position of immense power as the lessee of Drury Lane and could control details of decor and music in a way that anticipated today's notion of the director. But the theatrical and cultural conditions of the day meant this could never become the general procedure. Actors had a trade; if they could do it, then they didn't need to be taught by anyone else (unless that person was as powerful and talented as Garrick); if they couldn't do it they shouldn't be on the stage.

By the early 19th century many elements of this way of interpreting Shakespeare were still in place. But the theatres in which it had to be done were getting bigger. In 1660 only two theatres had been licensed, these becoming in due course the Theatres Royal at Drury Lane and Covent Garden. With occasional exceptions, this restriction remained in force throughout the 18th century; only two London theatres were permitted to play the spoken drama. The holders of these patents fought to retain their monopoly. At the same time they needed to make more money. So they enlarged the patent houses of Drury Lane and Covent Garden. Drury Lane, for example, was rebuilt in 1794 with a capacity of 3611. For a proscenium arch theatre, with the audience all on one side, this is large. The acting had to be impressive to make an impact. Edmund Kean (1787–1833), unstable, but capable of extraordinary power, could render Shakespeare in ways that burnt into the memory, as, for example, here with Richard III's dying moments, as recorded by William Hazlitt:

He fought like one drunk with wounds; and the attitude in which he stands with his hands stretched out, after his sword is taken from him, had a preternatural and terrific grandeur, as if his will could not be disarmed, and the very phantom of his despair had a withering power.

Great stars like Kean or his contemporary, Mrs Siddons (1755–1831) would go on playing their great roles for years. There was no sense of the interpretation of a particular role being inextricably part of an interpretation of the play as a whole. It seemed reasonable to them, for example, to arrive at a theatre when on tour, hand out a few notes to the resident suppporting company, run over any special business, and get on with the show without further ado.

In the course of the 19th century this began to change. In 1843 the London theatre monopoly was abolished. Old patterns persisted in many parts of the country, but there was a growing sense of the integrity of the play's effect. Changes were manifest in two ways: in the gradual stripping away of the accepted adaptaions of Shakespeare, and in the design. From Garrick onwards there had been attempts to restore Shakespeares's text. Garrick and, later, the actor John Philip Kemble (1757–1823), Kean's great rival and brother of Mrs Siddons, accumulated significant libraries of Shakespeariana. In the mid-19th century the restoration of Shakespeare's text picked up speed. At the same time a changed sense of history was reflected in the design of Shakespeare. In the 18th century, as in Shakespeare's own day, the sense of the otherness of the past was hazy. In the only surviving illustration of an original Shakespearian performance, a group of ancient Roman characters in *Titus Andronicus* are shown in a mixture of Roman and contemporary clothes. Similarly, pictures of Garrick and Mrs Pritchard (1711–68) as the Macbeths show them wearing 18th-century clothes. But there was an increasing sense that this was incongruous. Victorian Shakespeare tended to be mounted in his most prestigious London appearances with great attention to historical detail. It was not always the right period, but, at Charles (son of Edmund) Kean's theatre, the Princess's, it was elaborately researched. For example, the architectural historian George Goodwin advised Kean on the design for *Macbeth* (1852). Such procedures pandered to a Gradgrindian passion for fact, and the respectability of being learned, but they also fostered some sense of the world of the play having its on internal coherence, which needed to realized on stage with formidable planning and effort.

The Shakespearean productions of Sir Henry Irving (1838–1905) used such historically researched decor, but on a vast and splendid scale. Irving planned his productions meticulously, drilled his actors for weeks, and had command of armies of extras. He would study each play with immense care — and then cut and rearrange it to suit his purposes. His productions were lavishly pictorial. The sheer scale of the resources deployed meant that, in effect, Irving was working as a director (as Alan Hughes has argued) as well as the leading actor. However, he also looked back to such actors as Edmund Kean, whom he particularly revered, and to some extent sustained as a strand of his work the idea of the great actor interpreting his role in relative isolation.

Irving and his contemporary, Herbert Beerbohm Tree (1853–1917), carried quasi-realistic spectacle as far as it could go. In many ways they anticipated cinema. The acting in their theatres was now all upstage of the proscenium arch, which acted in effect as a picture frame behind which images of a separate world were created. So strong was Irving's sense of this separation that he even felt some qualms about delivering soliloquies out to the audience. Magnificent though Irving's Shakespeare was, he had been forced into the straitjacket of realism. It is a far cry from the Globe.

From today's point of view Irving looks like the last monarch of a toppled regime. The theatre of today is in many respects the creation of theatrical revolutionaries of the late 19th and early 20th centuries — men such as Ibsen, Strindberg, Stanislavsky and Antoine. In England Shakespearean production became caught up in the revolution.

William Poel (1852–1934) hit upon the simple notion that Shakespeare knew what he was doing. To prove it he built the best approximations he could manage to Elizabethan theatres, and mounted Shakespeare (and other early drama) in them. This meant no scenery, and, whatever the period in which the play was set, the costumes were Elizabethan with a few symbolic additions. In a sense Poel's historical reconstruction could not succeed. He might dress his actors as Elizabethans but his audiences remained late Victorian. One can never turn the clock back. But he did point the way forward in valuable respects. Heavy realistic scenery, which could impede the flow of the play, was cut. The stately ponderousness of Irving's Shakespearean delivery was cut.

Foremost of those who learnt from Poel was Harley Granville-Barker (1877–1946). He won commercial success for George Bernard Shaw in his new drama seasons at the Royal Court (1904–7). Having gained a foothold for the new drama in the new century, Barker set about doing the same for Shakespeare in productions of *The Winter's Tale* and *Twelfth Night* (1912) and *A Midsummer Night's Dream* (1914). He learnt Poel's lessons of simplicity and speed. Heavily encrusted late-Victorian decor was stripped away. He built an apron stage in front of the proscenium to bring his actors closer to the audience.

After the First World War Barker all but abandoned practical theatre, and turned scholar. He wrote his *Prefaces to Shakespeare*, which interpret Shakespeare's plays in the light of Shakespeare's stage. But he had already effectively pointed the way forward for what has become the dominant ideal in production of Shakespeare's plays in the 20th century. This involves the attempt to resolve a paradox: to be faithful to the play, while also making it modern. A production may be in period clothes, or modern clothes or clothes of no particular period at all, but it must speak to the audience.

In this process the director has become central. This is partly because the growing complexity of theatre equipment required that someone try to co-ordinate the performance. But it is mostly a question of cultural diversity and confusion. We evidently feel that Shakespeare needs to be interpreted by some co-ordinating intelligence — or rather that he needs to be re-interpreted, for Shakespeare's plays can now be seen again and again in many different productions. Sometimes this re-interpretation has resulted in a needless striving after novelty for its own sake. Often it has been revelatory.

The huge, publicly funded national companies of today, the Royal National Theatre and the Royal Shakespeare Company, are the inheritors of shoestring revolutionary ventures of the turn of the century and between the wars. Their very structures indicate how little we can agree upon. Both organizations retain proscenium-arch auditoria. But over the years they have had studio spaces (the Cottesloe, the National Theatre Studio, the Pit, the Other Place), and the huge Olivier in London, and the more intimate Swan in Stratford. It seems we cannot agree among ourselves on what a theatre is. We are conscious primarily of diversity. This is true of our approach to Shakespearean production. Though director's theatre is still dominant, it has not precluded the work of actor-managers such as Sir Donald Wolfit. Indeed, some actor-managers, such as Sir John Gielgud, Sir Laurence Olivier and Kenneth Branagh, have been able to work within directors' theatre. But directors' theatre is designed precisely to multiply the available interpretations. It is not itself a style.

Today we feel as if we live in a baffling matrix of many different voices and points of view. There is scarcely any sense of a single, dominant way of doing Shakespeare (though with hindsight future theatre historians may perceive patterns which we, being in the thick of it, cannot yet apprehend). Related to this is the sense of there not being any single audience for Shakespeare, with shared standards, values and expectations, but of there being a variety of audiences — ultimately of there simply being the many individual audiences that assemble night after night around the world, to let the theatre attempt to perform one of its most important function: that of taking a collection of diverse, separate individuals, and turning it into a group which enjoys a collective identity, if only for the duration of the play, so that we can test what values we share, and how we might live together.

## STRATFORD-UPON-AVON

Daniel Baker, the puritan High Bailiff of Stratford, banned players from the town in Shakespeare's lifetime, and for over a century after Shakespeare's death there were few performances in Stratford. In 1746 a touring company led by John Ward, grandfather of John Philip Kemble and Sarah Siddons, presented *Othello* in the old Town Hall and raised £17 towards the cost of repairing the Shakespeare monument in Holy Trinity Church.

The bicentenary of Shakespeare's birth in 1764 passed unnoticed, but in September 1769, David Garrick mounted a Shakespeare "Jubilee", an event dominated by pouring rain and containing no more than half a line written by Shakespeare.

The still-flourishing Shakespeare Club was formed in 1824 and in 1827 a small theatre opened in Chapel Lane, only to be demolished in 1872.

In 1874 Charles Edward Flower, son of a local brewer, gave as a site for a Shakespeare theatre two riverside acres, and a Shakespeare Memorial Association was founded. On Shakespeare's birthday, 23 April, 1879, a new theatre was officially opened, at a cost of £20,000, most of which Charles Flower had given himself. The opening play, *Much Ado About Nothing*, marked the beginning of Stratford as the world's centre of Shakespeare production. To begin with various minor companies provided the short annual season, usually a spring fortnight. In 1886 the tireless Frank Robert Benson took over the running of the "Festivals"; under him and his successor, W. Bridges-Adams (nicknamed "Unabridges" because of his fidelity to the text) the festivals grew in length until there was a month in the spring and another in the summer. In 1925 the Memorial received a royal charter.

On March 6, 1926 a mysterious fire destroyed the old building; only the library and picture gallery remaining. Generous donations from America made possible the building of the Memorial Theatre, opened by the Prince of Wales on 23 April, 1932 (*Henry IV, Part 1* in the afternoon; *Part 2* at night). Designed by Elisabeth Scott, it was much criticized, but it is now so weathered and familiar that early doubts are forgotten. Bridges-Adams was succeeded in 1934 by the scholarly director Ben Iden Payne, whose Elizabethan-style productions could be perilously dull. After Payne, two directors came and went, Milton Rosmer (1943) and Robert Atkins (1944–5). In 1946 Sir Barry Jackson controlled the first of three famous seasons. Surprisingly his contract was not renewed after 1948; the governors appointed Anthony Quayle, the actor, as his successor. Within the next 11 years — first under Quayle, then jointly (from 1952) under Quayle and Glen Byam Shaw, and from 1956 under Shaw alone — the Memorial Theatre was the home of a constellation of classical players, such as John Gielgud, Peggy Ashcroft, Michael Redgrave, Laurence Olivier, Edith Evans and Charles Laughton. It was during this period, in 1955, that with Peter Brook's production of *Titus Andronicus* (Olivier as Titus) Stratford at last completed the full Shakespeare canon. The interior of the theatre had been remodelled in 1951 and the chasm between actors and audience dwindled.

Peter Hall followed Shaw in 1960, aged 29. In 1961 the Memorial was rechristened the Royal Shakespeare. By now a Stratford season was lasting for nearly an entire year. The Company was formed round a core of associate artists; of actors, directors, and designers. Between 1960 and 1978 it had a London home, at the Aldwych Theatre;

thereafter it moved to the complex Barbican Centre. Trevor Nunn succeeded Hall in 1968, aged 28, and was largely responsible for the building of the Other Place, a subsidiary intimate studio-theatre, in 1974, where mainly non-Shakespearean work was presented, including Ford, Beaumont and Fletcher, O'Neill, Chekhov, Brecht, and Ibsen. Its London counterpart, The Warehouse (later the Donmar Warehouse) opened in 1977. Nunn was later joined as artistic director by Terry Hands; Adrian Noble, who became Artistic Director in 1991, to be succeeded by Michael Boyd in 2003.

# THE OLD VIC

The Old Vic, at the junction of Waterloo Road and The Cut, south of the Thames, was built in 1818 as the Royal Coburg. Renamed the Royal Victoria, it had a turbulent early history, but under the guidance of Emma Cons (1838–1912), it modulated in 1880 to the Royal Victoria Hall and Coffee Tavern, a kind of Mission, with wholesome entertainment for working-class Lambeth. In 1898, Miss Cons's niece, Lilian Baylis, arrived to help, aged 23. In 1914 she chose to present Shakespeare — as well as popular opera — in the cavernous theatre with its gaslit stage. The adventure went well under such directors as Ben Greet (1915–18) and Robert Atkins (1921–5). By the autumn of 1923, the tercentenary year of the First Folio, every play in the canon had been performed, by such actors as Sybil Thorndike, Ion Swinley, Edith Evans, and Baliol Holloway. From 1929 a new director, Harcourt Williams, had the young John Gielgud as leading man during two renowned seasons.

During the 1930s the theatre became established, with the help of such names as Peggy Ashcroft, Tyrone Guthrie, Charles Laughton, and Flora Robson. In 1937 Laurence Olivier's Hamlet and Henry V declared the rise of a major Shakespearian theatre. When Lilian Baylis died later that year she had seen the Vic become, in effect, a National Theatre.

In 1941 the theatre was bombed and the company moved to the New Theatre (today the Albery) from 1944 to the spring of 1950. Under the direction of the actors Olivier, Richardson, and the director John Burrell, these were the years of Olivier's famous *Richard III* (1944), the two *Henry IV* chronicles (1945), with Richardson's Falstaff and Olivier's Hotspur and Shallow; and in 1946 Olivier's own production of *King Lear*. In 1949 Hugh Hunt came from another Old Vic company at the Theatre Royal in Bristol, and directed Michael Redgrave in such parts as Berowne and Hamlet.

The Waterloo Road theatre reopened under Hunt on 14 November, 1950. Edith Evans, at the premiere of *Twelfth Night*, spoke Christopher Hassall's prologue "London, be glad! your Shakespeare's home again", with its line: "Illyria next stop after Waterloo".

From 1953 Michael Benthall controlled the Vic during a period that within five years covered every Folio play. In June 1963 the new National Theatre company, under Sir Laurence Olivier and as yet without a building of its own, took over the Vic and opened, with *Hamlet* — on 22 October. Internally, the Vic was still the theatre of what the writer Alan Pryce-Jones had called "gas-bracket rococo and plaster lace". In 1970 the Young Vic opened, also at the Cut; a theatre in the round, it presents Shakespearean and non-Shakespearean drama.

In 1975 the National company left for its new theatre; at the Old Vic, the Prospect Theatre company appeared under Toby Robertson. This seemed to be the theatre's natural tenant. In 1979, Prospect became known officially as the Old Vic Company. Since then the theatre has reverted to general use.

# THE NATIONAL THEATRE

From October 1963 for nearly 13 years the National Theatre company stayed at the Old Vic, awaiting the completion of their own theatre at the South Bank. Despite being first suggested in 1848, work did not begin on the building of a National Theatre until 1969 (after a false start in 1951). Despite protracted delays, each of the three theatres within the National, designed by Sir Denys Lasdun. was used as it became available. The Lyttelton (named for Oliver Lyttelton, the National's first Chairman, later Lord Chandos) opened in March 1976, the Olivier (named after the theatre's first artistic director, Lord Olivier) in October 1976, and the Cottesloe (named for Lord Cottesloe, first chairman of the South Bank Theatre Board, set up in 1962 to oversee the building of the theatre). The three theatres contain, in all, nearly 2,500 seats. Lord Olivier was director from 1963–1973; Sir Peter Hall took over until 1988, when he was succeeded by Richard Eyre. It was also in 1988 that the theatre gained a Royal charter. Nicholas Hytner became director in 2003.

# OPEN AIR FESTIVAL, REGENT'S PARK

The first performance in Regent's Park, masterminded by Australian actor, Sydney Carroll and director, Robert Atkins, was *Twelfth Night* in July 1932. Despite losses of £560, Carroll got permission to establish a theatre in the Inner Circle, adjoining Queen Mary's Garden; the first full season opened on 6 June 1933. The open-air stage then, as now, was backed by a screen of poplar, sycamore, and hazel, with a marquee on hand for inclement weather. Carroll reshaped the stage, transplanted trees, and hired deckchairs and park benches to seat more than 3000 people. The first season drew audiences of over

250,000, but lost £3,000. In order to secure its financial future, the New Shakespeare Company, a non-profit distributing company seeking subsidies, was formed in 1963, and successfully sought funding from the Arts Council, local councils, and several large companies. A year later came the Company's first overseas tour. The theatre continues to present professional open-air theatre throughout most of the summer.

## ENGLISH SHAKESPEARE COMPANY

The ESC was established in 1986 by the director Michael Bogdanov and the actor Michael Pennington. The inaugural production of the Henrys toured throughout the world to great acclaim and in 1987 the company added four new productions to form the *Wars of the Roses* — Shakespeare's complete history cycle — for which Michael Bogdanov won an Olivier award as Best Producer. Over the next six years the company performed over 15 productions, including a pioneering tour of four African countries with a specially adapted *Macbeth* and a four-week tour of India with *Coriolanus* and *The Winter's Tale*. In spring 1994 the company had played to over 1.5 million people across five continents, and ceased large-scale touring due to lack of Arts Council funding.

## THE GLOBE

The original Globe Theatre, in which Shakespeare was a sharer, opened in 1599 at Southwark on the south bank of the Thames, probably with a performance of *As You Like It*. In 1613 it burned down accidentally during a performance of *Henry VIII*. Rebuilt and reopened in 1614, it was described as "the fairest that ever there was in England". Only 30 years later it was pulled down by the Puritans.

The late Sam Wanamaker, Hollywood actor, Broadway director, and devotee of Shakespeare's plays, arrived in England in 1940 and sought the original site of the Globe. He was surprised to find the locals knew little about the historic site, and when he eventually found a plaque he had to clean it to read it. Wanamaker vowed to reconstruct the theatre, believing it more important than Shakespeare's birthplace, but he was to campaign for 20 years before he began to gain support. Legal and financial problems had to be overcome before a site, just 91.5 m (300 ft) from the original was obtained from Southwark Council. The Shakespeare Globe Trust, with Prince Philip as the Patron and Sam Wanamaker as Chief Executive, was set up to promote and raise funds for the project; fundraising committees were also set up in the United States, Canada, New Zealand, Australia, India, Japan, and Germany. With the help of the Friends of Shakespeare's Globe the financial hurdles were overcome, and the final phase of building started in June 1992. Tragically, Sam Wanamaker's death in late 1993 deprived him of his final dream, but the motto of the rebuilding plan, a line from *Henry VIII*, remains a fitting memorial to his efforts: "Our children's children will see this, and bless heaven". Mark Rylance was appointed director in 1995, and since 1997 the Globe has presented regular summer seasons. It has a flourishing Education Department.

# STRATFORD, ONTARIO

The mere coincidence of names first suggested to a local journalist, Tom Patterson, the possibility of an annual Shakespeare Festival in the Canadian Stratford, a small Ontario town by the Canadian Avon. Tyrone Guthrie, always tempted by unexpected ideas, agreed immediately to come from England to direct on an Elizabethan "thrust" stage evolved by Tanya Moiseiwitsch, so often his designer. Originally the festivals were held in a large tent where during the summer of 1953 Alec Guinness acted Richard III, and Irene Worth was Helena in *All's Well That Ends Well*, one of Guthrie's favourite plays. It was the beginning of an enterprise that through over half a century, and since 1957 in a permanent theatre, has been the main North American home of acted Shakespeare, under a variety of administrators — successively Tyrone Guthrie, Michael Langham, Jean Gascon, Robin Phillips, John Hirsch, John Neville, David William, and Richard Monette.

The main stage, in spite of alterations, remains basically the Moiseiwitsch-Guthrie creation. There are now three other stages. Stratford, during its 50-odd years, has worked through the Shakespeare Folio with consistent accomplishment by such visiting players as Irene Worth, James Mason, Paul Scofield, Douglas Campbell, Siobhan McKenna, Maggie Smith, Pauline Jameson, Brian Bedford, John Neville and Margaret Tyzack; and by a powerful group of Canadians for whom Stratford is, in effect, a National Theatre. Among them are Christopher Plummer, William Hutt, Douglas Rain, Frances Hyland, Pat Galloway, John Colicos, William Needles, Kate Reid, and Martha Henry. The summer festival has given international fame to its inconspicuous town, is directed by Robin Phillips, who went to Canada in 1974. Its repertoire is not confined to Shakespeare.

# INDEX

manikin puppet
mansionry abode
march-chick precocious youngster
marchpane sweetmeat, like
    marzipan
martlet house-martin
marybuds marigolds
maugre in spite of
mazard head
meacock cowardly, spiritless
mell become involved with
meridian highest point
metaphysical supernatural
mew cage up
miching stealthy
milch moist
mince make light of
minikin dainty
minion darling
misgraffed wrongly matched
mobled with head muffled
module image
moldwarp mole
mome blockhead
montant (fencing) upward thrust
moonish fickle
mop grimace
morisco morris-dancer
mountant lifted up
mousing mauling
mowing pulling faces
muddy-mettled dull-spirited
multipotent all-powerful
mumble-news gossip
mure wall
murrain plague
muss a scramble
mystery profession, craft

napless threadbare
natural idiot
nave hub of wheel
nayward denial
nayword password, byword
neaf fist
Nereides sea-nymphs
nervy sinewy
nether-stocks stockings
nightgown dressing-gown
nimble-pinion'd swift-winged
nole head
nook-shotten with many corners
    and angles
nuncio messenger

nut-hook beadle

ob a halfpenny
obsequiously with proper duty; as
    a mourner
occulted hidden
odds superiority, advantage
oeillades amorous glances
oes circles
operant active
opposing displaying
oppugnancy discord
orchard garden
ordinant provident; controlling
ordinary meal
orgillous proud
orifex opening
ort scrap
othergates otherwise, in a very
    different way
ouches ornaments
ounce lynx
over-peering looking with evil eye
over-topping over-ambitious
owe possess
oxlip the great cowslip

packhorse drudge
packing plotting
paddock toad
pain toil
painted specious
palliament robe of candidature
pantler pantry servant
parcel part, portion
parcel-gilt silver ornamented with
    gilt
partialize to be partial
partisan long-handled spear with
    double blade
partlet hen
passing exceeding
patch fool
peak droop, mope
pelting paltry
pennyworth bargain
perdurable lasting
peremptory presumptuous
perpend attend, ponder
phantasime fantastic fellow
phraseless beyond description
pia mater brain (lit. membrane
    covering brain)
picked finical

pickers thieves
pickthank toady, talebearer
pigeon-livered spiritless
pinch worry
pioner sapper, soldier of the lowest
    rank
pismire ant
pitch highest point of falcon's flight
pith strength
plausive plausible
pleasant jocular, facetious
point-devise precise in all
    particulars
points laces to hold up breeches
policy craftiness
politic cunning, scheming
pomander scent-ball
pomewater kind of apple
pomgarnet pomegranate
pompous ceremonious
portage porthole
possessed informed
posset (as a verb) to curdle
postmaster master of the post-
    horses
posy inscription inside a
    ring
pottle tankard; half a gallon
pouncet-box small perfume box
    with perforated lid
practice plot, treason
pranked up bedecked
pressure impression
prig thief
prime youth
primero card game
princox pert young fellow
probation examination
prodigy ominous phenomenon
prolixious superfluous
propugnation defence
proscription condemning to death
    without trial
proud-pied with many fine colours
psaltery stringed instrument
    resembling zither
puddled muddied
pudency modesty
puling whimpering
punk whore
punto (fencing) direct thrust
purblind totally or partly blind
purgation acquittal
purlieu land bordering forest

purveyor officer who goes ahead to make arrangements
puttock kite
puzzel drab, harlot

quaintly artfully
qualify to moderate
quantity scrap
quat pimple
quean hussy
quell slaughter
questant seeker, candidate
quietus settling debt, release from trials of life
quillets quibbles
quite requite
quittance discharge from debt
quoif close-fitting cap
quoted noted
quotidian a continuous fever or ague

rackers distorters
rampired fortified
rancours irritants
ravin gulp
reave rob by force
rebate make blunt
receipt prescription
recheat horn-call that summons back hounds
recordation remembrance
rector ruler
rede advice
red lattice windows of alehouse
re-edify rebuild
regiment government
rehearse narrate
reins loins
repugnancy resistance
repured purified again
rere-mice bats
reverend dignified
revolve ponder upon
rhapsody meaningless verbiage
rheumy dank
ribaudred lewd
riggish wanton
rigol ring, crown
rivage shore
rivelled wrinkled
road roadstead
roarers violent waves
romage upheaval

ronyon scabby creature
ropery roguery
rother ox
roundel dance in a circle
rowel spur-point
roynish rude, uncouth
rubious ruby-coloured
rudesby rude, boisterous fellow
runagate deserter

sack sweet white wine
Sackerson famous bear kept near Bankside theatres
sacring bell rung during Mass
salamander fabled lizard that lived in fire
sallet salad; also close-fitting helmet
samphire herb used in pickling
sanctuarize shelter
sarcenet flimsy silk
saucy importunate
saving no offence to
scaffoldage boards of the stage
scald mean, scurvy
scathe harm
scope full authority
scorch to cut
scotch a gash
scrimer fencer
scrip pouch
scrivener notary
scruple an apothecary's weight; a minute portion
scut tail of a deer
sea-coal mineral coal as opposed to charcoal
seconds coarse flour
septentrion north
sere withered state
serpigo skin disease
setter spy for thieves
sewer butler
shard wing-case
shark up gather up
shearman cutter of cloth
shent blamed
shive slice
shoal shallow
shoulder-shotten with a dislocated shoulder
shrewdly grievously
shrift confessional
shrine image
shuffling evasion

sicle shekel
simple (unmixed as in "simple of itself")
simples herbs
singular expert
sirrah form of address to inferior
skipping flighty
skirr scour
slab sticky
sleave skein of silk
sleeve-band wristband
sleided untwisted
slips leashes
slops wide breeches
slubber to scamp, do carelessly
smatch smudge
smoke smell out, suspect
smooth flatter
sneap snub
snow-broth melted snow
soft not so fast
sonance sound
sonties saints
soothing flattery
Sophy Shah of Persia
sortance agreement
soured pickled in salt
souse swoop down on
spanieled to follow like a spaniel
spaniel-fawning toadying
specialties special terms or documents
spilth spilling
spinster spinning woman
splenetive impetuous
spongy sodden with drink
sprag quick
sprat contemptible creature
springe snare
spruce affected
square quarrel
squash unripe pea-pod
squier foot-rule
staggers giddiness
staniel kind of hawk
staple fibre
state canopy
statist statesman
stigmatic marked with deformity
stint to stop, check
stithy smithy
stock-fish dried cod
stout bold